L6
.95

GW01553072

# THE CLASSICIST

## EDITORIAL COMMITTEE

ESSAYS:
Richard Wilson Cameron
Cecilia McIvor Hunt, *Copyediting*

PROFESSIONAL PORTFOLIO:
Courtney Coleman
Gilbert P. Schafer, III

ACADEMIC PORTFOLIO:
Donald M. Rattner

COMPETITIONS AND
SKETCHBOOKS PORTFOLIOS:
David T. Netto

GOOD PRACTICE:
Peter J. Talty

ALLIED ARTS:
Richard Wilson Cameron
Steven W. Semes

EX LIBRIS:
Steven W. Semes

MANAGING EDITOR:
Gabrielle Belson Rattner

SPONSORSHIPS:
Lawrence S. Dumoff

DISTRIBUTION:
Martin Brandwein

ART DIRECTION:
Seth Joseph Weine

FRONT COVER:
"Come, Let Us Build Ourselves
A City," by Jonathan Paul Lee.
Watercolor and pencil, 1995.
Logo by S.J.Weine.

FRONTISPIECE:
"View of the Basilica Ulpia in
Trajan's Forum" by Gilbert Gorski,
commissioned by archaeologist
James Packer, Northwestern
University. Colored pencil, 1988.

BACK COVER:
"Gate and Temple in Ruins"
Woodcut from the
*HYPNEROTOMACHIA POLIPHILI* by
Francesco Colonna, Venice, 1499.

## THE INSTITUTE FOR THE STUDY OF CLASSICAL ARCHITECTURE

### *"Fabrica et Ratiocinatio"*

For the building professional, the elements and ideas that define the classical system of architecture have long been acknowledged as a cornerstone of our cultural inheritance. Yet almost without exception institutions today fail to make available the kind of educational programs in traditional building which address the interests of the practitioner. Such instruction includes the opportunity to learn from the standpoint of the designer or builder the manual techniques, formal repertory, and theoretical and literary premises that constitute the classical tradition.

The Institute for the Study of Classical Architecture has been established to repair this educational shortcoming by providing current and future professionals with the chance to receive advanced training in classical building, in both its technical and artistic dimensions. Its programs have been formulated on the philosophy that a familiarity with traditional form is an objective which transcends stylistic debate, and that modern practitioners can only enhance the quality of their own work—*regardless of the idiom in which it is expressed*—for having learned about architecture through the classical perspective. We are therefore not a historical society, but an organization which aims to stem the erosion of cultural memory by presenting the achievements of the past as a resource for confronting architectural issues and tasks in the present.

### INSTITUTE ACTIVITIES

•**THE CLASSICIST:** An annual journal of artistic and architectural classicism.

•**The Summer Program in Classical Architecture:** A six-week intensive course of study in all aspects of classical design, held yearly in New York City.

•**Academic Year Courses:** Classes on *The Elements of Classical Architecture, Classical Architecture for Interior Design Professionals, Proportion,* and *Traditional Wash Rendering.* Courses are open to professionals and students.

•**Educational Seminars:** An annual two-day seminar and workshop on topics of professional interest, co-sponsored by *Traditional Building Magazine.* The 1995 seminar examines *The Ornament of Classical Architecture.*

•**Institute Series of Fine Books:** Reissued and new works on artistic classicism.

•**The Institute Salon:** An ongoing public lecture series at the Institute. Past guest speakers have included architects John Blatteau, Allan Greenberg, and Mark Hewitt; educators Carroll William Westfall, Tod Marder, and Jeffrey L. Cohen; Adele Chatfield-Taylor, James Howard Kunstler, and Deborah Nevins.

FURTHER INQUIRIES ARE WELCOME AT:

### THE INSTITUTE FOR THE STUDY OF CLASSICAL ARCHITECTURE

111 FRANKLIN STREET NEW YORK NY 10013
212.570.7374 (TELEPHONE) 212.627.5740 (FACSIMILE)

## TYPEFACES

TRAJAN (logo, cover text, and department heads) is based on the inscription carved on the pedestal of Trajan's column in Rome, 113 A.D.

BAUER BODONI (headlines) is derived from the designs of Giambattista Bodoni (1740–1813). This interpretation was cut in 1924 by Louis Hoell.

BEMBO (text face) is a twentieth century revival of a typeface cut by Francesco Griffo (c.1450–1518) at the Venetian printing house of Aldus Manutius.

*CASLON 540 ITALIC* (captions, author biographies) is inspired by the work of the English engraver and typefounder William Caslon (1692–1766).

DISTRIBUTED BY:
TRANSACTION PUBLISHERS
Rutgers–The State University of New Jersey, New Brunswick, NJ, 08903. Address all orders and business correspondence (including requests for reprint permission) to Transaction Publishers. Advertising information is available from the Advertising Director at 908.932.2280.

transaction

PRINTED BY:
THE STINEHOUR PRESS
Lunenburg, VT 05906-0159

© 1995
INSTITUTE FOR THE STUDY OF CLASSICAL ARCHITECTURE
All rights reserved.
ISBN 1-56000-850-4
ISSN 1076-2922

# NUMBER TWO: 1995-96
# CONTENTS

# LOGARCHAEOMACHIA POLYFOLLY

## (IN THREE PARTS)

**P**rologue » Historic:  *He was now alone in Rome, as Donatello had gone back to Florence, and even more intently and energetically than before he carried on studying the old ruins. There was no kind of building of which he did not make drawings: round, square and octagonal temples, basilicas, aqueducts, baths, arches, colosseums, amphitheaters, and all the brick temples, from which he noted the methods used in binding and clamping with ties and encircling the vaults. He recorded all the methods used for binding stones together and for balancing and dovetailing them; and he investigated the reason for there being a hole hollowed out in the center and underside of all the large stones, discovering that it was for the iron used to haul them up, which we call the ulivella. He subsequently brought this into use again and employed it himself. Then he distinguished the several orders, namely, Doric, Ionic, and Corinthian; and his studies were so thorough and intelligent that in his mind's eye he could see Rome as it had stood before it fell into ruins.*
– Giorgio Vasari, "The Life of Filippo Brunelleschi," in LIVES OF THE ARTISTS

**D**ialogue » Satiric:  Architecture and her old companion Archaeology were walking down a street in Pompeii one hot summer day not long ago. The dust had risen from the street and they were in an irritable mood, as old friends often are, having grown accustomed to and suspicious of one another through long acquaintance.

Archaeology, squinting through the heat and swirling dust at the scene of the destroyed street before them, stooped to examine a tiny fragment of paving at his feet. "You know," he said with evident pleasure, "the volcano has given us a unique opportunity in destroying this city. It has provided us with a large and complex puzzle, an enormous jigsaw with an infinite number of pieces—and to our unending delight, no evident solution. What could be more wonderful?"

Architecture, accustomed to her companion's pedantic ways, snorted loudly down her long nose in reply. Coming to a halt beside her friend, she cast a sweeping gaze over the entire scene of devastation before them. "What I see here is unparalleled opportunity," she declared. "Look at this magnificent site caught between the volcano and the sea. What is needed is a fleet of bulldozers, an army of workmen, some visionary developers. We must raze these dreary remains, fill in this useless ruin and build! Towers of glass and steel will glitter here in the mediterranean sun, condominiums and shopping malls, supermarkets and service stations, superhighways and pleasure parks will grow where now there is only dust and ruin. What splendid and brave opportunities for design are unleashed by this magnificent volcano's work!"

Archaeology, shook his head in horror and stood up from his examination of the paving fragment. "Architecture—it is ever thus with you now! Always this wanton disregard of study, of the

minute and rewarding examination of the past in favor of your garish novelties. Have you forgotten the days of our early friendship when we were constant companions, when we uncovered the splendors of antiquity and admired them together? I remind you of the words of that great English architect and scientist Wren—you do remember him, he was once one of your favorite sons— 'Architecture is now rather the study of antiquity than fancy.' You would destroy the work of decades with your fantasies. Each stone, each fragment, each molecule of this site must be located, measured, documented, and recorded with exacting precision, and then. . . ."

"And then what?" interrupted Architecture, impatient as ever. "Some pathetic diagram more like a medical chart or scientific diagram than a drawing or reconstruction, and some conclusions so circumspect as not to be worthy of the name!"

"Reckless dreamer! You are an ill-educated, unscholarly egotist and futurist!"

"I am an artist, you pathetic and dusty old fool—and you are nothing but an accountant of history. We have nothing left to say to one another!" With this pronouncement Architecture turned on her heel and headed for the parking lot. Archaeology, after pausing to replace his notebook with its carefully recorded data in his pocket, muttered "Hothead!" to himself and, hands clasped behind his back, walked deeper into the ruins of the ancient city.

**E**pilogue » **Analytic:** Do architects and archaeologists have anything to say to one another any more? Is there any longer any fruitful common ground for the two fields? Should architects be interested in the work of archaeologists—and vice versa?

For Donatello and Brunelleschi, the pursuit of archaeological and antiquarian knowledge had both a scientific and artistic purpose, and it was based on two premises. The first was their recognition that the work of the ancient Romans was in many ways superior to their own, and that they had much to learn technically and compositionally from studying the surviving fragments. The second and corollary premise was that the artistic achievement of Rome represented a challenge, again both artistic and technical, and a constant source of novelty and inspiration. Meeting and even surpassing the challenge of ancient Rome became the artistic project of the next three centuries.

In the eighteenth century, however, this approach—combining scholarship and inspiration—was increasingly replaced by a technical approach to the study of the remains, and pedantry in the artistic use to which the material was put. The Greek versus Roman controversy of the century attests to the increasingly divergent purposes of the two fields. And yet, the following century witnessed the career of perhaps the most distinguished practitioner to combine activities in both subjects, the English archaeologist and architect C.R. Cockerell. His precocious discoveries (made during his early twenties)

of the curvature of the columns of the Parthenon, the Aegina and Bassae marbles, and his restoration of the Temple of Zeus at Agrigento, are recognized as some of the most important archaeological work of the century. His subsequent career as the preeminent English architect and educator of his generation demonstrated the fertile ground in the combination of these two disciplines. Interestingly, it was Cockerell who argued *against* the pedantic use of archaeological material, recognizing in this pedantry the danger to architectural creativity of "archaeological correctness."

The beginning of this century had its moments of fruitful and rewarding collaboration. Thus the American archaeologist Gorham Stevens, who was investigating the masonry techniques at the Acropolis, provided casts of stone joints to Charles Follen McKim. McKim used them to achieve the precise joinery of the walls of the J. Pierpont Morgan Library in New York, which contributes so much to its monumental quality. The following decades also left us the last of the compelling archaeological reconstructions in the work at Colonial Williamsburg and the Stoa of Attalos in Athens.

With the full advent of the International Style in architecture, any direct interest which architects had in the investigations of archaeologists ended. The topic was relegated to history classes in schools of architecture. Archaeologists at the same time seem increasingly to have pursued the technical at the expense of the artistic. Thus, most archaeological drawings are at best fragmentary ciphers, which are more concerned with the accurate depiction of

broken remains than with the risk of attempting to produce conjectural restorations.

Yet, there is good reason for optimism. The revival of interest in the classical means a renewed interest in the researches of archaeologists by practicing architects. And while many archaeologists still continue to view architects with suspicion and skepticism, some may come to value the point of view which holds the work of preceding generations in high regard as a direct source of inspiration and artistic production.

Thus we can only hope that the sensational discovery, fifteen years ago, of drawings by architects working in the Hellenistic period, will prove of compelling interest to contemporary architects for what it has to tell us about ancient working methods—and perhaps informing our own approach to building. Equally we can hope that the compositional skill architects bring to archeological work might be valued once again, and we can struggle to see the ancient world in our mind's eye as Brunelleschi did. ❧

---

*The title of "The Classicist at Large" translates roughly as: "The Many Follies of an Ancient Debate (in Words)."*

*Opening quotation from the Penguin Edition of Giorgio Vasari's* LIVES OF THE ARTISTS, *translated by George Bull.*

*Figure: "Reconstruction of Large Theater in Pompeii" by Charles Robert Cockerell, 1824. Courtesy of the British Architectectural Library, RIBA.*

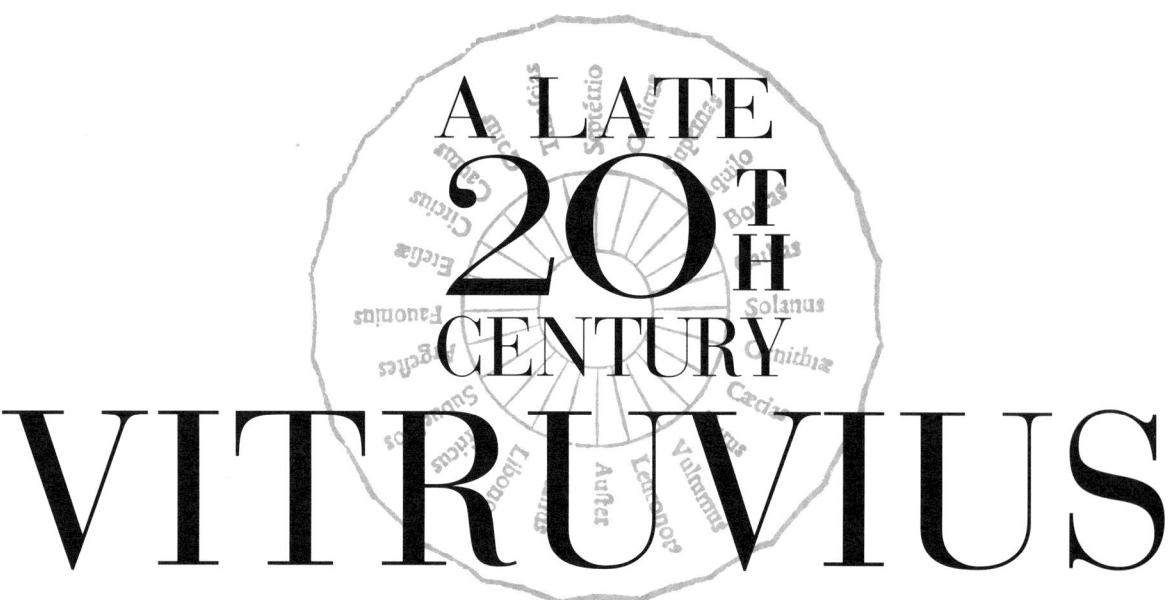

# A LATE 20TH CENTURY VITRUVIUS

## BY INGRID D. ROWLAND

Sometime between 30 and 20 B.C., at the very dawn of the Roman Empire, an elderly architect named Vitruvius Pollio offered ten papyrus scrolls of his writings on architecture to the man he called Imperator Caesar, and whom we call Augustus. Those ten scrolls, or "books," have been steadily read ever since, in different media, in different languages, and for many different reasons. There are two obvious reasons to reread Vitruvius at the end of the twentieth century. Recent developments in archaeology give his latter-day readers a substantially altered idea of what he might have been talking about and, in the aftermath of the modern movement, architects still look to him as the wellspring for design in the classical style.

Producing a modern translation of Vitruvius' work requires a bewildering array of specialized skills; not surprisingly, the forthcoming Cambridge University Press translation is a collaborative effort. My partner in this is Thomas Howe of Southwestern University, an architecturally trained field archaeologist whose research interests also include the history of architectural theory and of ancient technology, and who also has a good grasp of Latin. My own training includes a Ph.D. in classical Greek and classical archaeology as well as long experience with the study of manuscripts and a research speciality in the Italian Renaissance.

In approaching the work of Virtruvius, the initial task facing any editor, translator, illustrator, or commentator—and we aim to be all of these—is to determine what Vitruvius himself might have written. The 2,000-year-old text, originally set down in capital letters, without divisions between the words, on ten papyrus scrolls (the "books" of the traditional title *Ten Books on Architecture*), was composed in Latin but included a good deal of Greek, a language in which both Vitruvius and his ancient Roman readers were expected to be fluent. These Greek insertions range in length from individual technical terms to a phrase quoted from a play, now lost, by the ancient Greek dramatist Euripides (the *Phaethon*) and three complete poems about water.

This text has survived to the present day in somewhere between eighty and ninety separate manuscripts, no two of them presenting quite the same thing—mistakes happen, and although most of the differences between manuscripts are slight, some of them are not. The earliest preserved manuscript, MS Harleianus 2767, of the British Library in London, may have been drafted on parchment for Charlemagne in the eighth century. The latest versions were produced in the mid-sixteenth century, a good hundred years after Gutenberg's invention of movable type. (Our own handwritten Constitution shows the continued vitality of the manuscript in subsequent centuries.)

The scribes who copied the *Ten Books on Architecture* must have been a varied lot; certainly they came from widely disparate times and places. (Although female scribes were active throughout the Middle Ages and Renaissance, none to my knowledge can be specifically connected with Vitruvius and his manly arts of building and warfare. I have discovered that a number of contemporary scholars and architects remain skeptical of a woman's fitness to address such subjects!) Charlemagne's scribe was likely to have been a monk, perhaps Frankish; he was learned in Latin but ignorant of Greek, and so deeply Christian that he included a line drawing of a benevolent Jesus, hand raised in benediction, in one of the manuscript's margins. Two Italian paper manuscripts from the first quarter of the sixteenth century are the result of a three-way collaboration among the artist Raphael and two well-known scholars of Renaissance Rome; the impoverished old eccentric Marco Fabio Calvo and the wealthy socialite Angelo Colocci. Raphael knew only Italian, but Calvo knew Latin and Greek superbly well. Colocci certainly knew Latin and had a good reading knowledge of Vitruvius'

---

*"...To be educated, he must...*

second language. The manuscripts themselves, now preserved in the Bavarian State Library in Munich (MSS It. 37 and It. 37a), are virtually all that remain of the collaborators' hopes to produce the sixteenth century equivalent of our pending Cambridge edition—an illustrated, annotated translation into a modern language. Unfortunately, Raphael contracted a virulent fever in 1520 and died amid a spate of unfinished projects at the age of thirty-seven. On a less scholarly plane, but one of comparable aesthetic interest, a half-finished volume written on parchment in gold leaf and a blue of powdered lapis lazuli was intended to adorn a late fifteenth century Italian nobleman's table, but was likewise left unfinished.

Since at least the fifteenth century, classical scholars have made it their professional business to compare various manuscripts of Vitruvius in order to pick out the most plausible versions of the text, poring over it word by word, line by line, book by book. In 2,000 years of copying and recopying by people of widely varying backgrounds, competency, health, and degrees of interest, a whole range of errors have crept in. The Greek in the eighth century Harleianus manuscript looks somewhat like tortured Russian. Charlemagne's scribe clearly did not know the language and it is probable that the scribe who produced the long-lost manuscript from which he made his copy did not know Greek either. As the Greek technical terms became more and more obscure, scholars' and scribes' attempts to understand them became more and more imaginative. At the very least, terms may be mistranscribed and the rest of the sentence altered to "improve" its sense. Sometimes an explanatory definition, a gloss, might be inserted in the margin of the text or above the problematic word itself, and often these glosses have crept in to substitute for what Vitruvius himself had written. As a rule, manuscript scholars expect the oldest manuscripts to exhibit fewer errors, but even the venerable Harleianus, much of the time, no longer makes sense.

Not only can Greek pose a problem for copyists, but so can badly written Latin, or Latin written in a calligraphic style that is no longer current. Furthermore, no copyist is perfect, no matter their degree of interest or their level of education; my own transcriptions from manuscripts prove this time and again, as do those of my far more learned predecessor, the aforementioned Angelo Colocci. Letters

drop out by perverse magic, or reverse with a snap bout of dyslexia. If a transcriber has copied a phrase ending in a certain word, and that word appears again shortly afterward in the text, the eye may light on the second instance of the word, not the first, and suddenly a whole chunk of writing will be left out of the transcription.

Editors confront these problems by collation, the comparison of manuscript texts with others, and then by a process of educated guesswork in which mechanical errors are corrected, glosses relegated back to the margins, and the effect of more complicated transformations reversed—at least, so the editor hopes. When an editor believes that the ancient author may have used a word or phrase that no longer appears in any extant manuscript text, that conjectural substitution is called an emendation.

Emendation of Vitruvius, however, extends to image as well as text. The author of the *Ten Books* supplied his work with eleven illustrations at points where he felt incapable of explaining himself adequately in words. All but one of these illustrations seem to have been placed at the end of the individual papyrus scroll to which they were relevant, and all were long gone by the time the scribe of Harleianus 2767 put his own pen to parchment. Fortunately, there are other ancient texts on technological matters whose illustrations have been preserved, and Angelo Colocci, Raphael's collaborator, was one of the world's great collectors of such manuscripts.

Two kinds of ancient technical writings are of particular use for understanding Vitruvius. In Latin, there is a collection of treatises written by Roman surveyors known collectively as the *Corpus Agrimensorum*, its earliest components dating from about a century and a half after Vitruvius (the age of the Emperor Hadrian) and the latest from perhaps the third century A.D. Angelo Colocci once owned what is now the earliest known manuscript, which then passed through the hands of Erasmus of Rotterdam to arrive by a circuitous route in the Duke Augustus Library (Herzog August Bibliothek) at Wolffenbüttel in northern Germany.

Greek technological writers furnished the ancient world with information about a surprising array of machines, from steam-powered organs to catapults. Important manuscripts are preserved in Paris and in the Vatican Library, these last, again, legacies from the ubiquitous Angelo Colocci. The ancient diagrams pre-

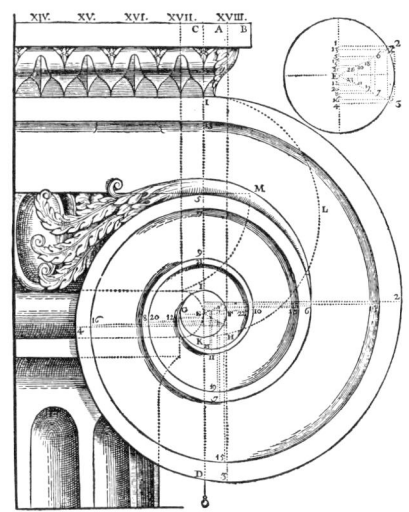

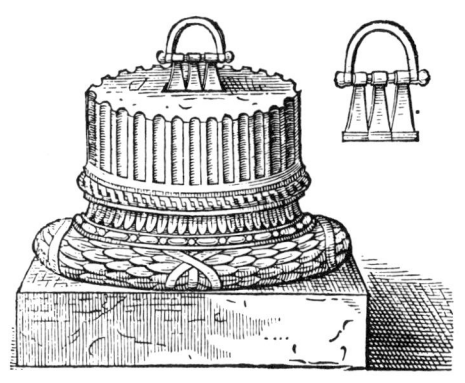

*...be an experienced draftsman...*

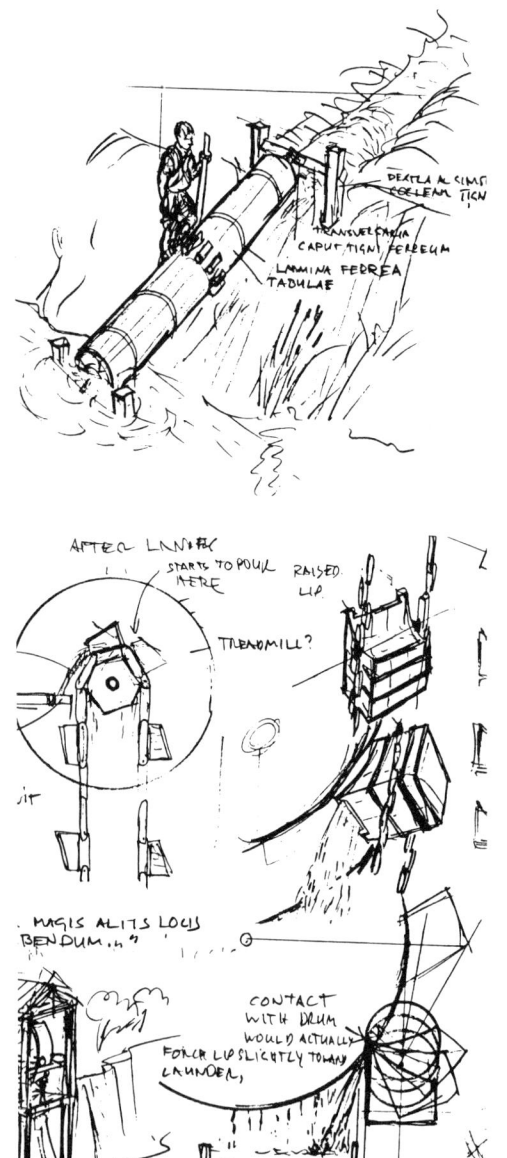

served along with these Greek and Latin works provide crucial evidence for what the drawings in Vitruvius might have looked like as well as clear graphic expression of his sometimes prolix verbal descriptions.

The text of Vitruvius was first committed to print in Renaissance Rome, in 1486, by an Italian grammarian named Giovanni Sulpizio da Veroli. For scholarly purposes he Latinized his name as Iohannes Sulpicius, and as Sulpicius he is usually known today. (Classicists now call such a first edition an *editio princeps* by a similar process of Latinization.) Sulpicius dedicated the book to a powerful cardinal, Raffaele Riario, whose own interest in architecture, ancient and modern, can be gauged by the monumental Roman palazzo he had commissioned in these same years, its facade a free interpretation of the Colosseum and built to a great extent with blocks looted from the site of that quintessentially Roman building.

The Vitruvius of Iohannes Sulpicius lacked two important features of the original Vitruvian *Ten Books*; its Greek passages and its illustrations. It hewed close to the manuscript texts that Sulpicius had at his disposal and probably was of interest only to litterati; people who, like Raffaele Riario, were thoroughly versed in Latin.

A far bolder and more ambitious Vitruvius emerged from the Venetian press of Giovanni Tridino in 1511. This version was dedicated to Cardinal Riario's cousin and onetime rival Pope Julius II. Illustrated with an extensive series of woodcuts, copiously emended and with Greek text firmly in place, it was produced by one of those proverbially versatile Renaissance men, the Veronese monk Fra Giovanni Giocondo, architect, scholar of Greek and Latin, and influential teacher.

Angelo Colocci's copy of the Fra Giocondo Vitruvius, with some of Colocci's own conjectures for emendation and a plethora of glosses, still remains in the Vatican Library. Using a set of coded symbols, Raphael's friend also collated the Giocondo text with two other Vitruvius manuscripts in his possession, one "very old indeed."

Our own Vitruvian text begins from a mid-nineteenth century German edition by Valentin Rose, published in Leipzig in 1867. Besides its judicious balance between loyalty to the manuscript text and informed conjecture, Rose's edition presents an important feature at the bottom of every page, the *apparatus criticus*, or critical apparatus, a line-by-line list of variant readings presented by other manuscripts of Vitruvius. This apparatus greatly eases our own work of collation and remains among the most copious ever compiled and is by far the easiest to use in quick consultation.

To an impressive extent Rose retains emendations first suggested by Fra Giocondo in 1511; we ourselves consult Giocondo in two versions—a photocopy of Angelo Colocci's copy of the 1511 edition, with all its scrawled marginalia, and a 1522 Florentine reprint like the one Valentin Rose used to create his Leipzig edition. We also keep several other Vitruvius editions on hand, from the sixteenth century translation of Daniele Barbaro to the up-to-the-minute ten volume *Belles-Lettres* edition of the Association Guillaume Budé, annotated and translated into French. (Appropriately enough, Budé, an early sixteenth century secretary to the king of France, was once a student of Fra Giocondo.)

We have rewritten the translation several times. Its penultimate version was composed in Rome in the summer of 1994, under circumstances similar to those of Renaissance publishing—"while you wait." I would draft a page of English translation, hand it to my colleague, who would try to draw what he read, all the while comparing my English with the Latin of Vitruvius. When we were confronted with problematic passages, we first tried to retranslate them with the help of our secondary literature and other editions. If that failed to make sense of them, we searched Rose's *apparatus criticus* for a more plausible reading and finally, as a last resort, we emended the Latin text. Like all our predecessors, we have emended, boldly going where none have gone before—except, we would like to believe, Vitruvius himself. We have inserted a new word, *collaxaria*, in a much disputed passage about safety valves in water pipes. We have traced a conjectural genealogy of scribal misconceptions and isolated a new meaning for the verb *calcare*—not only "to stomp," but, "to fill with quicklime." The great poets and orators of ancient Rome are of little help in penetrating the nitty-gritty of the Roman builder's world.

On a larger scale, we are also looking at the way in which Vitruvius defines his discipline. He offers a bracing perspective on the social relationships that generate architecture today, beginning with the most basic vocabulary surrounding the architectural act. Vitruvius

*...well-versed in geometry...*

worked in a world where the word 'client' meant an impoverished socialite who survived on the food and favors he begged from the wealthy families to whom he paid daily court—his patrons. The behavior of the new breed of architects in Vitruvius' day had come to resemble that of these clients, people for whom *ambitio*, literally, "making the rounds," had become a way of life:

*[If] our perceptions and opinions, and our knowledge of the various disciplines, were plain to see and thoroughly comprehensible, then influence and the currying of favor would be worth nothing. Instead, all commissions would be assigned voluntarily to the artist who had obtained the greatest knowledge in a field by true, reliable work. But because these things are not as clear and as self-evident as we think they ought to be, and I observe that the ignorant outdo the learned in charm, I have decided not to contend with them in making the rounds canvassing favor, but rather, by publishing these remarks, to display the excellence of our profession.* (III.PREF.3)

Vitruvius, in other words, decided to go about his profession in a new way by appealing to wealthy Romans' taste for edifying literature and producing the first comprehensive account of his profession. His contemporaries seem to have devoured texts that might look hopelessly unmarketable today—book-length works about astronomy (Manilius), atomic theory (Lucretius), and agriculture (Virgil), linguistic disquisitions (Varro), rhetorical handbooks, and introductions to philosophy (Cicero). What Vitruvius promised the earnest readers of such works as these was a comprehensive presentation of architecture as a worthy companion to the liberal arts. Appreciating good architecture, he would endeavor to show, played an important role in good citizenship.

Architecture as we define it takes up only about half of Vitruvius' treatise; the rest is concerned with presenting a series of applied principles that bring hydraulics, astronomy, and mechanics within the architect's sphere of competence. Still more significantly, the ancient author endeavored to present architecture as an organized body of knowledge that deserved full inclusion in a curriculum of liberal education:

*Architects who strove to obtain practical manual skills but lacked an education have never been able to achieve an influence equal to the quality of their exer-*

*tions; on the other hand, those who placed their trust entirely in theory and in writings seem to have chased after a shadow, not something real. But those who have fully mastered both skills, armed, if you will, in full panoply, those architects have reached their goal more quickly and influentially.*

*…Whoever puts himself forward as an architect…ought to have a native talent, and be amenable to learning the disciplines [of the profession]. For neither native talent without learning nor learning without native talent create the master craftsman. To be educated, he must be an experienced draftsman, well-versed in geometry, familiar with history, a diligent student of philosophy, know music, have some acquaintance with medicine, understand the rulings of legal experts, and have a clear grasp of astronomy and the ways of Heaven.* (I.I.2-3)

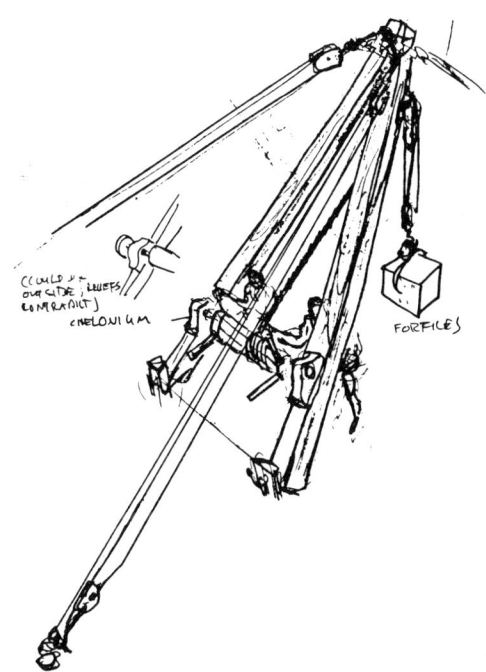

By integrating these various kinds of knowledge, Vitruvius' ideal architect made an essential contribution to society, creating cities, temples, public buildings, houses, hydraulic systems, clocks, and appliances that were both functional and attractive. Himself once engaged to make catapults for Julius Caesar, Vitruvius crowned his treatise at the end of the tenth book with heroic examples of quick-thinking architects who saved their cities from attack:

*These victories by besieged cities were not achieved by machines; instead, they were liberated by the cleverness of architects pitted against every kind of mechanical device.* (X.XVI.12)

Vitruvius' long excursion into mechanics was more than a personal footnote. After a set of introductory remarks about the liberal arts and architecture's rightful place among them, he frames his whole work between instructions for the foundation of cities (in Book I) and these final strategies for their defense; in effect, he sets all the rest of architecture, even the secrets of astronomy, exclusively within an urban context, and more particularly within the context of that unique combination of city and empire, the *Urbs Roma*.

Vitruvius wholeheartedly believed, with Aristotle, that human beings were meant to be city dwellers and that shared knowledge had been integral to that civic destiny from the beginning:

*Because…nature had not only equipped people with senses like all the other animals, but had also*

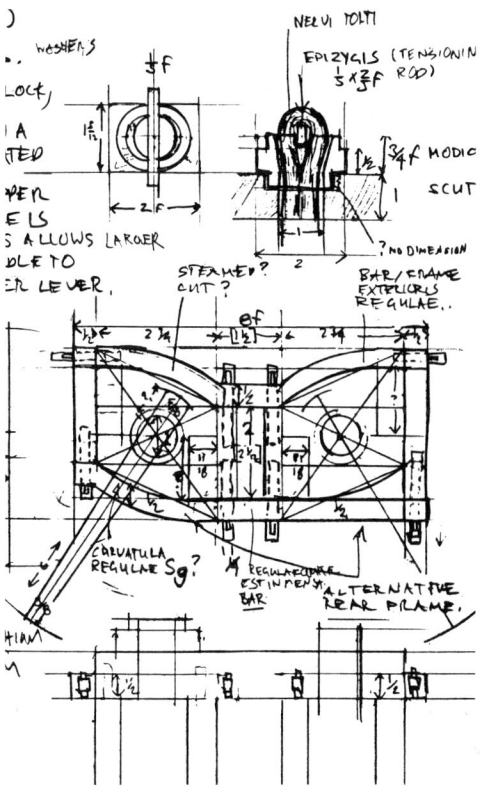

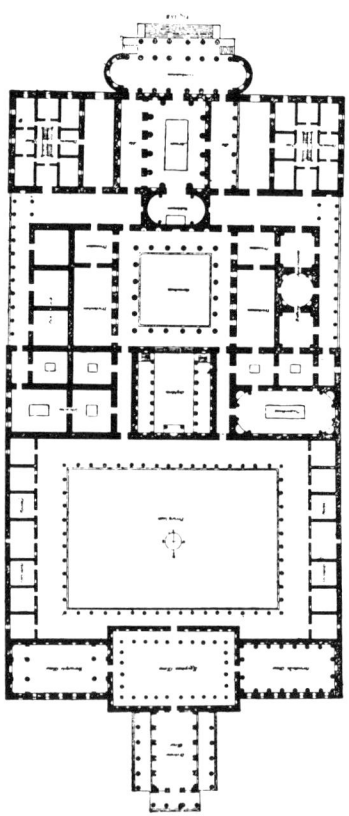

*armed their minds with ideas and plans and subjected all other creatures to their power, so from the making of buildings they progressed, step by step, to the other arts and disciplines, and thus they led themselves out of a rough and brutish life into gentle humanity.* (II.I.6)

Liberal education equipped people to face the increased complexity of society in the age of Augustus; Vitruvius hoped that his own treatise would serve his fellow Romans as one part of that equipment. He makes the case for the cosmopolitan practicality of liberal education in his famous tale about traces on the Rhodian shore:

*When Aristippus, a Socratic philosopher, had been washed up on the shore of Rhodes after a shipwreck, and noticed that geometric diagrams had been drawn there, he is said to have exclaimed to his comrades: "Let us hope for the best; I see human footprints!" and to have headed forthwith for the city of Rhodes. He came straight upon the gymnasium and after discussing philosophy there was rewarded with gifts sufficient not only to outfit himself, but also to allow him to provide clothing and the other necessities of life to those who were with him. When later his companions wanted to return home, they asked him what messages he would like to have relayed back. This is what he ordered them to report: children should be furnished with the sort of possessions and travel-money that can even survive a shipwreck in one piece.*

*For the real safeguards of life are those that neither the cruel storm of fortune nor political change nor the ravages of war can harm. In support of the same argument, Theophrastus put it this way, when he urged that people be well-educated rather than relying on money: an educated person is the only one who is never a stranger in a foreign land, nor at a loss for friends even when bereft of household and intimates. Rather, he is a citizen in every country, and may look down without fear upon the difficult turns of fortune. He, however, who thinks that he is fortified by the defenses of good fortune rather than learning will find himself a wanderer on shifting pathways, beleaguered by a life that is never stable, but always wavering.* (VI.PREF.1–2)

Humanity's need for a common store of shared knowledge has become still more acute in the 2,000 years since Vitruvius wrote; the geographic scope, social complexity, and sheer size of the present-day human population make the Roman writer's encyclopedic vision of a common education increasingly difficult to maintain, but increasingly important to our truly global society. Writing for an early version of the global village, Vitruvius well understood the dangers that fragmentation posed to such complex social organizations; he himself had lived through the terrors of civil war that preceded the Augustan *Pax Romana*. He also understood firsthand the importance of widespread education to the creation, and the continual unification, of the Roman world. Where Roman legions had marched, Roman schools followed, and, like the army, the educational system of ancient Rome allowed talented youth from every part of the Empire the opportunity to participate in what seemed to be the construction of civilization itself.

Part of this new construction involved appropriating the wisdom of the past and the wisdom of other cultures. Vitruvius makes specific remarks about his own relationship with his previous sources, both Greek and Roman:

*But I, Caesar, have neither substituted my name on a text while altering the indications that it is another person's property, nor have I sought approval for myself by slandering another's work; instead I offer infinite thanks to all those writers who, with outstanding wisdom and talent, have prepared abundant riches drawn from the ages, each of a different type, so that we may adapt them to our own enterprise, as if we are drinking deeply from a fountain, and have easier and more efficient access to them for our own writing so that, trusting in such authors, we may dare to prepare new principles.* (VII.PREF.10)

At least to his own mind, then, Vitruvius has adapted his readings to an entirely new undertaking, one that conspicuously involves the formulation of new principles, *rationes novae*. Chief among such *rationes novae* he counts the very structure of his book, in which he takes especial pride:

*When I observed, Imperator, that many writers had left behind them precepts and volumes of commentaries on architecture that were not in proper order but undertaken instead as if they were stray parts of something incomplete, I thought it would be a worthy and most useful contribution, first to set out the whole of such an excellent discipline in a comprehensive order and then in each volume to explain the particular qualities of each type of subject.* (IV.PREF.1)

*...a diligent student of philosophy...*

In the search for *rationes novae*, then, *perfecta ordinatio,* what I have translated as "comprehensive order," is the principal key to success. In his usual manner, Vitruvius here uses the word *perfectus* to mean a job completed rather than perfection attained. The difference in nuance between completeness and perfection has escaped twentieth-century translators into English such as M.H. Morgan and Frank Granger, leading to a general misconception among contemporary architects that the *Ten Books on Architecture* are a prescriptive tract for perfect buildings. Nothing, I hope to suggest, could be farther from what the text actually says.

Instead, Vitruvius, by his own estimation, differs from his Greek and Roman predecessors first, by having submitted his treatise to a comprehensive order; and second, by having treated each subject completely according to its type—to what he calls its *genus*. In effect, he has extended the literary convention of generic composition to a variety of other realms, not all of them realms that we would call artistic. This is a large creative step, and one pursued so effectively that it has frequently gone unnoticed by his critics, beginning in 1450 with Leon Battista Alberti.

Ironically, it is precisely these original qualities of structural completeness and generic clarity that seem to have induced some readers of the *Ten Books on Architecture* to discount the text as hopelessly anachronistic, to view it as a derivative account of Hellenistic stone masonry penned in the midst of the Romans' concrete revolution, with incongruous excursions into catapults, water clocks, plumbing, and sundials. Yet these anachronisms form an integral part of that comprehensive and innovative literary structure in which Vitruvius takes such conspicuous pride; they are key elements in his distinctively Roman sensibility. Indeed, the same compositional practices of structure and anachronism can be discerned in contemporary art.

For both ancient Greece and ancient Rome, the theory of artistic composition derived from the theory of rhetoric. Classical rhetoric employed an analytical vocabulary wherein the two predominant themes were those of genre and placement. This interplay of genre and placement is what I will mean when I refer to generic composition.

Genre, Greek *genos,* and Latin *genus,* must have been one of the catchwords in first century Rome; Cicero's *De Oratore* singles out the

invention of *genus* as the first step in human progress out of primal chaos. Greek *genos* meant "family," and among the Greeks the first genres were categorized as if they were distinctive expressions of the various Hellenic dialect groups or cities: Doric and Ionic architecture, Attic tragedy, the Lydian musical mode (all termed *genê* in Greek).

The word's broad range of applications by Vitruvius' time can no longer be conveyed in English; for this author, *genus* may denote a level of oratory (what we call the high, middle and low styles), a literary genre (tragedy, epic, love elegy), a musical mode (Lydian, Phrygian), or a column type (Doric, Ionic, Corinthian). It is *genus* that governed the sequence of decisions by which an argument, a temple, or an ode were designed, a process that both Greek and Roman theorists envisioned as placement, Greek *taxis* and Latin *dispositio,* whether that placement involved sections of an argument, syllables, notes, or marble blocks.

Roman artistic theory adopted Greek principles of generic composition along with the Greek genres, but always did so for Roman purposes. Thus the principles of Greek design might govern the ornamental details of a Roman temple, but they did not interfere with the temple's essential cult features of podium and deep porch. Even so Hellenistic a complex as the Forum Augustum is inalienably Roman in its layout, tightly coordinated where a Hellenistic architect would have let it sprawl.

So, too, Tibullus might adopt a Homeric caesura in his hexameter lines, but he did so in Latin and to write about the Roman Campagna. Roman art and education excerpted the Greeks, rather than imitating them wholesale. Hence the Romans developed a refined sense of the way in which the boundaries of Greek generic composition could be extended. This was accomplished first by their transferal into another culture, then by the juxtaposition of one *genus* with another. Verbal citations are examples of this—as are the visual "citations," such as the fourth century Greek painting and Egyptian sculpture contained within Roman wall paintings, or the application of trabeated architecture to the surface of arcuated construction, (as in the engaged orders of the Theater of Marcellus).

The Augustan building now known as the Farnesina House, for example, presents a series of artistic anachronisms as striking in their own

way as Vitruvius' description of Hellenistic Ionic temples amid instructions for pouring Roman concrete and laying in Roman lead pipe. A room decorated on a theme of cinnabar red displays a series of square white panels with white-ground vignettes painted in a style that differs markedly from that of the rest of the house. Comparisons with extant Greek paintings suggest that the white-ground panels in the Farnesina House are meant to imitate the work of Greek "old masters." Yet at the same time, these small *pinakes* are set within a comprehensive design in which the sophisticated modeling of columns and figures and the manipulation of perspective unequivocally declare the room's origins to be in the artistic sensibility of late first century Rome. Like his contemporary Vitruvius, the artist has deliberately adopted the conventions of Hellenistic Greece at the moment when Augustan Rome was undergoing its transformation from a city of brick to a city of marble. It is the same transformation of Augustan Rome, of course, that lies at the heart of the Vitruvian text itself:

*For I perceived that you [the emperor] had already built extensively, were building now and would be doing so in the future: public as well as private constructions, all scaled to the amplitude of your own achievements, so that these would be handed down to future generations. I have set down these instructions, complete with technical terms, so that by observing them you could teach yourself how to evaluate the works already brought into being and those yet to be. For in these pages I have laid out every set of principles for the discipline.* (I.PREF.3)

The last words in this passage, *omnes aperui rationes*, once again emphasize that the subjects Vitruvius chooses to discuss in his treatise are meant to be seen as components of a comprehensive rational system, and that their chief illustrative value stems from their placement within that system as a whole, not from particular specifications. That transformation, like the contemporary developments in art and literature, was guided, but not quite governed, by Greek generic principles. The technical terms set out in Vitruvius' Books I and III provide a good example of the kinds of Greek ideas on which Vitruvius built his treatise; they provide the building blocks, but not the overall design. The difference between Greek detail and Roman overview can be seen quite clearly from

the way in which Vitruvius approaches the generic composition of colonnades:

*In the third volume…I taught about the design of temples, and about the variety of their types, which species they have and how many, and what the distribution of the various components ought to be according to type. Of those three types whose proportions exhibit the most intricate modular systems, I taught the conventions of the Ionic. Now, in the present volume, I will speak about what have been set up as the Doric and Corinthian principles, and explain their distinctness and their special characteristics.* (IV.PREF.1)

Strikingly, all these descriptions focus on the temple in its elemental form, a colonnaded box, when actual temple construction in Italy had long included elaborate complexes like that of Fortuna at Praeneste. Vitruvius seems to make no explicit mention of engaged orders of columns, yet these, too, had been part of the Roman architectural vocabulary for generations. The reasons for this apparent omission are probably the following; in the first place, the principles of trabeated architecture did not shift their essential character when bent inwards or outwards—as at Praeneste or in a Roman wall-painting (like those in the House of Livia on the Palatine)—or upwards as in a serliana. Columns scarcely change their proportions when applied to a facade, or paired, or expanded into a giant order as in a fanciful scene from Oplontis or in Vitruvius' own Basilica at Fano. Both Vitruvius and his intended readers knew perfectly well that such things could be done with orders of columns, but that all these modifications were adventitious to the *rationes,* that is, the placement of elements and the relative proportions, of the columnar system itself. On the level of proportional *rationes,* there is no difference between the *eurythmia* of the functional columns in the Basilica at Fano and the ornamental columns of the Theater of Marcellus. Structural duty and ornamental duty make the same demands.

Furthermore, when the time came for actual designing, Vitruvius could be as bold as any of his contemporaries. His Basilica at Fano exhibits striking peculiarities, from its giant interior order, its unusual roof construction, and its orientation toward the temple of the Deified Caesar to its cheap materials. The description itself may seem dull, but a translation into images shows how innovative Vitruvius could be:

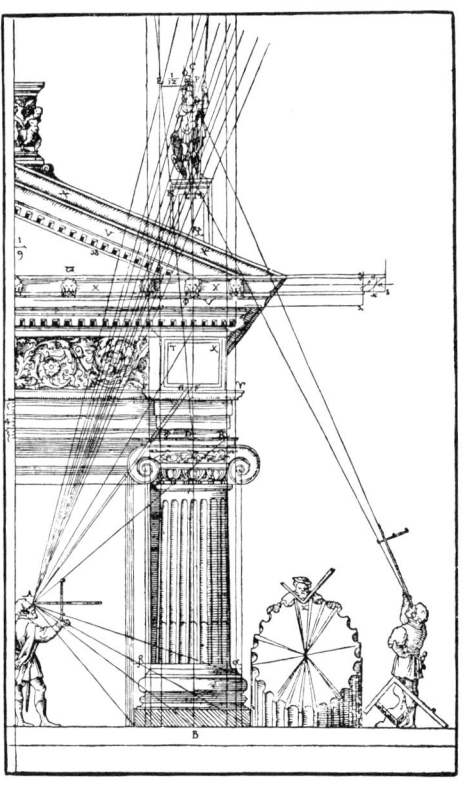

*...have some aquaintance with medicine...*

*The central hall, between the individual columns, is one hundred twenty feet long, and sixty feet wide. Its portico, which surrounds the central hall, is twenty feet wide between columns and walls. The columns are of a uniform height: fifty feet including their capitals, and five feet in diameter.[1] Behind them, they have pilasters twenty feet high,[2] two and one-half feet wide, and one and one-half feet thick. These hold up the beams onto which the upper floor structure of the porticoes is carried. Above these are a second set of pilasters of eighteen feet, two feet wide, one foot thick, and these, too, receive the supporting beams for the rafters and the ceilings of the porticoes[3] that are set underneath the main roof. The areas remaining between the beams spanning columns and pilasters, that is, the areas along the intercolumniations, are left for the windows. The columns along the breadth of the central hall, including the left and right corner columns, number four; along the length nearest the forum, still including the corner columns, eight; on the opposite side, including corner columns, six, because the two central columns along that side have not been set in place; they would block the view from the front pronaos of the shrine of Augustus, which has been placed at the center of the wall surface of the basilica facing the forum and the temple of Jupiter....*

*Above the columns, beams are set all round, made of three two-foot timbers fixed together, and these beams turn inward from the third column in on each side toward the antae that project from the pronaos of the shrine; these antae touch the hemicycle on right and left. Above the beams, in line with the capitals of the columns, posts three feet high have been placed as supports; these measure four feet on every side. Above these, sloping beams[4] made of two two-foot timbers have been set in place; above these, in turn, the tie-beams with their king-posts, placed in line with the bodies of the columns and the antae and the walls of the front portico, come to one ridge over the interior of the basilica, and to a second ridge above the center of the pronaos of the shrine.*

*Thus the double-ridged design created by placement of the roofline on the exterior and the top of the ceiling on the interior presents an elegant aspect. In addition, the removal of the ornamentation of the epistyles and the apportionment of attics and upper columns relieves us of labor and annoyance, and greatly reduces the sum total of the expenses. Indeed, the uninterrupted extension of the columns themselves to just under the beams of the vault seems to increase both the magnificence of the expenditure and the authority of the work. (V.I.6–10)*

One of the most peculiar features of this most peculiar building is the roof, where Vitruvius uses an enigmatic phrase, *trabes everganeae*, "sloping beams," whose interpretation requires the best efforts of Latin manuscript studies, archaeological experience, and architectural know-how. *Everganeae* is what classicists call a *hapax legomenon*, a "thing once spoken," that is, a word that appears only once in preserved ancient literature—in this case, in Vitruvius. Because most of the eighty-odd surviving Vitruvius manuscripts preserve the word *everganeae* despite its uniqueness, it is unlikely to be a mistaken transcription of something else. The rarity of the adjective stems from the fact that most ancient Roman authors—indeed, all but one— did not write about the nuts and bolts of roofing systems.

Where do the "sloping beams" go? The roof of the Pantheon porch provided a clue; its wooden beams and braces are still preserved from the second century A.D. A system of knee braces seemed to correspond both to the Vitruvian text and to the evidence from the Pantheon, but the resulting interior differs almost as significantly from ancient Greek architecture as the Pantheon differs from the Parthenon.

With the Basilica at Fano, Vitruvius characteristically assumes a great deal of tacit knowledge on the part of his readers, whom he assumes to be ancient Romans. Again, the fact that Vitruvius takes a great deal for granted need not imply that he resists new developments in architecture. He mentions the porticoes of the Theater of Pompey, but not the theater itself because he can generate theater design from any number of examples but can find lavish public gardens with porticoes attached to theaters only in Rome itself. He feels no need to specify that the Basilica at Fano had walls and windows because basilicas invariably did, a fact that was lost on that literal reader Palladio when he went about his own reconstruction of the Vitruvian basilica. *Caveat lector* (let the reader beware).

Furthermore, as sacred architecture, temples represented especially vivid examples to set before the busy *patres familiarum* at whom Vitruvius aimed his treatise:

*When [the ancients] were handing down proportional sequences[5] for every type of work, they did so especially for the sacred dwellings of the gods, as*

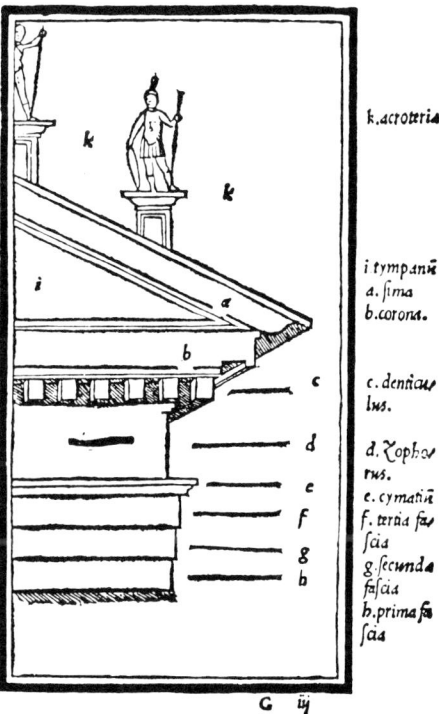

k. *acroteria*

i *tympanū*
a. *sima*
b. *corona.*

c. *denticu-
lus.*

d. *zopho-
rus.*

e. *cymatiū*
f. *tertia fa-
scia*
g. *secunda
fascia*
h. *prima fa-
scia*

G ij

*the successes and failures of those works tend to remain forever.* (III.I.4)

All the Vitruvian examples are meant to perform this same function, to be concisely memorable:

*As I employ these esoteric names and the proportions derived from the components of architectural projects, I shall explain them so that they may be memorized. In this way, readers' minds shall be able to absorb the information more quickly. And no less emphatically, because I have observed that the city is thronged with people wholly engrossed in their business, public and private, I have decided that it is better to write concisely, so that people reading in their restricted leisure time may understand these points quickly.* (V.PREF.2–3)

Vitruvius means, in other words, to be comprehensive, not exhaustive, and he anticipates readers who drive quickly to the point:

*No one tries to undertake any other craft at home, like shoe-making, fulling, or those that are easier—no craft but architecture, for the reason that those who profess it are called architects not on account of real skill, but falsely. This is why I thought that I should record the body of architecture and its governing principles as thoroughly as I can, thinking that this will be no unwelcome gift for every person of good family.* (VI.PREF.7)

Bettina Bergmann's recent article in the *Art Bulletin* of June 1994 postulated an intimate relationship between the rhetorical practice of artificial memory and the painted decoration of Pompeiian houses, many of which would have been commissioned by *patres familiarum* who employed the artificial memory in their work. Vitruvius clearly assumes a similar connection between his readers' experience of their visual world and the visual world they create in their memories. His ancient Greek temples function as memory images connected with their respective *genera*, their vividness further enhanced by association of these various *genera* with human figures: Doric with a youth, Ionic with a matron, Corinthian with a young girl. In the same way, images of Egypt such as the Nile mosaic in Praeneste or the Isis figures on Roman walls fix the mental life of ancient Romans in a larger Mediterranean context.

Like memory figures, the Vitruvian *exempla* draw their real life from their *dispositio,* the way in which their placement contributes to an overall design. It is the presence of overarching *rationes* that sparks the development of hybrid *genera* in Roman creative practice, whether in literary efforts such as the love elegies of Tibullus, Propertius, and Ovid, or the didactic satire of Horace's *Ars Poetica,* or in artistic efforts such as those enumerated by Vitruvius:

*Some designers take the column placement from Tuscan types and apply these to the gridding of Corinthian or Ionic works[6].... By so doing, they effect a common reasoning for Tuscan and Greek work.*

*Others, removing the walls of the temple and applying them to the intercolumniations, are able to create a spacious interior for the cella by taking away the areas reserved for the colonnade. However, in retaining all the other particular and systematic proportions they seem to have created a new type of temple—the pseudoperipteros.*

*These types of temples are devised for the purposes of sacrificial ritual. Temples should not be made according to the same principles for every god, because each has its own particular procedure for sacred rituals.* (IV.VII.5-6)

In each case, therefore, the innovation in temple design has been undertaken for a practical reason—the accommodation of cult—and according to rational principles. Indeed, when Vitruvius, in Book VII, and Horace, in his *Ars Poetica,* decry monstrous hybrids in art, it is the violated logic of *dispositio,* not innovation per se, that has made these artistic monsters monstrous. After all, Vitruvius and Horace themselves wrote as creators of new literary hybrids—the encyclopedic architectural treatise and the didactic satire—in which they set out systematic principles of generic composition to make these principles valid for an exuberantly eclectic age. Artistic invention, in their view, should be ordered and communicative—that is, it should command the qualities of successful rhetoric. For the Greeks, rhetorical success had been gauged by the power of persuasion, *peithô,* whereas the Romans evaluated success by the rather different criterion of *auctoritas,* a concept that implied nurturing as well as persuasion and ascribed considerable moral responsibility to its possessor.

Vitruvius is acutely aware of the extent to which the moral weight of *auctoritas* was con-

*...and have a clear grasp of astronomy...*

which the moral weight of *auctoritas* was conveyed by adherence to the subtleties of compositional convention:

*Those, Imperator, who have set out their own thoughts and their researches in volumes more engaging than these, have contributed the greatest and most outstanding authority to their writings. So, too, with our own enterprise, the subject will obviously prove to be one whose authority would be enhanced by more engaging presentation, but this is not so easy as one might think.* (IV.PREF.1)

In his first book, the fledgling author pleads for some indulgence on the part of his readers:

*I request, Caesar, both of you and of those who will read these volumes, that they forgive anything that has not been composed according to the rules of literary style. For I have striven to write them not as a great philosopher or an eloquent orator, nor as a grammarian trained in the finer points of his art, but as an architect, with an architect's knowledge of literary style. But on the power of my own art and the sytems of reasoning included in it, I promise that, as I expect, in these pages I will without a doubt prove myself possessed of the greatest authority—not only for those who intend to build, but also for all learned men.* (I.I.17)

Despite this plea, many readers of Vitruvius have continued to judge him on his sometimes tenuous adherence to Ciceronian prose style. In his own time, as we all know, architecture had become a particularly expressive art form in Roman hands, capable of assimilating a wide variety of stimuli, both visual and technological, into its formal repertory, and Vitruvius has also been much maligned for seeming to ignore many of these processes in his treatise. Yet if we take him at his word, he seeks to provide an outline of architecture as a compositional system, rather than an exhaustive account of details, and in fact he has done so with such effectiveness that many of his readers now assume it had all been done before.

It will take more than a brief essay to restore this innovative *auctor* to his rightful *auctoritas*, especially when the areas of his greatest creative energy may well be those books on hydraulics, astronomy, and mechanics, where he has extended the principles of generic composition to embrace technology. We, on the other hand, no longer refer to these Roman *artes* as art. Instead, we have left the *rationes novae* of our environment to the particle physicists and molecular biologists and relegated our architects to specialized schools in which half of what Vitruvius discussed is no longer considered architecture. Is it really he who cast a blind eye on the world around him? As Giordano Bruno, another writer in the vein of *perfectaordinatio*, would muse in 1584:

*The point on which we should fix our mind's eye is this: whether we abide in the daytime with the light of truth above our horizon, or in the regions of our adversaries, our antipodes? Whether we stand in the shadows, or they? Whether, in conclusion, we, who begin to renew the ancient philosophy, stand in the morning to put an end to the night, or in the evening to put an end to the day?*[7] ❧

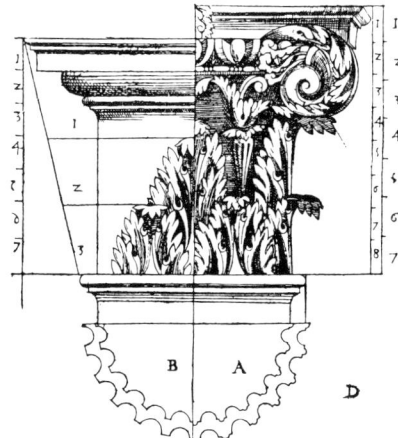

## NOTES

1. Because of the re-entrants and the return on one colonnade, these columns must be Corinthian.
2. The numbers here are problematic, as the pilasters fall 12 feet short of the height of the colonnade.
3. Reading, with Giocondo, *porticuum* for MS *porticum*.
4. Knee braces.
5. *Ordines.*
6. Note the absence of Doric.
7. Giordano Bruno, *La Cena de le Ceneri*, Dialogue 2, 27: *"Quello dunque, al che doviamo fissar l'occhio de la consideratione, é si noi siamo nel giorno, et la luce de la veritá é sopra il nostro orizonte: overo in quello de gl' aversarii nostri nostri antipodi? si siamo noi in tenebre, o' ver essi? et in conclusione si noi che damo principio a' rinovar l' antica philosophia, siamo nela mattina per dare fine á la notte: o' pur ne la sera per donar fine al giorno?"*

*The illustrations for this article, except for the figures on pages 8-9, are taken from a number of editions of Vitruvius published since the Renaissance. The figures on pages 8-9 are preparatory sketches by Thomas Noble Howe for the new edition of Vitruvius undertaken with the author.*

*Ingrid Rowland is Assistant Professor of Art at the University of Chicago.*

*...and the ways of Heaven." —Vitruvius*

# C.R. COCKERELL
## AND · THE · ROLE · OF
# ARCHAEOLOGY
## IN · MODERN · CLASSICAL
# ARCHITECTURE

### BY DAVID WATKIN

Charles Robert Cockerell (1788-1863) is an inspiring example of an architect who was dedicated to the ideal expressed by the classical language of architecture, but who was appalled at the pedestrian character of contemporary classical buildings in Britain. By studying Greek architecture at firsthand, he made revolutionary discoveries about its sculptural freedom, color, and poetry that overturned eighteenth-century conceptions of its character. These had been part of the myth of Greece that had been promoted in the age of the Enlightenment by influential theorists and antiquarians such as Marc Antoine Laugier, Carlo Lodoli, and J.J.Winckelmann. None of these men had visited Greece, however, and so had constructed an idealized image of it.

Though Laugier knew nothing firsthand of Greek architecture when he wrote his celebrated *Essai sur l'Architecture* (1753), he felt able to argue that "Architecture owes everything that is perfect to the Greeks." Perfection to him was his analogy of the temple as hut, a trabeated construction of load-bearing members in which there was no ornament, no sculpture, no color. Like Winckelmann's belief that Greek architecture was pure and colorless as water, this vision was in harmony with the Enlightenment belief in a return to origins and first principles through the study of reason and nature. This was the view Cockerell inherited, but which his archaeological studies led him to believe was romantic fiction. His failure fully to publish his discoveries, however, led some contemporaries to misunderstand his attempts to incorporate the fruits of them into his own buildings.

Why was he so hostile to the products of the Greek Revival, in which he was ostensibly a leading

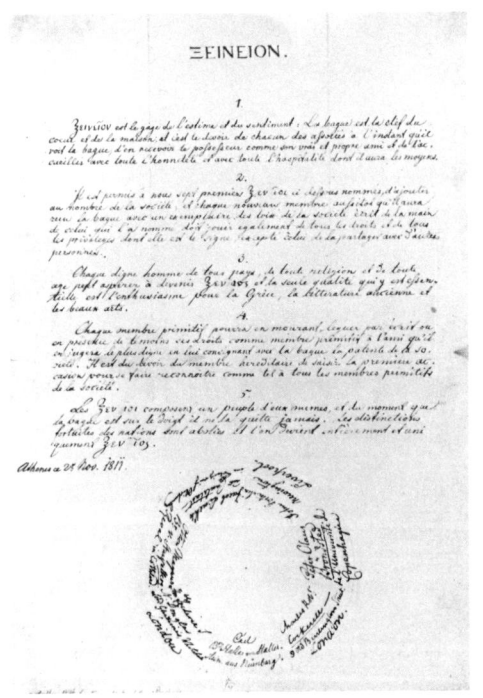

*FIGURE 1, ABOVE: Founding document of the Xeineion, November 1811.*
*FIGURE 2, RIGHT: Restoration drawing by C.R. Cockerell of the Temple of Aphaia, Aegina, showing its polychromy.*

participant? One early possible influence was that, before leaving England for his Grand Tour in April 1810, he almost certainly attended the four lectures John Soane delivered that year in his capacity as Professor of Architecture at the Royal Academy.[1] It was in his fourth lecture, delivered on 29 January 1810, that Soane made his celebrated condemnation of the Royal Opera House, Covent Garden, which had been completed in the previous year from designs by the young Robert Smirke. The building represented all that Soane found most offensive about modern architecture: he complained that it lacked not only meaning and character, because the Doric was a solemn sacred order inappropriate to a theater, but also architectural coherence, because there was no relation between the design of its front and its flanks.

Nonetheless, works such as Covent Garden Theatre and George Dance the Younger's Royal College of Surgeons, essentially routine Palladian buildings with fashionable and scholarly Greek trim, provided a formula that became the norm for official architecture after Waterloo. Cockerell, at the age of twenty, had worked on Covent Garden Theatre when he was in Smirke's office in 1808. He sharply censured it on his return from his remarkable Grand Tour of 1810-17[2] because by then he had made vital discoveries about the use of polychromy, sculpture, and entasis in Greek architecture.[3] These discoveries demolished for him the Enlightenment ideal of Greek architecture as timeless, pure, and truthful, as it had been promoted by Winckelmann.

Two of Cockerell's watercolor views of Corfu and Sparta[4] reveal the impact on him of the Greek landscape as a setting for architecture. His panoramic technique recalls that adopted by Karl Friedrich Schinkel in the views he had drawn in Italy a few years earlier. Cockerell reached Athens late in 1810, where he met the German architect and archaeologist Carl Haller von Hallerstein, with whom, so Cockerell wrote to his sister, he later swore eternal friendship. This was in the context of the remarkable but little-known Xeineion, a fellowship that Cockerell and a small group of international scholars formed in November 1811. The group consisted of, in addition to Cockerell and Haller von Hallerstein, the Liverpool architect John Foster, Jakob Linckh (from Württemberg), the Hon. Frederick Douglas (later Lord Guilford), Baron Otto von Stackelberg, and the Danish archaeologist Peter Brondsted. They gave each other bronze rings inscribed "Xeineion" (token of friendship) and depicting the owl of Minerva. The foundation document,[5] written in French, is worth translating for its charming blend of high archaeological idealism and *Boy's Own* chumminess:

*Xeineion is the measure of esteem and feeling. The ring is the key of the heart and the home, and it is the duty of each associate as soon as he sees the ring to receive the possessor as his true and own friend and to welcome him with all the honesty and hospitality which he can provide. It is permitted to us, the first Xenioi named below, to add to the number of the society (each new member will be given a ring and a copy of the rules). Every worthy man of every country, every religion and every age can aspire to become a Xenios, the only essential quality being enthusiasm for Greece, ancient literature and the fine arts. On his death every original member can bequeath his rights in the society to a friend who will receive the ring and introduce himself to the other original members. The Xenioi themselves constitute a nation or people, and the moment the ring is on the finger it never leaves it. The arbitrary differences between the nations are abolished and one becomes wholly and uniquely a Xenios.* (FIGURE 1)

In April, 1811 Cockerell, Foster, Hallerstein, and Linckh made the short sea expedition from Athens to the island of Aegina to study the late archaic temple

16th May 1843

that they believed was dedicated to Jupiter (or Zeus) Panhellenius. This magnificently sited and well-preserved temple, built in about 510–490 B.C., was in fact dedicated to Aphaia, the old goddess of the whole earth, protectress of sailors and hunters. It was not built of marble, as the Parthenon was to be, but of local limestone faced with cream-painted stucco, like a building by John Nash! Moreover, its many ornamental features, including the pedimental sculpture, acroteria, lion mask, and griffins, were richly painted in bright colors, though these faded on exposure to the air after excavation in April, 1811. Cockerell was among those who in that month made these exciting discoveries of consistent architectural polychromy and archaic sculpture of Homeric battle scenes at Troy. The use of color by ancient Greek architects had, in fact, been noted in passing by earlier archaeologists, beginning with James Stuart and Nicholas Revett, who illustrated, in black and white, a colored anthemion frieze from the upper fascia of the archi-

trave of the pronaos at the now-demolished temple on the river Ilissus in Athens.[6] Stuart attached little importance to this feature: indeed, the engraving is barely an inch square.

The temple on Aegina also displayed numerous refinements of proportion: for example, apart from the Temple of Athena at Paestum, it is the first in which all the columns tilt inward, while those on the corners are slightly thickened; the columns also have entasis, and the stylobate has an upward curve. Cockerell certainly noted the entasis but perhaps not the other features. It was his intention at this time to publish his discoveries in a book illustrated by J. M.W. Turner, who, of course, shared his interest in color. In 1816 Turner painted a romantic view[7] of the temple with young persons dancing the Greek national dance, the Romaika. Turner had been inspired by the Byronic interest in Greece, which involved seeing it as a place where Englishmen could parade their liberal consciences and fight for national liberation from the Turks. The collaboration between Cockerell and Turner failed, though Cockerell did include a lithograph by Turner in his belatedly published book on Aegina and Bassae of 1860.[8]

Cockerell was to first publish his discoveries at Aegina in brief articles in an obscure journal, in 1819.[9] In them, he showed that polychromy was integral to Greek architecture from the start, and that both the marble and the stucco on the Aegina temple were colored. By this time, Bertel Thorwaldsen and Johann Martin Wagner were busy in Rome restoring and painting the Aegina pedimental sculpture that had been bought by Crown Prince Ludwig of Bavaria for his Glyptothek in Munich.[10] Cockerell regretted this, both because he had tried to acquire the sculpture for England and because he felt that Thorwaldsen was going too far in adding color to it. The architect Leo von Klenze created an appropriate setting for the sculpture in the Glyptothek, in 1830 devising a coloured plaster version of its facade on the wall of the room in which it was displayed. This version is itself important as an early monument in the revival of architectural polychromy. Cockerell's own arresting restoration of the color on the Aegina temple, doubtless initially prepared in about 1816-19, was not published until 1860 (FIGURE 2). He had been beaten to it by the French archaeologist Abel Blouet, a positivist in the circle of J.I.Hittorff and Henri Labrouste, who published nearly thirty years earlier.[11]

As if these striking discoveries were not enough, Cockerell followed them by further important excavations at the Temple of Apollo Epicurius at Bassae (FIGURES 3-5). He was there with a small group in 1811 for ten days in August, the hottest time of the year. Unknown at the time when Stuart and Revett visited Greece, this temple is one of the most fascinating of all, partly because there are so many mysteries about its date, architect, and even dedication. Attributed by Pausanias to the architect Ictinus, it is generally supposed to have been designed in about 429-427 B.C.. and completed in about 400 B.C. Apart from its marble roof-tiles, the temple is of local gray limestone; its external Doric colonnade has a certain archaic or old-fashioned flavor and also lacks the optical refinements of the Parthenon, save for entasis. So if the exterior seems an improbable work for Ictinus, the interior has a number of striking innovations that more than justify that attribution. The cella is flanked by impressive Ionic half-columns taller than the Doric columns outside and connected to the cella walls by curious spurs that perhaps recall those in the early archaic Temple of Hera at Olympia, not all that far away. The strange half-columns seem to be struggling in Michelangelesque fashion to emerge from the walls in which they are embedded. They also have extravagantly flared bases, which are echoed in the unusual three-faced capitals with their two canted volutes and curved tops. These are a development from the end capital of a Greek Ionic colonnade, which was always carved with one diagonal volute at the corner. There was no precedent for this Bassae Ionic order nor for the Corinthian capital that crowned the central column along the south short end of the cella. The capital has since been destroyed and we know it only from drawings made on the spot by Cockerell's friend Haller von Hallerstein. The curving tendrils of the double rows of acanthus leaves on this capital are the origin of the Corinthian order so beloved of the Romans. It was used in the Greek and Hellenistic period only for interiors, especially sacred ones.

Another novelty in the cella was the continuous figured frieze that ran round all four sides of the interior. It represents in carved marble the battles between the Greeks and the Amazons, Lapiths and centaurs, and is more vigorous and forceful than the Parthenon frieze. Thanks to Cockerell's efforts, it was bought for the British Museum. Cockerell suggested that the cult statue may have stood, unexpectedly, in the inner adytum, or sanctuary, on the west wall, for there is an oddly placed door in the east wall, which would allow sunlight to flood onto the statue. (The temple, unusually, faces north not east.) Cockerell's restoration drawing of the interior shows his unique response to

TRANSVERSE SECTION OF THE TEMPLE OF JUPITER OLYMPIUS AT AGRIGENTUM.

*FIGURE 3, ABOVE LEFT: Interior view of the Temple of Apollo Epicurius, Bassae, by C.R. Cockerell.*

*FIGURE 4, BELOW LEFT: Section of the Temple of Jupiter Panhellenius, Agrigento, by C.R. Cockerell.*

*FIGURE 5, ABOVE: Ionic order of the Temple of Apollo Epicurius, Bassae, by C.R. Cockerell.*

its proto-Baroque elements and the picturesque drama of light and shade in the sanctuary. In a remarkable personal response to the aesthetic intentions of Ictinus, Cockerell explained that the "peculiarities of this work exhibit the perspective science of the architect, and show how freely and confidently he could deal with his materials, regardless of the reproach of anomaly and caprice."[12] The temple seems, indeed, to have been the first Greek building to have had an aesthetically composed interior, though its revolutionary implications were not fulfilled until the Roman period.

The ten-day excavation of August 1811 was followed by a much fuller one from June to August the next year, in which Cockerell did not take part. He was already making new discoveries at yet another temple, this time the Temple of Jupiter Olympius (or temple of the Giants) at Agrigento on Sicily (FIGURE 6). The largest and in some ways most remarkable of all Doric temples, it was built during the fifth century but left uncompleted on the sack of Agrigento by the Carthaginians in 406 B.C. It is memorable for the mysterious male figures, or telamons, twenty-five feet high, carved on the outer walls with their arms above their heads, apparently supporting the entablature. In order to help carry the enormous weight of the entablature, which was also strengthened with iron bars, the outer columns were not freestanding but were half-columns engaged against a continuous solid wall. These external half-columns and the pilasters that answer them on the inside wall create the kind of molded wall-mass that is supposed to be typical of Roman not Greek architecture. So, just as the discovery of polychromy, a decorative element of an essentially transitory nature, overthrew the Winckelmannesque idea of timeless Greek purity, so the use of decorative engaged columns and concealed iron supports challenged the doctrine of Laugier (in his *Essai sur l'Architecture*, 1753) that required all columns to be truthful, that is freestanding and load-bearing. The same feature of engaged columns appears in Temple F at Selinunte in Sicily, which Cockerell also visited in 1812.[13]

Cockerell spent the winter, from December 1812 to February 1813, in Sicily at Syracuse, preparing the plates for the book on Aegina and Bassae he proposed publishing with Haller von Hallerstein. It was later arranged that Haller should come to England for this purpose, but he died in 1817, having given his notes on Bassae to Cockerell. Cockerell spent much of 1813 in Athens, where he suffered from a long fever; in 1814 he traveled in northern Greece but later in the year returned to Athens, where he stayed until 1815, the year in which Haller sent designs for the Walhalla inspired by the Parthenon to Munich. (Thus the Walhalla, as eventually built near Regensburg from von Klenze's designs in 1830–42, emerged from the circle of the Xeineion founded by Cockerell and his friends in 1811.

From Athens, Cockerell sent a letter to Smirke on December 23, 1814 in which he enclosed a strip of paper, twenty-one inches long and six wide, showing the entasis on the columns of the Parthenon. He also noted the entasis on the columns of the Erechtheion and the temple at Aegina. Previous archaeologists, including Stuart and Revett, had shown the Parthenon, Theseion and Erechtheion with all their columns straight. Cockerell generously gave Francis Cranmer Penrose what the latter called his "Athenian sketches of measurements." Penrose used these in his great book, *Investigation of the Principles of Ancient Architecture: Optical Refinements in the Construction of Ancient Buildings in Athens* (1851). Cockerell did not publish his discovery of entasis on the Parthenon, but he did publish an account of the Temple of the Giants (or Olympeion) at Agrigento in a supplementary volume to Stuart and Revett, entitled *Antiquities of Athens and other Places in Greece, Sicily, etc.* (1830).[14]

Just as Cockerell gave his notes on the Parthenon to Penrose, so he kindly allowed T. L. Donaldson, an architect just seven years his junior, to publish in 1830 the account of the temple at Bassae in the supplementary volume to Stuart and Revett, even though Donaldson had not been present at either of the excavations. Donaldson, in return, praised Cockerell's scagliola capitals in the Bassae Ionic order in the hall at Oakly Park, Shropshire, and in the dining room of 1823 at Grange Park, Hampshire. Donaldson obviously regarded these capitals as a happy example of that fruitful interaction between archaeology and modern design that went back to Stuart and Revett. Donaldson was important in the history of polychromy because he had investigated the painted decoration in the Theseion in Athens in 1820, even bringing scraps of it back to England.[15] It was patterns such as these that were used by designers like Leonard Collmann, who employed them in his decorative scheme of 1847 for the great staircase at the British Museum.[16] Like Hittorff, Donaldson became a keen champion of polychromy, though always in theory and not in practice. Cockerell, significantly, did not take up the cause of polychromy nearly so strongly. In his opinion, it was ill fitted for external use in a northern climate such as that of Britain.

In March, 1823, eleven years after Cockerell's visit to Selinunte on the south coast of Sicily, two English architects, William Harris and Samuel Angell, visited the site and discovered metopes from the so-called Temple C. This exciting discovery brought Hittorff to Selinunte in July, 1823.[17] Here he excavated the remains of the tiny Temple B, which had, and still has, remains of color.[18] Carried away by his determination to find justification in Greek architecture for his own passionate love of

color, Hittorff jumped to three erroneous conclusions about the dedication, decoration, and date of Temple B. He wrongly claimed that it was a temple of Empedocles, that it combined Ionic columns with a Doric frieze, and that it was Greek in date, whereas in fact it is Hellenistic. He first published his discoveries in his book with Karl von Zanth, *Architecture antique de la Sicile*, in 1827-30, and then more fully in his great work of 1851, *Restitution du temple d'Empédocle à Selinonte; ou l'architecture polychrome chez les Grecs*. Hittorf used color, not entirely successfully, in his own Parisian buildings, such as St. Vincent de Paul of 1830-56, a twin-towered neo-Grec church that, as we shall see, may have been inspired by Cockerell's

---

## "...something imposing, grand, massive and high is wanted in our buildings at present."

---

Hanover Chapel of a few years earlier (FIGURES 7-8). In 1844 the Ecole des Beaux Arts for the first time allowed its students to make records of Greek rather than Roman buildings. This led to a flood of grandiloquently polychromatic Hittorffian restorations, such as the exotic, even barbaric, images of the Parthenon prepared by Benoit Loviot in 1879-81.[19]

Earlier, a commission had been appointed in London in 1836 to investigate the Elgin Marbles and fragments of Greek temples in the British Museum to establish whether they were colored. The architects on this committee included Cockerell, Donaldson, and Hittorff, who, incidentally, had first visited London in 1820 in order to see the Elgin Marbles. The committee met in 1836 and 1837, and Donaldson published its results in 1842, with a bold colored plate of painted architectural details from the Erechtheion and Theseion.[20]

In his diaries, begun in 1821, four years after his return from Greece and Rome, Cockerell gave a clear picture of what he thought modern architecture ought, and ought not, to be, as, for example, when he wrote of Dance's Royal College of Surgeons (1806-13):

*The Ionic portico the gravest I have seen most severe...[but] ill-applied to the paper front of a house with which it has no connection either by ornamental architectural style, solidity, character, lines or material...what is now most essential is to appropriate the Greek style, engraft it on our wants and recast it for our necessities. The Italian architects did this, particularly Palladio.[21]*

He also condemned the interior of Dance's building, just as Soane had condemned the exterior for the lack of relation between its facades. Taking up Soane's criticism, Cockerell leveled it at Greek Revival buildings in general: "We stick a slice of an ancient Greek temple to a barn which is called breadth and simplicity, than which nothing can be more absurd."[22]

Cockerell was also hostile to the most striking Greek Revival church in London, St. Pancras, Euston Road, designed in 1818 by W. and H.W. Inwood. The younger Inwood was in Athens in 1818-19, where he studied the Erechtheion, on which he subsequently published the standard archaeological monograph.[23] The form of the church is based on the tripartite plan of the Erechtheion, though the Inwoods could not resist tidying it up and making it symmetrical. The west tower is inspired by both the Tower of the Winds and the Choragic Monument of Lysicrates in Athens, while the portico below is modeled on the west portico of the Erechtheion: indeed, actual casts of the Erechtheion door surrounds were shipped from Athens to London to enable exact copies to be made.[24] The round apse at the east end is a rather un-Greek form, though the caryatids in the flanking pavilions are closely modeled on those of the Erechtheion. However, the caryatids are not exact copies, for they "carry water ewers and inverted torches to symbolise their function as presiding over the entries to burial vaults."[25] The work of the sculptor John Rossi, they are of terra cotta, though the church itself is of Portland stone. At a cost of nearly £77,000, it was supposed to have been the most expensive London church since St. Paul's Cathedral.

None of this impressed Cockerell, who wrote in his diary:

*Simple Greek Greek Greek—radiates bad taste through the whole...ignorance and presumption of Mr Inwood attempting to impress on one an idea of his importance. Mr Inwood and his boys have tormented themselves to invent du nouveau and have planned a most minute research into every moulding, wherever their authorities have ceased they as usual have been aground. It is anything but*

---

*FIGURE 6: Frontispiece from C.R. Cockerell's* THE TEMPLE OF JUPITER OLYMPIUS AT AGRIGENTUM, COMMONLY CALLED THE TEMPLE OF THE GIANTS *(London, 1830).*

*architecture—the inside trite, the apse is flat roofed and the whole ceiling low and unmeaning.*[26]

To underline Cockerell's point, we might compare St. Pancras Church with a reconstruction of the Erechtheion submitted in 1848 by Jacques-Martin Tétaz as his Envoi to the Ecole des Beaux Arts in Paris.[27] Tétaz's poetic watercolor gives a very different impression of antique architecture from that given by the Inwoods, for, following the recent discovery of Greek polychromy, he shows the building as a vivid slice of life, animated by strong coloring.[28]

Smirke's British Museum of 1823–46, with an Ionic order inspired by that of the great Hellenistic Temple of Athena at Priene, is another key monument of the Greek Revival. After a visit to it in October, 1824, Cockerell noted: "Exterior architecture is an expense much thrown away in this climate, especially in a corner so little seen [as Great Russell Street], fine effect of wide steps leading up to portico." He recalled Aristotle's definition of beauty as consisting of magnitude and order, but noted that magnitude is relative and that he "did not like the taste of any part of the build-

ing,"[29] though he was impressed by Smirke's use of cast iron corbels.

Cockerell also condemned Smirke's Physicians' College and adjacent Union Club in Trafalgar Square, writing of them in April 1822:

*The flank totally out of character with porticoed front. Thin, flat, attempt at play, confused in consequence, and that vicious mode of composition of lapping under and over, a cornice or frieze sometimes appearing, sometimes concealed, somewhat French in composition. Want of strength and character, a something imposing, grand, massive and high is wanted in our buildings at present.*

Visiting the interior in 1825, he noted: "total deficiency of character, nothing like a public building, nothing monumental, staircase contracted."[30]

In 1825-26 Cockerell entered the competition for University College, London. His design, echoing one for a college published by J. N. L. Durand in 1802,[31] has a noble courtyard in the form of a cloister approached through Greek Doric propylaea and flanked by quadrant wings with horseshoe-shaped lecture rooms. Unlike his contemporaries, Cockerell did not consider the provision of a high portico to be the way to echo the spirit of Greek architecture. It is thus instructive to compare his design with the less imaginative winning design by William Wilkins, executed in 1827-28. This was dominated by a monumental

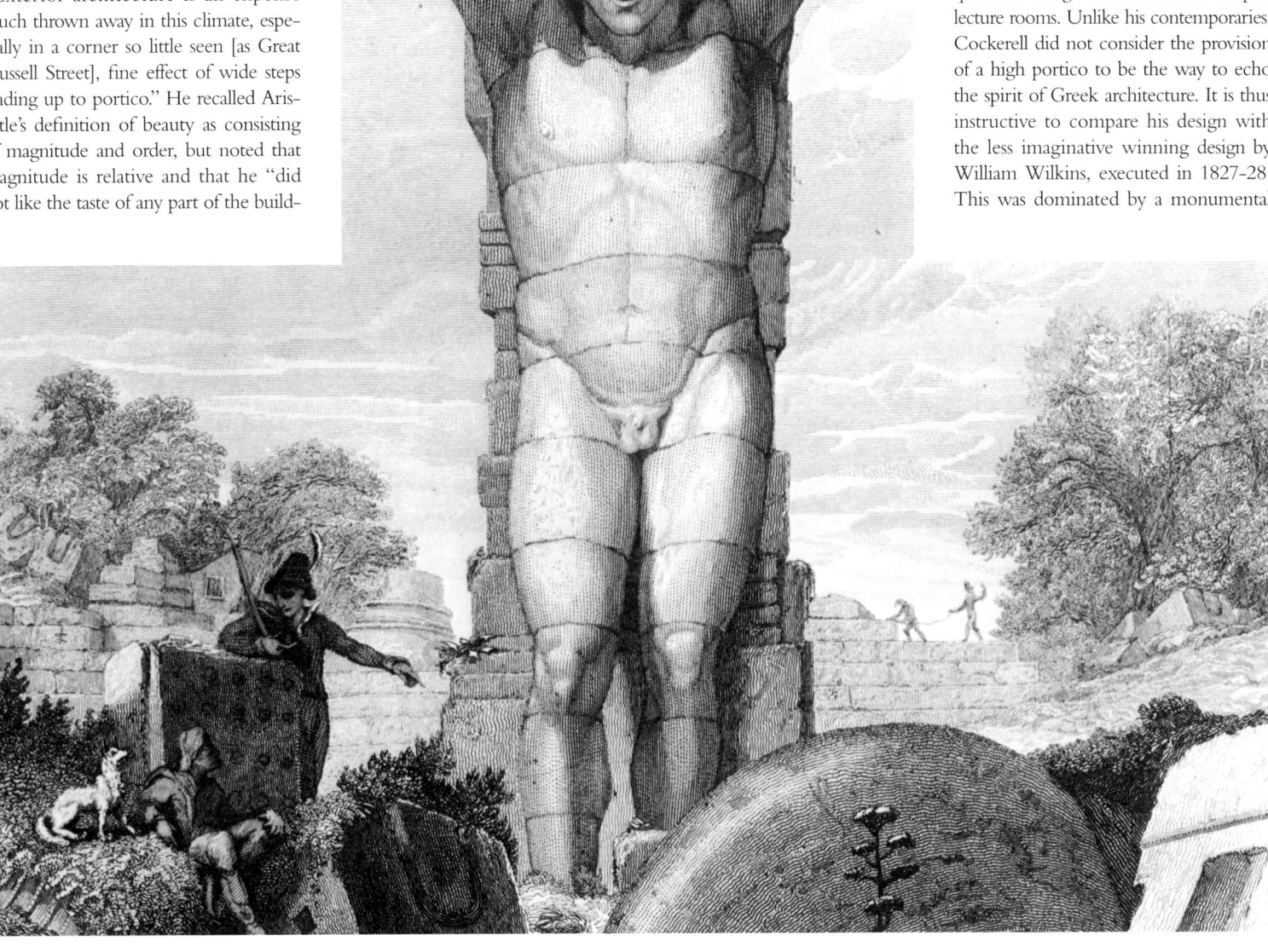

but perfectly useless portico modeled on the Olympeion in Athens.

Cockerell's own Hanover Chapel, Regent Street, London[32] (designed 1821-22, executed 1823-25, and demolished 1896), was a remarkable anticipation of the twin-towered west front of Hittorff's St. Vincent de Paul. Cockerell tried to achieve in it something of the richness and variety he had admired at firsthand in Greece. The proportions of the portico were based on the Temple of Athena Nike in Athens, while the Ionic order was taken from the large-scale Asiatic Ionic Temple of Athena at Priene; the pilaster capitals came from a similar Hellenistic source, the great temple of Apollo at Didyma, near Miletus. More important than the sources of these elements is that they are incorporated into a building that has towers, which are Gothic in implication though wholly classical in detail. Soaring above the adjacent commercial properties in Nash's Regent Street, these were the result of Cockerell's belief that "something imposing, grand, massive and high is wanted in our buildings at present."

Cockerell went on to develop a richer and more plastic classicism in his masterpieces: Cambridge University Library, designed 1836-37, executed 1837-40[33] (FIGURES 9-10); the Ashmolean Museum and Taylorian Institute, Oxford, 1839-45 (FIGURES 11); and the branches of the Bank of England at Bristol and Liverpool, designed in the mid-1840s. The one executed range of his Cambridge University Library has an entrance front cast in the form of a triumphal arch in which the arch breaks dramatically through the entablature. This originates in the proto-Baroque forms of late Roman architecture in Syria and Asia Minor, but in the hands of Cockerell, who had contemplated the massive stones and delicate lines of Greek architecture, this language appears neither Greek, nor Roman, nor Baroque, but timeless. Certainly it is architecture that it is extremely hard to date.

The great end pavilions of the Ashmolean Museum develop the Cambridge theme in a more sculpturally ambitious way. Here the swelling flared volutes of the Bassae Ionic order set the tone for a rhythmic composition, rich with freestanding and relief sculpture, which proclaimed Cockerell's belief that "sculpture is the voice of architecture." He similarly echoed the polychromy of the ancient Greeks in a novel way by using stone of three contrasting colors: for the plinth and massive retaining wall he chose a reddish brown Whitby stone; for the principal facades, a bright golden Bath stone known as Box Ground; and for the columns, pilasters, and entablatures, the gleaming white Portland stone. The effect in sunlight is breathtaking.

On the entrance front of the Ashmolean Museum, he showed how the classical language of architecture can articulate a largely blank wall, a solu-

FIGURE 7, TOP LEFT: *East front elevation of Hanover Chapel.*
FIGURE 8, MIDDLE LEFT: *Perspective view of Cockerell's Hanover Chapel, Regent Street, London, 1823-25.*
FIGURE 9, BOTTOM LEFT: *Cockerell's project for Cambridge University Library, 1836-37 (model by Gavin Stamp).*
FIGURE 10, ABOVE: *Cambridge University Library, east entrance front, 1836-37.*

tion architects in the modern movement deprived themselves of unnecessarily. The organization of the wall surface with pilasters may be inspired by similar features at the Temple of the Giants at Agrigento. In the staircase hall Cockerell boldly unites Greek Doric columns with Roman arches, a combination he might have justified by Ictinus' use of Corinthian in the Doric temple at Bassae, a cast of whose frieze he incorporated round the top of the stairwell.

It should now be apparent how Cockerell's hostility to the Greek Revival was related to his discovery that ancient Greek architects, especially in their use of the orders, of color, and of sculpture, did not conform to the theories of Laugier and Winckelmann, or to the practice of Wilkins and Smirke. However, despite his awareness of how an architect such as Ictinus could "freely and confidently... deal with his materials, regardless of the reproach of anomaly and caprice," Cockerell's reluctance to publish his views on Greek architecture meant that his own buildings were sometimes misunderstood.

His Liverpool bank was criticized in the *Civil Engineer and Architect's Journal* in 1849 by someone who was unaware of what Cockerell had discovered in Greek architecture, even though the intellectual level of this journal was higher than that of its principal rival, *The Builder*. Attempting to describe Cockerell's handling of the Doric order, the anonymous critic complained that Cockerell:

> ...applies it illogically and quite contrary to its nature, when he introduces it—as he has done—as mere decoration in fenestrated fronts, consequently essentially different in their general physiognomy from anything in ancient Greek architecture.... [He] has forcedly introduced a Greek-Doric order (considerably modified, it is true), whose columns are mere ornamental expletives in the structure—architectural rhetoric without architectural logic; for being attached to the wall, they not only serve no real purpose, but lose the greater part of the effect that would else attend them, and are reduced to mere embellishment.[34]

The author of this criticism had failed to understand the richly plastic yet linear weave that informed the treatment of columns embedded in a wall mass, as at the Temple of the Giants at Agrigento. Such an antique building lay behind Cockerell's expressive handling of decorative orders at Liverpool and elsewhere. His critic in the *Civil Engineer and Architect's Journal* had simply inherited a view of Greek architecture, at once mechanistic and idealist, that went back at least to the theories of Laugier in the 1750s and which is probably still widely held today. Recently, however, in the large new Library, Cast Gallery, and Classics Center which Robert Adam has designed at the rear and side of the Ashmolean Museum, he has brilliantly responded to the breadth and freedom with which Cockerell, though an archaeologist and a scholar, handled the orders as an expressive language. Adam's work, to which reference is made later in this issue of THE CLASSICIST, is also a model of how to fit new, large-scale buildings harmoniously yet imaginatively into a complex of existing ones—an area in which the arrogant iconoclasm of the modern movement caused it to make many of its most disastrous mistakes.

The imposing new library, a huge rotunda resembling the Caldarium of the Baths of Caracalla, squats like an unexploded bomb at the heart of this great complex of buildings, radiating lines of force around the whole site and reaching out to the Cast Gallery, a half-Pantheon with an iron and glass dome. Adam has planned three new entrances to his extensive additions, each making a reference to discoveries by Cockerell at Bassae: in St. John's Street, there is a one-storied, top-lit, rotunda, its entrance guarded by Greek Doric columns; in Pusey Lane, the high and narrow entrance facade is a composition of gripping dynamism, dominated by a single column of the Bassae Corinthian order. Centrally placed in the facade, this breaks with conventional notions of classical practice, but follows the unusual disposition of the single Corinthian column in the cella of the temple at Bassae; finally, the St. Giles Street entrance celebrates the rhythmic poetry of the Bassae Ionic order.

This powerful contemporary work reminds us that the classical language, properly handled, is a liberating force, and not a restricting one, as the Modernists used to tell us. In every way a worthy complement to Cockerell's brilliantly conceived buildings, Adam's addition will make the Ashmolean an even more compelling place of pilgrimage to lovers of architecture than it already is. ❧

*FIGURE 11: Stair hall of Cockerell's Ashmolean Museum, Oxford, 1839-40 .*

### NOTES

THIS PAPER IS A REMODELED VERSION OF ONE DELIVERED AT A SYMPOSIUM ON LATE GEORGIAN CLASSICISM, WHICH I CHAIRED AT THE GEORGIAN GROUP, LONDON, IN 1987.

1. See my forthcoming book, *The Mind of Soane: Enlightenment Thought and the Royal Academy Lectures of Sir John Soane* (Cambridge, 1996).
2. See Pieter Broucke, *The Archaeology of Architecture: Charles Robert Cockerell in Southern Europe and the Levant, 1810-1817.* Exhibition catalogue, Yale Center for British Art, 1993.
3. David van Zanten, *The Architectural Polychromy of the 1830s* (New York and London, 1977) is a useful study, but does insufficient justice to the role of British archaeologists.
4. Reproduced in Sotheby's sale catalogue, *18th and 19th-century British Drawings and Watercolours.* 12 March 1987, lots 52-3.
5. See Hansgeorg Bankel, ed. *Carl Haller von Hallerstein in Griechenland: 1810-1817.* Exhibition catalogue, Berlin, 1986, pp. 188-89.
6. J. Stuart and N. Revett, *The Antiquities of Athens,* Vol. I (1762), chapter II, pl. VIII, fig. 3.
7. On the history of this painting, see John Gage, "Turner and the Greek Spirit," *Turner Studies,* Vol. I, No. 2, (1981), pp. 14-25.
8. C. R. Cockerell, *The Temples of Jupiter Panhellenius at Aegina, and of Apollo Epicurius at Bassae near Phigaleia in Arcadia* (London, 1860) pl. II. Although this did not appear until 1860, it was announced for publication in June 1835 in *Loudon's Architectural Magazine,* Vol. I (1834), p. 86.
9. C. R. Cockerell, "On the Aegina Marbles," *Quarterly Journal of Literature, Science and the Arts,* Vol. VI (1819), pp. 327-31, and "Additional Remarks relating to the Aegina Marbles described in the Sixth Volume of this Journal," ibid., Vol. VII (1819), pp. 229-38.
10. See *Glyptothek München 1830-1980.* Exhibition catalogue, Munich Glyptothek, 1980.
11. G.-A. Blouet, *L'expédition scientifique de Morée,* 3 Vols. (Paris, 1831, 1833, and 1838).
12. Op.cit., p. 48, C. R. Cockerell, *The Temples of Jupiter Panhellenius....* Cockerell's suggestion as to the placing of the cult statue is not now generally accepted.
13. Other Greek buildings on Sicily featuring engaged

columns are the temples of Asclepius at Agrigento and of Serapis at Taormina. These should not be regarded as provincial aberrations, for such columns also appear on the Greek mainland in the west wall of the Erechtheion and in the stoa at Epidaurus.
14. The remarkable hall at Kingston Lisle, Berkshire, surrounded by piers and columns capped with caryatids, may be a rare instance of influence from Cockerell's restoration of the Temple of the Giants at Agrigento. The architect is unknown.
15. See Richard John, "T.L. Donaldson: The Last of the Old Gods?," BA thesis, Cambridge, Department of History of Art, 1987.
16. This handsome neo-Greek work has been long since obliterated, but it is hoped that it will eventually be reinstated.
17. On Hittorff's contribution to the polychromy debate, see Donald Schneider, *The Works and Doctrines of Jacques Ignace Hittorff 1792-1867,* 2 Vols. (New York and London, 1977).
18. A section of the entablature, apparently with original colour, can be seen today in the archaeological museum in Palermo.
19. See Ecole Nationale Supérieure des Beaux Arts, *Paris, Rome, Athènes: Le voyage en Grèce des architectes français aux XIXe et XXe siècles.* Exhibition catalogue, Paris, 1982, pp. 230-37.
20. *RIBA Transactions,* Vol. I, No. 2, 1842, pp. 101-8.
21. Cockerell's diary, quoted from David Watkin, *The Life and Work of C.R. Cockerell* (London, 1974), p. 66.
22. Ibid., p. 65.
23. H. W. Inwood, *The Erechtheion at Athens: Fragments of Athenian Architecture and a few remains in Attica, Megara and Epirus* (London, 1827). Inwood dedicated some of the plates to Thomas Hope, to whom he addressed a flattering letter, explaining that he had learned from Payne Knight that Hope "had been pleased to express much approbation of the church lately completed on the model of the temple of Erechtheus".
24. J. Britton and A. C. Pugin, *The Public Buildings of London,* 2 Vols. (London, 1825-28), Vol. 1, p. 160.
25. *Survey of London,* Vol. XXIV, King's Cross Neighbourhood, Part IV, 1952, p. 3.
26. Watkin, op. cit., p. 67.
27. See Ecole Nationale Supérieure des Beaux Arts, *Paris, Rome, Athènes,* op. cit., pp. 178-87.
28. In fact, the interior of St. Pancras Church was given a similarly rich decorative treatment by the Crace firm in 1880, though, sadly, this no longer survives.
29. Watkin, op. cit., p. 73.
30. Ibid., pp. 73-74.
31. J. N. L. Durand, *Précis des leçons donnés à l'école polytechnique.* 1825 ed., (Paris, 1802), Vol. II, pl. 8.
32. See G. L. Carr, "C. R. Cockerell's Hanover Chapel," *Journal of the Society of Architectural Historians,* Vol. XXXIX (1980), pp. 265-85.
33. See David Watkin, "Newly Discovered Drawings by C. R. Cockerell for Cambridge University Library," *Architectural History,* Vol. 26 (1983), pp. 87-91.
34. *Civil Engineer and Architect's Journal,* 1849, p. 323.

*David Watkin is a Fellow of Peterhouse and Lecturer in the History of Art at Cambridge University.*

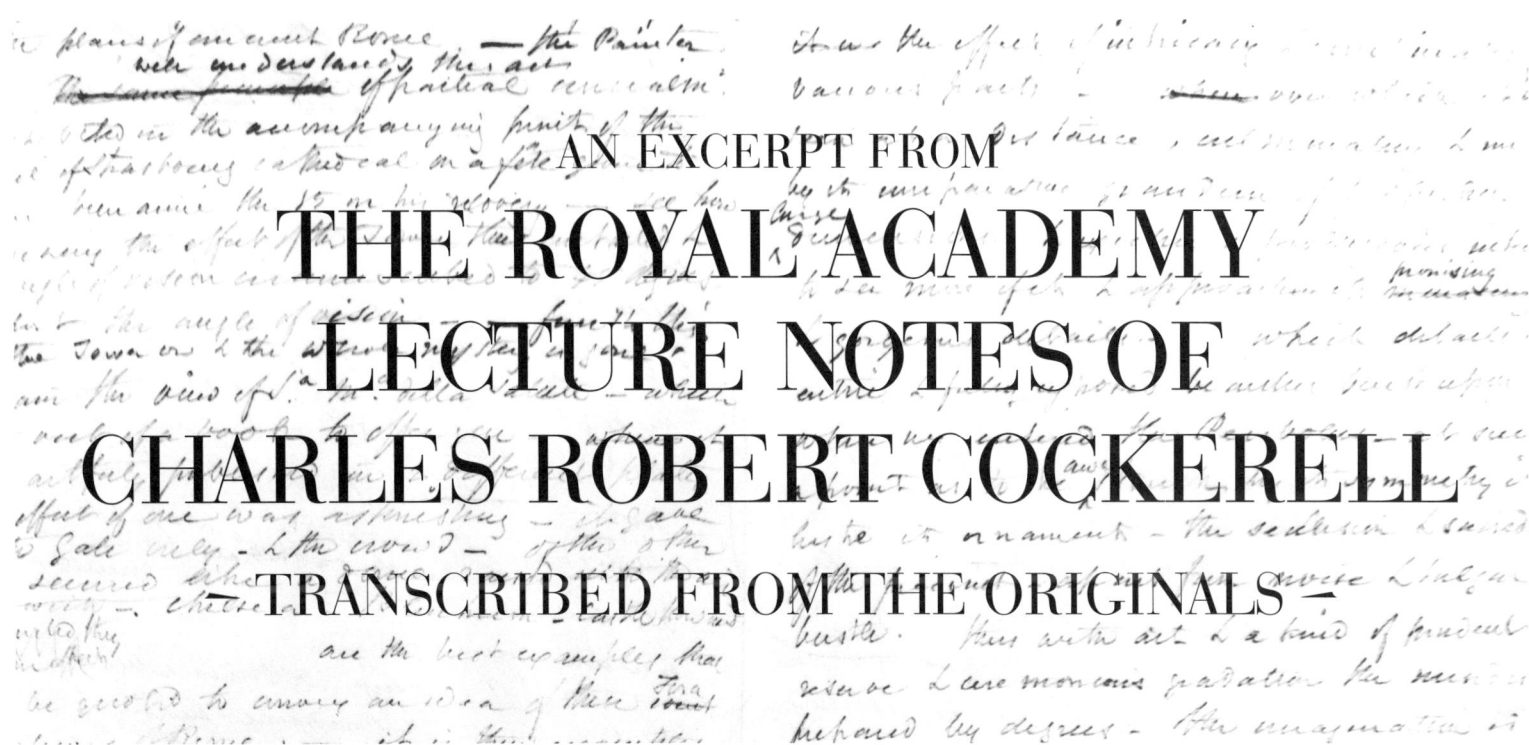

# AN EXCERPT FROM
# THE ROYAL ACADEMY LECTURE NOTES OF
# CHARLES ROBERT COCKERELL
## TRANSCRIBED FROM THE ORIGINALS

## INTRODUCTION

### BY RICHARD CAMERON

In 1839 Charles Robert Cockerell became the fifth Professor of Architecture of the Royal Academy of Arts following Sandby, Dance, Soane, and Wilkins. The position required the delivery of six lectures annually to the students of the Academy. Although Cockerell spent only a year and a half in preparation for his first series of lectures, which he began to deliver in January 1841, he had in fact spent the better part of his life in preparation for the task, and in many ways was better suited to it, both academically and temperamentally, than any of his predecessors.

Cockerell's lectures, which were delivered over a fourteen year period from 1842 to 1856, are preserved in part today in the library of the Royal Academy of Arts, with a single lecture from 1842 housed at Trinity College library in Cambridge. They are written in a fine light pencil hand, which resembles Cockerell's delicate pencil draftsmanship, into a series of school exercise books with a number of small pages inserted into the main text as addenda. Summary reports of the lectures were given in contemporary architectural journals of the period (like *The Builder*) but Cockerell refused verbatim publication of the texts. In reading the texts of the lectures it becomes clear that unlike Soane's lectures—completely scripted

presentations which were then read to the students of the Academy—Cockerell's notes are just the opposite. While there are extended passages which have complete sentences and paragraphs, much of the text is in point form and was fully elaborated only in the final oral presentation. This may explain, at least in part, Cockerell's reticence in having the lecture notes published.

While Dr. David Watkin gives an extended treatment of the lectures in his pioneering monograph of Cockerell (published by Zwemmer in 1974), and makes reference to them in his essay for this issue of THE CLASSICIST, it is nevertheless unfortunate that some effort has not been made to make the texts of these lectures available. Although Cockerell has remained somewhat obscure in this century, he was undoubtedly one of the most learned and insightful architects of the nineteenth century—and his combined activities as archeologist, practicing architect, and professor exemplify the relationship of theory to practice in the field of architecture. The lecture notes, even in their fragmentary form, are filled with innumerable insights into the theory and practice of classical architecture and its relation to the other architectural styles. Cockerell's first hand knowledge of ancient architecture and his broad reading of the literature were unparalleled in his day and remain an inspiration for anyone aspiring to practice in the tradition

today. A.E. Richardson, in his introduction to *Monumental Classic Architecture in Britain and Ireland*, gives us some idea of the importance of Cockerell the teacher and architect:

*An archaeologist of the first rank, Cockerell knew the limitations archaeology imposed on creative impulse, especially if a vain display of learning were persisted in. Deeply versed as he was in the knowledge of Hellenic art, he forbore the interpretation of its forms in any spirit other than that of freedom. He was eminently modern in the catholicity of his tastes, he carried the excellences of Sir Christopher Wren's buildings back to meet the Italian motif, and infused them with the true Promethean fire of old Greece and Rome.*

As a complement to Dr. Watkin's article on Cockerell and the Greek Revival, THE CLASSICIST publishes here several excerpts from Cockerell's lecture notes transcribed from the notebooks by the author, with the generous permission of the Librarian of the Royal Academy of Arts and the Librarian of Trinity College, Cambridge. ❧

*The editor spent the period of February to May, 1994 in England as the recipient of the first prize in the Royal Oak Foundation's inaugural competition in the architectural arts, engaged in a study of the building, drawing, and writing of the English architect C.R. Cockerell.*

# Mr. President & Secretary & Students of the Royal Academy;

**1845**

The method which I have adopted in the present course has been to illustrate some of the principles of our art by taking into re-view the Greek & Roman remains & more particularly the Greco Roman (as that style which uniting the arched with the trabeated system is best suited to our practical purposes)—and I beg leave to repeat that which I have more than once had occasion to observe to you that it is not for the mere purpose of displaying erudition of the authors whom I have cited so frequently, or to entertain you with antiquarian wonders & curiosity that I have adopted this course but under the persuasion of the practical utility of this survey or review of ancient monuments, & to incite your study & diligent research into those sources of instruction upon these subjects which so many learned men & such expressive publication during the last 300 years have placed at your disposal, stores of ideas & wealth for the imagination of the architect which the last half century has more especially enriched by the zealous enterprises of students & the excavations made in different regions of the ancient classical world.

To make these lectures antiquarian discourses merely, would be an abuse of your valuable time as well as my own—for the architect should regard these researches solely for the purpose of seeing how he can elevate his conception by them & multiply his resources, give grace & elegance to his works in short to see how he can borrow & steal from them—in order to engraft it to his own mind & ameliorate his ideas & his practice.

We know that when the brightness of classical literature was confessed & became a passion in the 15th & 16th centuries that the artists all & the architects especially confessed the superiority of those models to any conceptions of the middle ages. Their remains were studied with the enthusiasm of a newly discovered truth of eminent beauty & ability—the learned Alberti wrote his admirable work treating largely of the whole subject, "I found no subject" says he "more worthy of the zeal & study of an enlightened man than the noble principles of ancient building and the endeavor to emancipate this magnificent art from the wretched state in which it had fallen during the middle ages." Bramante & his scholar Raphael practically studied Vitruvius & executed works in imitation of the ancient model encouraged by all the most accomplished men of Europe. Balthasar Perruzzi carefully measured & laid down the remains of Rome afterwards published under the patronage of that illustrious Prince Francois Ist of France by his scholar Serlio—Palladio, Vignola & many others of great merit followed in those footsteps & acquired a fame & laid down principles derived from those remains which can never be controverted & which have become the accepted models of imitation during more than 250 yrs. since those great men lived & laid down their principles.

Such was at that time the admiration & zeal applied to ancient researches in the graces of ancient art & the delight which they communicated that the learned Colonna who had retired in the convent of S. Peter & S. Paul's at Venice occupied his leisure in composing his famous novel the love–dream of Poliphelus– in which his principal scope was to describe poetically a great variety of ancient masterpieces in the three sister arts of architecture, sculpture & painting illustrating his works with admirable wood cuts describing inventions some ancient & many

of his own derived from ancient art of such merit & beauty that they were quickly adopted by succeeding artists & have since been almost all embodied in the subsequent works of the revival. It would be hard to say whether this ingenious dream of Colonna was calculated most to satisfy the love of antiquity or to promote it, so many beautiful images of ancient art does it present & so many more of inquiry & of invention does it suggest—imbued with all the sentimentality of a lover of the beautiful he makes you wander with him into the solitudes of wasted cities, he describes to you the scattered fragments of by–gone glories, he occupies you with himself in reconstructing the fallen parts & reestablishing the whole; he stimulates your taste & invention, gratifies you with the exercise of your own ingenuity & with your assistance he solves the problem of grace & beauty which the divided portions of architecture he describes would scarcely arrive at in other hands. We may say that as Robinson Crusoe made many a sailor in the hope of being cast away on a desert Island—so Colonna made many an architect full of ardor to investigate antique inventions & burn with the hope & desire of attaining new discoveries in antiquity of beauty & ingenuity—Colonna's work became universal, & it was then as now ever fresh & delightful—{our contemporary the ingenious Mr. Whightwick has written a beautiful work in the same idea called the Palace of Architecture —but he has not like Colonna interested our natural feelings by interweaving with it the story of a passion of the heart namely the adventures of a love of flesh & blood—together with the cooler love of antiquity.}

But which literature & science found in the investigation into classical remains the true fountain of taste & advancement, how would it be otherwise with fine art—where such coincidences produced a Shakespeare, a Bacon & soon after a Milton, how could they be unaccompanied with fine art in its other form of lineal beauty.

Since those fair beginnings each age has added something of its own to surprise & improve them & in antiquity (as already observed) great things have been done for our arts of which the review of the learned Canina is one of the last & most important. & with respect to progress he makes this reflection applicable to our subject—the investigation & labors says he of the 15th century having been embodied into a system by those of the 16th century & beginning of the 17th centuries as Scamozzi & others, those consequences which inevitably arise from laws too rigidly determined upon a limited range of examples, followed—first that invention became fettered & chilled by rules so as to lose all freshness & vigor in the works of the subsequent period—& to determine secondly that a revolt as with them altogether produced great extravagances in Borromini, Bernini &c. Secondly—new resources were wanted… & the investigations undertaken in Egypt, Syria, Greece & Southern Italy have added largely to our means & probably a new era of taste will follow from a better intelligence of ancient models & ancient writers as Vitruvius especially—of which I have given in former lectures the most signal proofs—Vitruvius indeed will gain in credit immensely by these investigations which confirm his dicta so remarkably. The ancients will be more than ever confessed our masters in all that refers to optics perspective and form which their practice of more than 1000 years perfected & reduced to a system of certainty.

Of them according to the simple dictum of Wren the study of architecture is rather to be promoted by the investigation of antiquity than the cultivation of fancy—our review of Greek & Roman works with Canina for our guide can never be otherwise than a profitable occupation & in employing these lectures for the present year in their investigation we cannot be reproached with the mere gratification of wonder and curiosity. ❧

*Forum by the Temple of Castor and Pollux, by C.R. Cockerell,*
*pencil and watercolor, 1815-1817. British Architectural Library, RIBA.*

# FRANCIS H. BACON

## Master Draftsman
## as Archaeologist

### BY CHRISTOPHER THOMAS

The shift to be observed in American architecture in the late nineteenth century from realistic, bodily modes of design to idealized, classical ones perhaps owes more to the practice of classical archaeology in the period than is generally recognized, as the career of Francis Henry Bacon, brother of the better known Henry Bacon (designer of the Lincoln Memorial in Washington), suggests.[1]

Francis Bacon, known to his contemporaries as Frank, was born in 1856 in Chicago to a family proud of its deep New England roots and respectful of education. After studying engineering in Maine, he enrolled as a two-year special student in William Robert Ware's architecture program at the Massachusetts Institute of Technology, the first of its kind in America. From Ware he imbibed respect for classicism and Beaux Arts methods of training and design.[2] On graduating, he worked for Ware on drawings used as teaching aids and as a draftsman for architects in New York City and Albany. In the latter capacity Bacon did some moonlighting for

McKim, Mead & Bigelow in New York, and there formed a friendship with Stanford White, who would soon join them to form the memorable partnership of McKim, Mead & White. These contacts later proved crucial to both himself and his brother Henry (who went by the name of Harry).

Frank's true interests lay elsewhere than the practice of architecture, however, and in 1878 he and a friend, Joseph Thacher Clarke, set off to visit "the sites of all the important Greek temples as [they] intended to write a history of Doric Architecture."[3] In an adventurous two seasons sailing a small craft they christened *The Dorian*, they enthusiastically explored, studied, and sketched their way

through the Aegean basin. At Hissarlik in Asia Minor, Heinrich Schliemann, the eccentric and rather savage amateur archaeologist, showed Frank the remains of what he was convinced was Homer's Troy; and at Turkish Behram, opposite Mytilene, they explored the site of the Greek colonial city of Assos, astounded at the wealth of its remains. Landing up "stone broke" in Athens in August, 1879, they had their passage home paid by Charles Eliot Norton, professor of fine arts at Harvard, who on their return agreed to seek ways to underwrite a campaign of excavation at Assos. To accomplish this Norton founded the American Institute of Archaeology.

While the campaign was being organized Frank again worked as a draftsman for McKim, Mead & White and then for Herter Brothers, the crème de la crème of American interior decorators. In Herters' drafting room he formed friendships with some of the most promising young architects in America and, in the evenings, helped form a draftsmen's sketch-club that later became the Architectural League of New York.[4]

In January, 1881, armed with money and a mandate from Norton's new institute, Clarke and Bacon returned to Assos to excavate the site thoroughly. Besides the remains of an unconventional Doric temple (having a Doric frieze combined with a figured epistyle, or architrave), they found traces of secular and civic structures and of a Street of Tombs outside the western gate that was among the finest yet to have come to light. This trove was hailed as extremely important in its time, and Frank's mentor Ware said the campaign at Assos "revealed the most complete collection of secular Greek buildings as yet discovered."[5] Because of his fluent draftsmanship, especially in ink, Frank took charge of recording many of the finds and later assumed responsibility for editing and publication of the report on the campaign, titled *Investigations at Assos* (2 Vols., 1902 and 1921). His drawings of structures at Assos—and elsewhere, for comparison—were considered marvels of their type and, in some cases, are still reproduced.

The expedition also gave Frank precious opportunities to travel throughout the Mediterranean basin, visit museums there and in northern Europe, and form links with archaeologists with similar interests, especially Robert Koldewey, a young Prussian scholar who dug with them at Assos and later became famous as the discoverer of what remained of Babylon's fabled hanging gardens. In Frank's personal life, too, the campaign had crucial results. At Chanakkale in the Dardanelles he met the American consul and noted antiquarian Frank Calvert, whose niece Alice he later married.[6] (Later still, Harry wed her sister.) So, in a remarkable way that was both personal and professional, and that belied the nineteenth-century myth of modernity, the Bacons absorbed and, so to speak, relived Greek antiquity.

Frank Bacon's lasting importance, however, lies in how he applied the Greek models he studied to his own contemporary designs and how he influenced others by his teaching and example. On his second return to America, in 1883, he went to work in Brookline, Massachusetts, for H. H. Richardson, then the leading American architect, who valued Frank's razor sharp draftsmanship and his flair for interior design.[7] At Richardson's urging he joined A.H. Davenport, a noted Boston furniture maker with whom Richardson often collaborated, as a designer and rose to become Davenport's head designer[8] and vice president. For Davenport (until 1908) and thereafter on his own, Bacon designed furniture that looked hand made—as Arts & Crafts pieces were intended to—but were in fact factory pro-

*LEFT: The Acropolis, Athens, seen from the Temple of Jupiter Olympus, 1879.*
*ABOVE: South side of Parthenon, Athens. Column overthrown by explosion.*

NDE Sept: 17·1878·
s Hôtel de Ville) ✕
D· 1567

TOP RIGHT: "Shrine" housing the Declaration of Independence and the U.S. Constitution in the foyer of the Library of Congress, Washington, D.C.; designed in 1923. Present whereabouts unknown.
BOTTOM RIGHT: Cabinet, an example of Bacon's furniture design.
LEFT: Termonde, tower of the Hôtel de Ville. Travel sketch from 1878.

FIG. 1  PERSPECTIVE SHOWING CONSTRUCTION—ALTERNATIVE SCHEME OF RESTORATION

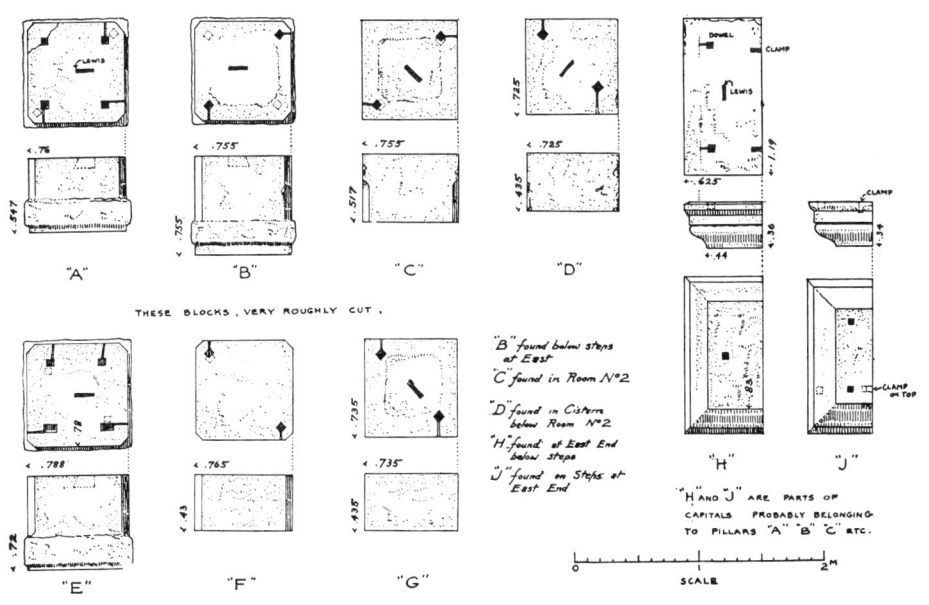

FIG. 2  EXISTING FRAGMENTS

*Conjectured reconstruction and excavated fragments of the Bazaar at Assos, from* INVESTIGATIONS AT ASSOS.

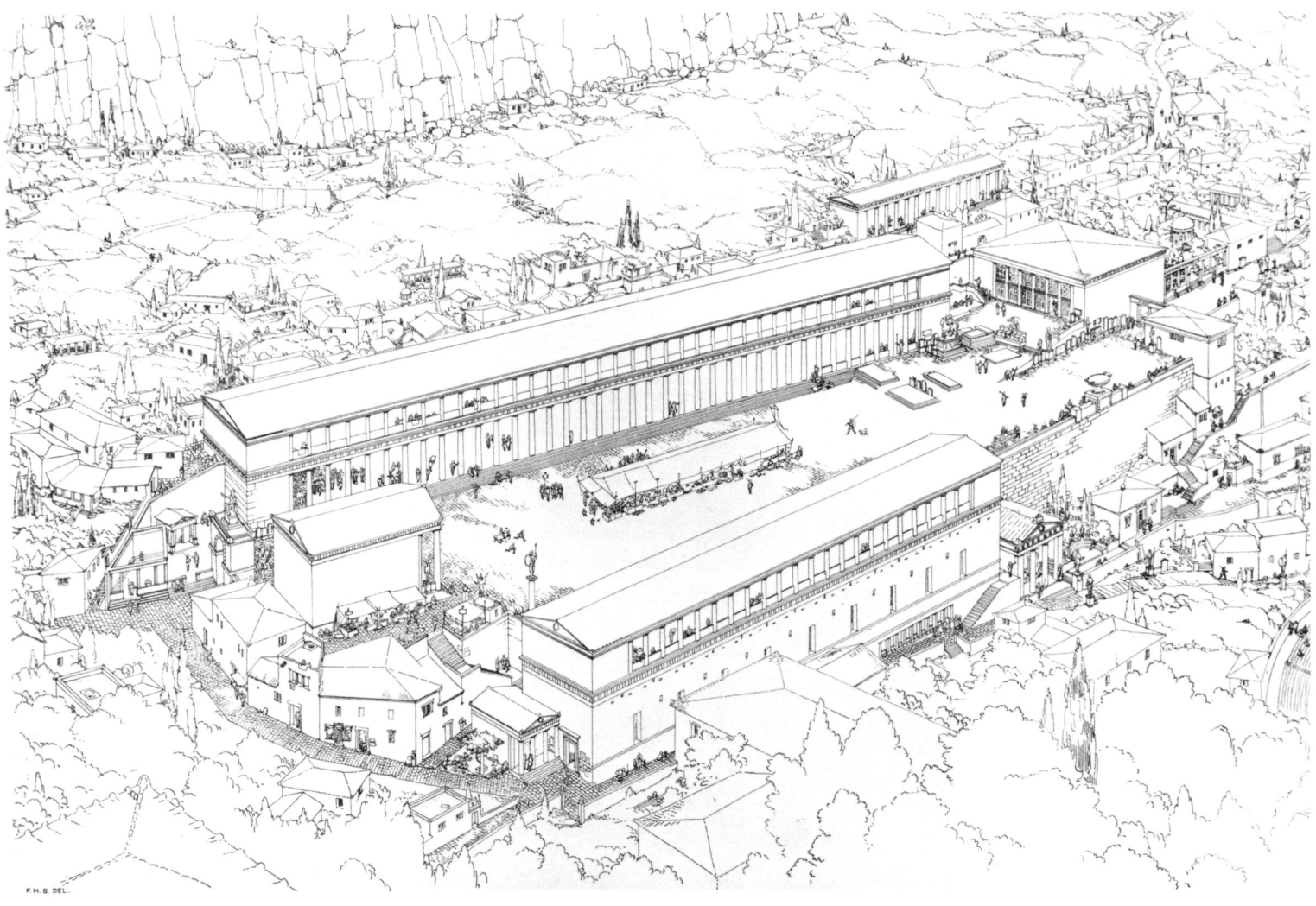

*ABOVE: The Agora at Assos, restored.*
*RIGHT: Cut-away perspective of a vaulted tomb.*
*Both images from* INVESTIGATIONS AT ASSOS.

duced. Claude Bragdon called him "the first great American emancipator from mid-Victorian stuffiness,"[9] whose work was marked by decorative probity that surely derived from the elemental Greek designs that so inspired him. Frank designed furniture for some of the outstanding academic classical buildings (public and private) of the period 1885 to 1925, in collaboration with such architects as McKim, Mead & White; Peabody & Stearns; and Shepley, Rutan & Coolidge. In Washington, where sophisticated classical design was at a premium, he designed furnishings for the White House (1902), the Secretary of the Treasury's offices (c. 1910), and the Caucus Room of the Russell Senate Office Building (1910-11), as well as members' benches for the House of Representatives (1913) and a marble "shrine" for the Declaration of Independence and U.S. Constitution in the foyer of the Library of Congress (1923).[10] He specialized in pieces emulating Greek classical and eighteenth century British and American models.

Indirectly, too, Frank influenced a generation of American classical architects, as tributes to him later in life suggest. In 1924 Frank Swales said, "His intimate study of Greek architecture has made him a leading authority upon the subject and one whose counsel and criticism has been sought by the very best of our scholarly designers of classical architecture."[11] For instance, one wonders if the sanitary white purity of design of key features of the 1893 World's Columbian Exposition—such as Charles Atwood's terminal peristyle of the Court of Honor—owed a debt to Frank's advice, as he and Atwoot had worked together at Herters'. Further research is needed to document connections like this, but not to observe the scholarly, archaeological character that crept into much American official and semi-official design from the 1880s on.

A link to Frank is clear, however, in the case of his brother Harry, whom Frank taught to draw, had placed as a draftsman in the offices of architects who were his friends, and inspired to study the remains of ancient Greece. Not surprisingly, Harry's specialty became the design of monuments and memorials based on Greek models—one reason he was chosen to design the memorial to Lincoln in Washington (1911-22).[12] Thus, Frank's knowledge of and taste for the Greek contributed to the design of the nation's tribute to its most American of presidents and, indirectly, to the turn of the century academic classicism that is among America's finest architectural expressions. ❧

## NOTES

1. This article is based on material in my Ph.D. dissertation, "The Lincoln Memorial and its Architect, Henry Bacon (1866-1924)," Yale University, 1990, mainly in Vol. 1, pp. 8-30. Archival sources on Frank Bacon, an inveterate diarist, include Bacon family papers, especially a typescript autobiography called "An Outline for the Family," and collections of his papers and drawings in MIT Archives and Special Collections, Harvard University's Houghton Library, the Boston Museum of Fine Arts (Classics Department), and the Avery Library of Columbia University.

2. Though his own work was not always classical, Ware knew students' need of training in conventional design modes and, to that end, published several texts, including *Greek Ornament* (1878) and the influential *American Vignola* (1902-5). See David G. DeLong, "William R. Ware and the Pursuit of Suitability," in Richard Oliver, ed., *The Making of an Architect, 1881-1981: Columbia University in the City of New York* (New York, 1981), pp. 12-20; and John Andrew Chewning, "William Robert Ware and the Beginnings of Architectural Education in the United States, 1861-1881," Ph.D. thesis, MIT, 1986.

3. FHB, unpublished reminiscences in Bacon family papers. Frank's wonderfully warm and humorous log of the journey, now in MIT Archives, appeared in excerpts in *Architectural Review*, n.s., 1 (July-Dec. 1912), 73-7, and passim.

4. On Herter Brothers see Doreen Bolger Burke, *In Pursuit of Beauty: Americans and the Aesthetic Movement,* Ex. cat., New York, 1986, pp. 438-40 (entry by Catherine Hoover Voorsanger). The American Decorative Arts department of the Metropolitan Museum of Art is currently organizing an exhibition on Herters. On the sketch club see Francis S. Swales, "Master Draftsmen, V: Francis H. Bacon," *Pencil Points,* 5, (Sept. 1924), 51-54, and records of the ALNY in the Smithsonian Institution's Archives of American Art.

5. In his foreword to the article "American Explorers in Assos," *The Century,* n.s., 10 (1886), 848. On the temple of Athena there see A.W. Lawrence, *Greek Architecture,* 4th ed. (Harmondsworth, 1983), pp. 147-8; and Bonna D. Wescoat, "The Temple of Athena at Assos: 1982—1985,"*American Journal of Archaeology,* 90 (1986), 194-5. On the remains more generally, especially of the civic agora, see Lawrence, op. cit., 295-6 and 346-7.

6. See Marcelle Robinson, "Pioneer, Scholar, and Victim: An Appreciation of Frank Calvert (1828-1908)," *Anatolia,* 44 (1994), 153-68. At the conference in Boston in March 1995 [co-sponsored by the Institute for the Study of Classical Architecture and Boston University's Institute for the Classical Tradition] at which a version of my article was delivered, Mrs. Robinson gave a version of her article as a paper, too.

7. William Welles Bosworth, "I Knew H.H. Richardson," *AIA Journal,* 16 (Sept. 1951), 125. It turns out that Frank was the author of the designs of much "Richardson furniture" built in the mid-1880s.

8. On the three-way relationship between Richardson, Davenport, and Bacon see Burke, *In Pursuit of Beauty,* p. 418; Anne Farnam, "A.H. Davenport and Co., Boston, Furniture Makers," *Antiques,* 1009 (May 1976), 1048-55; and idem, "H.H. Richardson and A.H. Davenport: Architecture and Furniture as Big Business in America's Gilded Age," in Paul B. Kebabian and William C. Lipke, eds., *Tools and Technologies: America's Wooden Age* (Burlington, Vt., 1979), pp. 80-92.

9. "Francis H. Bacon, 1857 [sic]-1940: An Appreciation," *Architectural Forum,* 72 (March 1940), 190.

10. The shrine went out of use when the documents were moved to their present home in the south chamber of the National Archives in 1935.

11. Swales, "Master Draftsmen: FHB," p. 54.

12. See Thomas, "The Lincoln Memorial and Its Architect" (cited in n. 1), and idem, "The Marble of the Lincoln Memorial: "Whitest, Prettiest, and...Best," *Washington History,* 5, no. 2 (fall/winter 1993—4), 42—63.

*Christopher Thomas is Assistant Professor in the Department of History in Art at the University of Victoria.*

# ARCHAEOLOGY AND INNOVATION IN THE BUILDING OF ROMA CAPITALE

## By Hugh Petter

Architects working in the Eternal City have, from the Renaissance onwards, drawn inspiration from antiquity for the design of their buildings. This architectural tradition of taking both compositional devices and decorative details from antique sources, breathing new life into them, and incorporating them into fresh designs can be appreciated readily by anyone visiting Rome today. And yet many of the buildings which one might admire on such a pilgrimage are the under-valued buildings of Roma Capitale, erected in the late nineteenth century by a forgotten generation of young Roman architects working to construct the new capital of a united monarchical Italy.

The survival of this particularly Roman architectural tradition into the twentieth century is remarkable, for the frantic transformation of the Eternal City into a modern European capital after 1870 brought with it a demand for a whole series of new building types, together with a bewildering palate of new materials and technology. But these challenges were tackled by the architects of the day with the confidence which one can only expect from those who possess a profound grasp of their cultural traditions, and the results of their labors are worthy additions to the rich architectural heritage of Rome.

Before focusing upon specific architects and buildings, however, it is instructive to consider for a moment the physical state of Rome in 1870. The population of the city at this time numbered some 230,000, seventy percent of whom were illiterate, and within the Aurelian walls only half of the area was occupied by the urban fabric; the rest was divided into secluded gardens for grand Renaissance villas and agricultural land.[1] Sheep and goats were a common sight in the streets and piazzas, and the Tiber regularly burst its banks, which it had done since antiquity. This was the Rome so lovingly described by the guide books of Augustus Hare, the novels of Francis Marion Crawford,[2] and the evocative watercolors of Ettore Roesler Franz.[3]

The breach of the Aurelian Wall at Porta Pia by the royalist troops of the House of Savoy on September 20th, 1870 was the crowning act of unification for the State of Italy. Soon afterwards the

*Master plan of Rome and its vicinity, 1873. Photo by M. Sanfilippo.*

capital of the nation formally moved from Florence to Rome, and with this shift of power came an urgent need for radical action to transform the picturesque but backward and decayed city into a modern capital of a suitable scale and grandeur to compete with Paris, Vienna, and the other great European capitals.

Within two weeks of the breach of the Aurelian wall at Porta Pia, a committee was set up to prepare a master plan for the "expansion and embellishment of the city."[4] After several abortive attempts, a master plan was finally approved by the city council in 1873 and, although never formally sanctioned by the State, this plan was used to control much of the urban activity of the early years of Roma Capitale. Within the historic center a number of existing streets were widened to open up the heart of the city. The Master Plan Commission[5] pronounced that these new streets need not be straight or uniformly wide, but could be irregular and discontinuous for the sake of sparing bits of extant construction.[6]

Before 1870, the majority of architectural commissions for those practitioners working in Rome were connected in some way with the Roman Catholic Church. But the shifting of the capital to Rome, and the consequent divide between the "black" and "white" aristocracy[7] presented the established architects with a dilemma. Should they, on the one hand, retain their allegiance to the Vatican and the black aristocracy or should they align themselves with the white aristocracy and new Royalist regime and vie for the many lucrative and exciting commissions which formed a part of the ambitious plans for the new capital? When faced with this situation, many of the established architects of the day remained *nerissimo* and, in so doing, effectively left the stage vacant for a rising generation of young architects to make their names in the building of Roma Capitale.

The architecture erected in the early years after 1870 can be broadly divided into two distinct categories. The Neo-High Renaissance or Neo-Cinquecento style was used predominantly by those architects working on commissions controlled by the city council and indeed the majority of the buildings erected in this period are designed in this manner. But a significant number of architects

> *"There is no need to call upon the 'charm' of modern foreign architecture, nor any of the 'beauty' of the medieval period, because the past of Rome and the creative fantasy of the artist are sufficient for everything." —Camillo Boito*

worked in a Neo-Antique style, particularly those whose commissions which came under the direct supervision of the State. Unlike the Neo-Cinquecento buildings, many of those in the Neo-Antique style incorporated cast iron elements, a building material which had only become widely available after Italy had estab-

*Arcaded palace at the Piazza dell' Esedra, by Gaetano Koch. Photo by Hugh Petter.*

lished her own heavy industry for the development of her navy and the railways.

Neo-cinquecentismo had been in vogue constantly in Rome since the High Renaissance, a fact which, in itself, is indicative of the pace of change in the city before 1870.[8] The majority of the architects working in this style had been trained at the notoriously reactionary and antiquated Accademia di San Luca in Rome. The curriculum of this Papal Academy, founded in 1577, had remained largely unchanged since its formation[9], and was described by Camillo Boito[10] in an article on the teaching of architecture[11]:

> *…The Genius can prove himself later when he has learned as a young man to imitate well, that is, when he has learned the elements…. The talented, when he has mastered these principles, does not pain himself by following in the footsteps of another, nor does he attach himself to the arm of anyone, but instead he develops his own technique. The teaching at the famous Accademia di San Luca follows precisely this principle. As soon as the young know how to copy from life, from paintings and from Sculpture, they turn to that great museum that is Rome, learning, seeing, imitating….*

In another article[12] on the hotly debated choice of an appropriate style for buildings in the new capital, Boito pronounced that,

> *In the city, where the antique tradition has made itself so strongly felt…to import a "Foreign" or "Italian" style to Rome out of the blue would be a blot in its history. In Rome, today's architects can, with the elements of Roman architecture, put together the modern style, creating a new organization and a new aesthetic. From the time of Bramante on, without leaving Rome or moving from ancient sources, an integral world of artistic concepts and ornamental forms is to be found. There is no need to call upon the "charm" of modern foreign architecture, nor any of the "beauty" of the medieval*

*period, because the past of Rome and the creative fantasy of the artist are sufficient for everything.*

This article, so clearly putting the case for a modern Roman architecture, caught the mood of the time and was often quoted by the architects of Roma Capitale in their own writings.[13]

The great architectural treatises of the High Renaissance, such as those by Serlio[14] and Vignola,[15] had been constantly in print in Italy from the time of their original publication. These texts formed a crucial part of the curriculum for the students at San Luca and were to be found on the shelves of the studios of all the architects working in Roma Capitale.[16] Serlio, as a young man, had worked with Peruzzi[17] in Rome, and his architectural treatise provided students with a rich diet of forms and details inspired by antique precedents. He took, for example, the cyma reversa bracket from the frieze of the crowning tier of pilasters on the Colosseum and reworked it to form a bracketed version of the Doric triglyph which he showed in a plate for a doorcase designed in that order.

Vignola, another seminal architect of the High Renaissance, also drew heavily from Roman antiquity for inspiration in his architectural treatise.[18] For example, he took the Doric order from the fornix of the Theater of Marcellus, notable for its unusual dentil cornice[19] with a crowning cavetto molding, added an idiosyncratic double torus base, and published it in his treatise. From the time of its publication, Vignola's treatise was unceasingly popular with Roman architects and consequently his Doric order is used widely in the city, even, as Krautheimer[20] has identified, in the baroque architecture of Bernini.[21]

By far the most skillful exponent of the Neo-Cinquecento style was Gaetano Koch[22] who, when he died prematurely in 1910, was acclaimed by his contemporaries as "without a doubt, the prince of contemporary Roman architects."[23] Upon graduating from the Accademia di San Luca, Koch quickly established himself in the young capital and within a few years was enjoying some of the most prestigious commissions of the day.

The project to design the arcaded palaces in the Piazza dell' Esedra at the head of the via Nazionale provided Koch with a splendid opportunity to display his talents. It was decided that the line of the exedra from the Baths of Diocletian should be retained with the building of two symmetrical crescents on the antique foundations, which would function as a grand gateway into the new capital from the railway station at the side of the antique bath complex.[24] For the engaged columns of the arcade, Koch reworked Vignola's

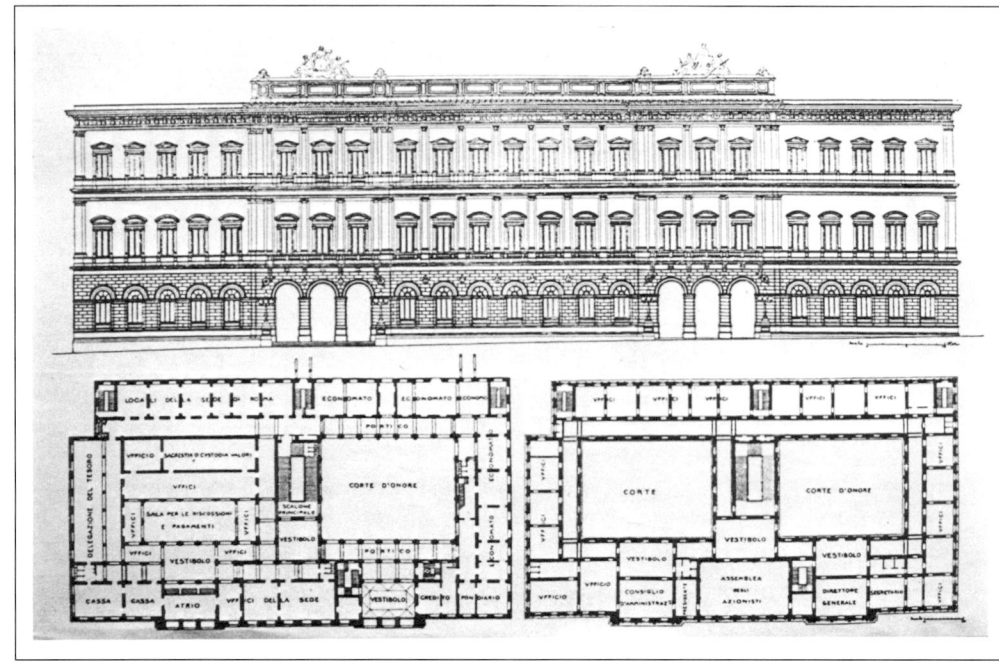

*ABOVE LEFT: Plans of the Palazzo della Banca d'Italia, designed by Gaetano Koch. Photo by L'Edilizia Moderna.*

*LEFT: Palazzo delle Esposizione, on the via Nazionale, designed by Pio Piacentini. Photo by Hugh Petter.*

*ABOVE RIGHT: Elliptical hall of the Aquarium in the Piazza Mandredo Fanti, designed by Ettore Bernich, 1883. Photo by Hugh Petter.*

*NEAR RIGHT: Maritime refrences in the Aquarium's design, as exemplified by rostrae brackets supporting the internal balconies. Photo by Hugh Petter.*

*FAR RIGHT: Engraving of an ancient Roman design, from Luigi Canina's influential book, L'ARCHETTURA DOMASTICA DI SVELTE FORME.*

Doric order, but with Serlian cyma reversa triglyph brackets over the arches in the end pavilions. The majority of the remaining architectural details, however, take their cue from Vignola.

Antique victories bearing laurel wreathes are used as caryatids and replace the uppermost tier of pilasters on the pavilions at each end of the two crescents. Above these figures, broken segmental pediments contain cartouches surrounded by allegoric groups, and the composition is dramatically completed with victory

eagles standing on pedestals on each corner. It is clear from this composition that Koch possessed a solid grasp of the symbolism of the decorative forms commonly found in antiquity which he had undoubtedly gained whilst at San Luca, and the rich embellishment of these structures clearly indicates their perceived importance in the hierarchy of new buildings erected in the city.

Half way down the via Nazionale on the left hand side is arguably Koch's finest public building, the Palazzo della Banca d'Italia, the seat of

leaf and scroll brackets into the frieze, and these support modillions in the cornice. The resulting unification of these two parts of the entablature enabled Koch to reduce the overhang required to provide a satisfactory crown to the whole composition. For the design of the acanthus and scroll brackets in the frieze, it appears that Koch may have drawn inspiration from the soffit of the cornice of the Temple of Castor in the Roman Forum[27] and it is quite feasible that, especially in light of his training, Koch would have decided to draw inspiration for his innovative detail from an antique source.

Koch gained great respect from his peers for his pioneering work in modifying the traditional Roman palazzo formula to provide simple apartment blocks for the large numbers of middle class bureaucrats pouring into the new administrative offices of the capital. The composition and decoration of these buildings, unsurprisingly, relies heavily upon the treatises of Serlio and Vignola,[28] so giving his designs a peculiarly appropriate Roman flavor. One can appreciate, both from visual evidence and from contemporary accounts such as that supplied by Marcello Piacentini, that these sources from the High Renaissance were clearly used by the majority of architects working in Roma Capitale, albeit often with less grace and skill than Gaetano Koch.

Another architect of similar caliber was Pio Piacentini.[29] His Florentine design for the Banca d'Italia[30] was rejected in favor of Koch's more Roman design, but on the other side of the via Nazionale, Piacentini was commissioned to design the Palazzo delle Esposizione, a grand new public building to provide a venue to exhibit the fine arts of the new nation.

The blind walls of the galleries are articulated with Corinthian pilasters which, in the center of the building, break forward to become freestanding columns framing the grand triumphal arch entrance.[31] The forest of columns leading up the grand staircase forms a subtle light filter to help the eye adjust from the intense light of the Roman summer to the more gentle light in the galleries.[32] The spandrels of the triumphant arch contain Victories bearing laurel wreaths and the central keystone supports a victorious eagle also with a wreath. Above the main cornice line, an attic over the entrance supports an allegorical group which crowns the whole composition.

The majority of Piacentini's work is in the more sober neo-cinquecento style, but the commission for the Palazzo delle Esposizioni fell under the umbrella of the State administration, and this may account for the more Neo-Antique flavor of the design.

the new central bank of Italy. The overall form of this long building, with two courtyards separated by a central staircase, takes its inspiration from Fuga's eighteenth century Palazzo Corsini in Trastevere which in turn draws inspiration from a design in Ammanati's unpublished treatise from the High Renaissance, "La Citta."[25] The handling of the long elevation looks to Bernini's Palazzo Odescalchi, with unadorned walls at either end, framed by pilasters and engaged columns across the central bays. The proportions

of the main group of rooms on the piano nobile, as Meeks has identified,[26] look to Palladio's work at the Palazzo Chiericati in Vicenza, which was inspired by the latter's detailed study of the Baths of Caracalla in Rome.

The crowning cornice of the Banca d'Italia presented Koch with a problem, since a conventional entablature of an appropriate size to cap this enormous structure would clearly have resulted in cantilevered stones of an unmanageable size. So instead Koch introduced acanthus

Let us turn now to consider the second category of building which I identified earlier, namely those designed in a Neo-Antique style. Compared with the quantity of buildings designed in the Neo-Cinquecento style, the Neo-Antique buildings are far fewer in number and all of them were erected by only a handful of architects working in the capital.

One such man was Ettore Bernich[33] who, in 1883, designed the aquarium in Piazza Mandredo Fanti near the center of the new Esquiline Quarter of the city. This building, intended as a place for public education, was one of a number encouraged by Quintino Sella, a Piedmontese statesman and Comptian Positivist who, when asked what were his plans for Rome replied simply, "knowledge."[34]

The Aquarium building consists of an elliptical hall, around the edge of which are grouped the tanks linked internally by a cast iron gallery[35] which allows the viewer to promenade and view the fish. Externally, a grand triumphal arch forms the entrance to the aquarium, with a large apsidal portico flanked by Doric aedicules.[36]

The Doric order on either side of the entrance portico is of particular interest. The soffit of the brackets or mutules in the cornice contain little pegs called guttae as is commonly found with the Doric order, but Bernich added an additional row of guttae to the edge of these mutules. This idiosyncratic detail bears close resemblance to the antique "Doric of Albano,"[37] from the church of S. Maria della Rotunda in that town. In antiquity this round building had been the nymphaeum of Domitian's villa, built by Rabirius in the second century AD.[38] The related character of Rabirius' nymphaeum and Bernich's Aquarium would provide a neat conceptual link which might explain the latter's use of this particular antique order.

Below the curved echinus of the capital of the Doric order, an unadorned disc forms another distinctive feature. A similar detail may be found on the Doric order of the Basilica Julia in the Forum, the excavation of which coincided with the erection of the Aquarium. It is possible, therefore, that Bernich consciously used this detail from a great public building of antiquity to adorn his own public building.

In the early 1880s Bernich had assisted the English archaeologist Parker in the excavation of the Baths of Agrippa behind the Pantheon, during the course of which the beautiful dolphin, trident, and palmette frieze, visible today, was discovered.[39] Having already identified Bernich's predilection for drawing inspiration from appropriate antique sources, it comes as no surprise to

see Agrippa's dolphin frieze reworked in the crowning entablature at the Aquarium.

Cast iron was rarely used in buildings in Rome before 1870, as it had to be imported. But with the rapid program of industrialization after the unification of the nation, this material became more readily available, and for architects the arrival of cast iron provided a wealth of new structural and decorative possibilities.

In his book entitled *L'architettura domestica di svelte forme,*[40] the distinguished architect and archae-

*Quintino Sella... when asked what were his plans for Rome, replied simply: "knowledge."*

ologist Luigi Canina encouraged those of his colleagues who were wrestling with the detailing of "thin forms" in either wood or iron to look to the fantastical and theatrical architectural compositions in Pompeian Second and Fourth Style wall paintings for inspiration. The pages of Canina's book are full of exquisite engravings of such scenes from antiquity, including those to be found at Nero's Domus Aurea, and other examples from Rome.

Bernich drew heavily from Canina's publication in the internal decoration at the aquarium, where many of the details have playful maritime references. For example, dolphins with curling tails take the place of conventional volutes on the capitals of some of the pilasters. This theme is continued with fish scale iron railings on the staircase, modeled on antique transennae, and with a balcony supported on large rostrae on the first floor which displays the House of Savoy coat of arms. The remaining wall areas are covered with painted panels which portray a variety of well known subjects from classical mythology and important scenes from the building of Roma Capitale.

Although the exterior fabric of the Aquarium was relatively poorly constructed, its scholarly detail, its innovative use of cast iron, and its rich internal color scheme make it one of the most interesting and imposing Neo-Antique buildings constructed in the early years of the capital.

Bernich's other buildings in Rome exhibit a similar delight in the reworking of antique details. For example his palazzo facing the Colosseum fuses Vignola's Doric order from the Theater of Marcellus with Rabirius' Doric of Albano in the cornice crowning the rusticated ground and first floors. The giant order which unites the piano nobile and second floor is Corinthian, with an eagle replacing the usual rosette under the abacus of the capital, similar to that found on the Corinthian order of the Portico of Octavia. The overall form of this palazzo, however, with a rusticated base, a giant order, and pavilions above the main cornice line owes more to the High Renaissance and Serlio's idealised palace facades from his *Five Books of Architecture.*

Giulio de Angelis[41] was one of the few architects working in Roma Capitale who, although Roman by birth, had received his architectural education at the Polytechnic of Milan. At that time, Milan was the most prosperous and industrialized city in the peninsula, and this fact, combined with the proximity to the rest of Europe, resulted in many of the early Italian cast iron buildings being erected there.[42] These revolutionary structures appear to have fired the imagination of the young De Angelis for, after graduating, he returned to his native city and produced many of the finest iron buildings in Rome over a short period in the early 1880s. His Rinascente department store on the via del Corso was the first such building in the new capital. De Angelis' composition has striking similarities with that of the antique gates of Verona as illustrated in Serlio's treatise, where a giant arcade is surmounted by two smaller arcaded galleries. The open facade proudly displays the iron structure, while also providing ample space for elaborate window displays. The interior of the building boasts a light cast iron structure with the various floors of the shop united by a central atrium, the detail of which draws inspiration from the plates of Canina's *Svelte Forme.* Externally the bronze rostra on the corner pilasters emphasize the triumphant air of the building sited on the corner of Piazza Colonna, the heart of the new administration.

Sadly, however, De Angelis' clients were all badly affected by the financial crash in the 1880s and he was forced to abandon architectural practice for a career in conservation, during which he restored a number of antique monuments.[43]

TOP:
Palace of Justice,
designed by
Guglielmo Calderini.
Photo by Hugh Petter.

LEFT:
Palace facing
the Colosseum,
designed by
Ettore Bernich.
Photo by Hugh Petter.

RIGHT:
Rinascente depart-
ment store,
designed by
Giulio de Angelis. Photo
by Hugh Petter.

Arguably the best known and most criticized building in Roma Capitale is the monument to King Victor Emmanuel II in Piazza Venezia. Much has been written about this pompous, self-conscious monument, although most of this criticism is, as David Watkin has correctly identified,[44] focused upon the position of the building rather than the architectural form and detail.

Those who care to look beyond the obvious criticisms of Sacconi's creation are rewarded with a highly articulate architectural design. Externally the decoration of the various terraces draws heavily upon antique sources with, for example, rostra, victories, military trophies, and garlands of oak leaves; the latter are without their acorns, which, in antiquity, was a recognized funereal motif. The labyrinthine interior contains an extraordinary sequence of vast exhibition halls, modeled upon ancient Roman bath buildings; these are linked by a grand staircase which gently winds up through the various floors before arriving, finally, at the crowning colonnade from which one is rewarded with remarkable panoramic views of Rome. In front of the extraordinary theatrical backdrop a pedestal supports the huge bronze equestrian statue of Victor Emmanuel, facing north across the piazza Venezia towards the via del Corso.

The monument can be seen as one of the most brutal anti-papal acts of the new administration and it is significant that its siting, its decoration, and the overall composition, which draws heavily on the ancient necropolis of Praeneste,[45] are deliberately connected with antiquity. For it was the conscious forging of this link with the antique which formed a key part of the new administration's attempts to loosen the grip of St. Peter on the new capital.

Aside from the monument to Victor Emmanuel, the other well known and much maligned building of the early years of Roma Capitale is the vast Palace of Justice, on the Prati di Castello near the Vatican.[46] The palazzo is approached on axis via the Humbert I Bridge which, it has been suggested, emphasizes that it was the House of Savoy which had brought law and order to the capital. The architect of the Palace of Justice, Guglielmo Calderini,[47] skillfully manipulates the orders[48] to weave together this vast composition, the heavy rustication, and ornamentation of which owes a good deal to Piranesi's fantastical engravings.

The extraordinary development of Rome after 1870 is an enormous subject which has, for too long, remained in the shadows of the history of the Eternal City. The period is often only referred to in passing and under such derogatory titles as "The Rape…" or "The Third Sack." But while the building of Roma Capitale is by no means the most distinguished period in the architectural history of the city, many of the architects of this frantic period of urban activity

*The results of this ingress of modernist ideology into Rome is the ever thickening crust of concrete blocks which have neither the architectural nor the urban qualities of their nineteenth century ancestors.*

did manage to carry the long established architectural traditions of their city into the twentieth century. It can only be lamented that in more recent times, Roman architects have self-consciously abandoned the traditions of their city, preferring instead to root their work in the barren soil of international modernism.

The results of this ingress of modernist ideology into Rome is the ever thickening crust of concrete blocks which have neither the architectural nor the urban qualities of their nineteenth century ancestors. And yet while the suburban sprawl of Rome today continues at an alarming rate, the center of the city remains trapped in a time warp with the prohibition of any new development in the heart of the capital. Such paralysis, though widespread throughout the world, is clearly not healthy for the life of any town, and it is particularly tragic that even Rome, the Eternal City, has succumbed finally to this disease.

However, the rich architectural fabric of the center of Rome clearly demonstrates that working within the spirit of the traditions of the city by no means stifles the creativity or imagination of the architect, while at the same time ensuring that the contribution of each generation respects the established architectural character of the extant buildings. If only those responsible for the development of Rome today could be reunited with the threads of their rich architectural heritage, one could be sure that these would be woven in new and interesting ways, and that archaeology and innovation could be fused again in the development of the Eternal City. ❧

## ACKNOWLEDGMENTS

I am most grateful to the Faculty of Fine Arts and Architecture of the British School at Rome for the award of a Scholarship which enabled me to undertake a substantial program of research into the development of Rome post 1870; to Valerie Scott, Richard Hodges, Amanda Claridge, and to Maria Pia Malvezzi, whose wizardry in gaining access to obscure places and archives was invaluable. In addition, I should like to express my thanks to Emanuela Fabbricotti, whose generosity in allowing me access to her family archives gave me a profound insight into the work of her great uncle Gaetano Koch; to ARCUK for their generous financial support in the form of the William Kretchmer Award; to Geoffrey Broadbent and Robert Adam who guided my program of research and, with Peter Hodson, were constant sources of encouragement. I am greatly indebted to my fellow scholars Robin Williams, Terry Kirk, and Francesco Garofalo who know far more about the political manipulation of the antique than I ever shall and who drew my attention to many of the points made in the latter part of the essay, and all my other friends and family who have assisted me in the course of my labors. Finally, I should like to thank my long-suffering fiancée (and now wife) Chloe, for her endless patience as I wrestled with these words, and to whom I became engaged during the preparation of this essay in Michelangelo's piazza on the Capitoline Hill—what finer spot than the center of the ancient world!

## NOTES

1. Lanciani, R., *Notes from Rome* (London, 1988), 171-4.
2. Francis Marion Crawford was an Italian-American author whose contemporary novels such as *Don Orsino* (1892) give a unique insight into the mood of the period in Rome.
3. Ettore Roesler Franz (1845-1907) painted some 120 views of Rome before the rude awakening of the city, after 1870. This collection, known affectionately as "Roma Sparita," is on view at the Museo di Roma, and in published form by L.B. Dal Maso and A. Venditti, *Rome the Picturesque* (Terni, 1981).
4. For a full discussion of the early master plans see I. Insolera, in *Urbanistica* 27.
5. "Sul Piano Regolatore di Roma: Relazione della Commissione Esaminatrice al Consiglio Comunale," Rome, 1873, 6-7.
6. The relatively sensitive approach to carving new arteries through the extant fabric of Rome contrasts strongly with that adopted in Paris where points were connected with straight lines and with little concern for what stood in the way of these new axial routes.
7. The Black aristocracy retained their allegiance to the Pope and refused to have anything to do with the new administration. See the novels of F.M. Crawford; J.R. Glorney Boulton, *Roman Century* (London, 1970); and C. Hibbert, *Rome: The Biography of a City* (Harmondsworth, 1985).
8. I am indebted to Dr. Janet Delaine for helping me to establish that the main sources for building materials (for example brick, travertine, pozzolana, and pepperino) in the early years of Roma Capitale were the same as those which had been in constant use since antiquity.
9. A common misconception is that the architectural training in Rome at this time was merely copying that at the

Ecole des Beaux Arts in Paris. The reality, in fact, is that the reverse is true: see D.D. Egbert, *The Beaux Arts Tradition in French Architecture* (New Jersey, 1980), 19.

10. Camillo Boito (1836-1914) has been described as the Italian Ruskin. See C.L.V. Meeks, *Italian Architecture 1750-1914* (New Haven, 1966), 207-9 for a discussion on the man, his ideas on architecture, and his influence. To read some of his numerous articles, see M.A. Crippa, ed., *Camillo Boito: Il Nuovo e L'Antico in Architettura* (Milan, 1988).

11. Boito, "L'architettura odierna e l'insegnamentodi essa," 1860. See Crippa, op. cit. p. 147.

12. Boito, "Rassegna Artistica," 1875. See Crippa, op. cit., pp. 63-66.

13. For example see G. Koch, 1883, *Palazzo por La Banca Nazionale da costruizi in Roma. Relazione sul secondo progetto redatto dall'architetto Gaetano Koch* (Roma, 1983), p.4.

14. For a full discussion of the publications and influence of Sebastian Serlio (1475-1554), see C. Thoenes, ed. *Sebastiano Serlio* (Milan, 1989).

15. Vignola, *I Cinque Ordini di Architettura Civile,* 1563 (Rome, 1861).

16. See M. Piacentini, *Le Vicende Edilize di Roma dal 1870 ad oggi* (Rome, 1952), p. 72.

17. Serlio worked with Baldassare Peruzzi (1481-1536) from 1514 until the sack of Rome. Peruzzi was a considerable scholar of antiquity, and his master's enthusiasm for the antique clearly rubbed off on Serlio. His treatise was the first to codify the five orders, together with information on how to construct them and examples of compositions from antiquity, from the Renaissance and of his own designs.

18. During the 1860s Vignola's treatise was published in special Roman editions including examples of the author's works in Rome and northern Lazio.

19. Anyone who has attempted a design in the Doric order will inevitably have encountered problems in spacing the triglyphs and metopes in the frieze. The triglyphs, which are half a diameter wide should be centered over the order and the metopes between these triglyphs should be square. In the cornice, mutule brackets align over the triglyphs. In the abstract this sounds straightforward enough, but the problem becomes evident when one tries to integrate this rigid horizontal proportioning system with arches and other vertical elements, as at the Theater of Marcellus. The solution in this particular antique example adopted by Vignola is brilliant in its simplicity. By using an essentially Ionic entablature with the Doric order, the problem of the triglyph spacing disappears, and the horizontal proportioning becomes infinitely flexible to coordinate easily with other elements of the design. It is this neat solution to one of the most taxing problems facing architects working with the Doric order which has ensured that Vignola's treatise has remained so popular since its original publication.

20. See R. Krautheimer, *The Rome of Alexander VII, 1655-1667* (New Jersey, 1985), pp. 37-47.

21. For example, the details from Bernini's Palazzo Odescalchi in Piazza SS. Apostoli are all taken directly from Vignola, as is the Doric order used in the famous piazza S. Pietro, albeit in this latter example, the order itself is stretched to an Ionic proportion.

22. Gaetano Koch (1849-1910). I should like to acknowledge my debt of gratitude to my friend Emanuela Fabbricotti, whose great uncle, Ottaviano, was Gaetano's brother. The two shared a studio and worked together.

23. Obituary in *La Tribuna,* May 15, 1910, p.6.

24. Palimpsest is when the buildings of one age take on a new significance or function in another age. This phenomenon is one of the characteristics of the architecture of Rome, where many of the surviving buildings from antiquity have been reused in subsequent rebuildings of the city. Obvious examples include the Pantheon or the Borsa. One

*Grand interior staircase of the monument to Victor Emmanuel II in the Piazza Venezia, designed by Giusseppe Sacconi. Photo by Hugh Petter.*

could argue that this phenomenon is also present in the decision to retain the line of the exedra with the new curved palaces which surround the Piazza dell' Esedra.

25. See M. Fossi, *Bartolome Ammanati: La Citta, appunti per un trattato* (Rome, 1970).

26. Meeks, op. cit., 1966, p. 334.

27. The entablature of the Temple of Castor was published by Palladio in his *Four Books of Architecture*, 1570 (1965 ed.) although the temple was not actually excavated fully until the early years of the twentieth century.

28. We know from M. Piacentini, 1950, that Koch and his contemporaries also had copies of Letarouilly's famous three volumes in their studios. In addition, Emanuela Fabbricotti recalls that Koch had a complete set of Piranesi's prints as a working copy in the studio. Consequently we can be rea-

sonably sure that the libraries of these architects contained a fairly comprehensive collection of the history of Roman architecture.

29. Pio Piacentini (1846-1928). See V. Sgarbi, *Dizionario dei Monumenti Italiani e dei Loro Autori* (Milan, 1991), pp. 200-201.

30. Pio Piacentini's design for the Bank of Italy is illustrated in Piacentini, op. cit., 1952.

31. For a full discussion of Piacentini's composition, refer to Meeks, op. cit. 1966, 332. Meeks correctly points out that Piacentini's triumphal arch with the trabeated side openings is in fact a reworking of a Palladian motif, although of course its roots lie, ultimately, in the triumphal arches of antiquity.

32. E. Lavagnino, *L'Arte Moderne dai Neoclassici ai Contemporai,* I (Turin , 1956), 609.

33. Ettore Bernich (1848?-1890). See Scarbi, op. cit., pp. 43-44.

34. B. Croce, *A History of Italy, 1871-1915* (Oxford, 1929).

35. The cast iron galleries of the Aquarium are one of the earliest examples of the use of this material in Roma Capitale. The cast iron was manufactured at Castell Maggiore near Bologna.

36. Apsidal porticoes such as that on the Aquarium are a common feature of antique bath complexes; the related nature of these two types of buildings would form a neat conceptual reason for Bernich's use of the detail on this building.

37. I am indebted to Peter Hodson for drawing this point to my attention.

38. A fragment of this particular Doric order had been drawn by the great High Renaissance architect Pirro Ligorio at the church of S. Maria della Rotunda in Albano in the sixteenth century. A Frenchman, Roland Fréart de Chambray, in the mid-seventeenth century included the Doric of Albano in his influential *Parallel of Orders* after which time it has been used all over the world, but is rarely found in Rome. It is to be lamented that all trace of the order today has vanished from Albano, although there is possibly one surviving fragment fixed to the wall in the cloister of S.S. Quattro Coronati in Rome.

39. See R. Lanciani, op. cit. 1988, p. 99.

40. See L. Canina, *Particolare genere di Architettura Domestica decorato con ornamenti di svelte forme* (Rome, 1852).

41. De Angelis (1845-1906). See Sgarbi, op. cit., 1991, pp. 86-7.

42. Meeks, op. cit., 1966, p. 29.

43. De Angelis went to restore historic buildings in Lazio and the Abruzzo and directed the conservation works at the Baths of Caracalla.

44. D. Watkin, *A History of Western Architecture* (1986), p. 43.

45. The antique necropolis of Praeneste at Palestrina had recently been restored by Luigi Canina.

46. I am indebted to my fellow scholars Robin Williams and Terry Kirk for first drawing my attention to this juxtaposition.

47. Guglielmo Calderini (1837-1916). See Sgarbi, 1991, p. 69.

48. See Meeks, op. cit., 1966, p. 354.

*Hugh Petter is a Foundation Course tutor at the Prince of Wales's Institute of Architecture and a Fellow of the British School at Rome.*

# ARCHITECTURE & ARCHAEOLOGY

# THE PRACTITIONER'S VIEW

The dialogue between archeology and architecture may be central to the classical tradition, but opinion on the matter has been anything but unanimous. The uses of historical precedent—and which precedents to use—have been debated at least since the time of Vitruvius. Before it was interrupted by the ascendancy of the International Style, the battle of the "ancients" and the "moderns" split the academies, with some voices questioning the value of any study of historical models. Of course, both freedom and scholarship are equally valuable in maintaining a living tradition. Let us hope the debate continues far into the future, with much passionate oratory, and no clear winner. Here are three views. —S.W.S.

---

## ERNEST FLAGG

*Ernest Flagg (1857-1947) studied architecture at the Ecole des Beaux Arts and is best known as the designer of the Singer Building in New York.*

The Greeks labored for a thousand years in perfecting the design of their temples, always engaged on a single type of building without the admixture of any foreign element.

The builders of western Europe, in like manner, labored with their aim constantly in view —almost from the time of the downfall of the Roman Empire until the end of the twelfth century, a period of about eight hundred years, before their efforts were crowned with complete success.... During the later development of styles in France, from the Renaissance to the Revolution..., changes in fashion followed each other in regular and orderly sequence, all minds engaged... in adapting [and] improving what they saw about them.

CONTINUED ON PAGE 43

---

## THOMAS GORDON SMITH

*Chair of the School of Architecture at the University of Notre Dame, Smith is the author of* CLASSICAL ARCHITECTURE: RULE & INVENTION.

In the early 1970s, when I first began to study architecture as a graduate student at Berkeley, I presented a program to my advisor which involved the simultaneous study of architectural history and design. This was met by the good natured retort, "So you want to do applied archaeology?" This holdover from the polemics of the 1920s, with its anti-*envoi* attitude, shocked my sensibility. Seen from a more remote perspective, however, he was right.

If we are to retrieve an unselfconscious relationship to old architecture, and break down the psychological barriers that modernists impose between dead people and our age, then we certainly should be enthusiastic about applying the

CONTINUED ON PAGE 44

---

## STEPHEN FALATKO

*Stephen Falatko currently practices architecture in Singapore. His design work was featured in* THE CLASSICIST NUMBER ONE.

When a designer confronts the facts of life, it's best to realize that things are not just what you think they are or would have them be. To have your preconceptions dismantled and rebuilt is a source of strength. That is the value of classical archaeology to architects.

My involvement with archaeology began with a part-time student job in the expedition room at Princeton's Department of Art and Archaeology. I worked with William Childs, Shelley Stone, John Kenfield, and Barbara Tsakirgis on a variety of tasks.

I did very little actual excavation, though I was around it and assisted all the time. My main tasks were to record existing finds and advise on

CONTINUED ON PAGE 45

ERNEST FLAGG
CONTINUED FROM PAGE 42

The nineteenth century opened a most disastrous epoch for western architecture. The fundamental principles upon which it had always rested and to which every truly great production had been due now began to give place to architectural archaeology—a practice which…has sapped the art of its vitality and undermined its very foundations.

Reason, which had hitherto governed, no longer held sway. The orderly evolution of styles or fashions ceased and the copying of former styles was substituted…. Invention was succeeded by imitation, and with it the progress of architecture as a fine art, in great measure ceased, for the practice of archaeology in the guise of architecture became common.

…Guadet, speaking of French church architecture, says: "The architect of today puts to himself in good faith this monstrous question, the mere statement of which at any other epoch would have branded him who made it a fool. 'Shall I, artist of the twentieth century, make my building of the twelfth, thirteenth, fourteenth, fifteenth, or sixteenth centuries?' And so deeply has the evil penetrated, that he does not even comprehend the idiocy of the proposition." What applies here to churches only in France, applies to all architecture in most other countries.

When one looks for the cause of this strange and disastrous manifestation, he finds it originated in the enthusiastic admiration for classic remains as revealed by the discovery of Pompeii, the publication of the many works on classic architecture which followed, and most notably Stuart and Revett's *Antiquities of Athens*. The beautiful examples of architecture thus revealed engendered a desire to copy them; that is to say, to practice archaeology instead of architecture; and progress in art stopped, as if by a blight, for reason, an essential element of good design, was discarded.

In this country, up to that time, builders had been engaged in adapting the classic forms inherited from the mother country to the materials employed here in building, and the structures to their uses. The classic proportions were modified to make them suitable for wood, and new forms in great variety, invented by so doing. All this…gave place to the slavish imitation of Greek models, with the result that archaeology was substituted for good architecture. The light, fresh, and graceful forms and details which they had created when following the sound principles of design, were succeeded by heavy imitations of stone architecture carried out in wood; the structures were no longer adapted to their uses; but the

Greek temple became the model for every kind of building, and queer imitations of it sprung up all over the land. It seemed as if everyone had suddenly become obsessed with the desire to live in a Greek temple, and the same form was used for churches and public buildings of all kinds. The Colonial style was killed at a blow.

…The publication of Pugin's and Rickmann's works, and others on Gothic architecture, started a new era of archaeology, and the desire to live in Greek temples was succeeded by a similar desire to live in what were supposed to be Gothic buildings. …The multiplication of illustrations and the introduction of photography led to the copying of all kinds of styles, and building became a veritable archaeological salad, the like of which the world

*Singer Tower, New York, 1908; demolished 1970. Ernest Flagg, architect. Photograph courtesy of the Singer Sewing Company.*

had never seen on earth—Egyptian, Italian, Tudor, Queen Anne, Romanesque, Colonial, French, and a hundred other imitations, but nothing that could be called American, unless it be the comic mixture produced.

Slavish copying leads nowhere in art. Every production that has stood the test of time, and is regarded as a masterpiece, was, when made, strictly modern; that is, in the style of its time and place.

…When a pupil at the Ecole des Beaux Arts, I was once engaged on a design for three houses on an irregular plot. I had recently made a tour of the provinces and became enamored of the beautiful remains of sixteenth century architecture which I had visited. In my design I drew inspiration… from the Hôtel d'Ecoville at Caen. Working next to me in the studio was a young Frenchman, engaged on the same problem, but doing so without the aid of archaeology. His design was unmistakably French of the nineteenth century, and very ugly it appeared to me. He often expressed his admiration of the beautiful motives I was so freely borrowing, and spoke in no very respectful terms of the style he himself was using. I asked him why he did not do as I had done, and take for a model something good-looking. "Nothing I should like better," said he, "and tomorrow I shall ask the Patron to let me do so." But when the morrow came, "the Patron" would have none of it.

He did not say it in so many words, but his meaning was plain. For me, a foreigner, it did not matter. I might practice archaeology if I chose; but for a Frenchman, No—emphatically NO!

Monsieur Blondel was right. He knew, as every other eminent French architect knows, that the road of archeology in architecture leads nowhere. To yield to the temptation is to abandon progress; to detach oneself from the evolution of modern art and go backward, not forward. The logical Frenchman understands this thoroughly and cannot be beguiled into the ways of archaeology. The national style of the time may be ugly, fashions often are; but then it is the duty of everyone using it to contribute…toward its beautification. But to abandon modern architecture for some bygone fashion which reflects neither the spirit nor civilization of the time…is to confess defeat and enter a blind alley. The national style, for the country fortunate enough to have one, is a priceless heritage from the ages—a living thing—an evolution in progress,

ERNEST FLAGG
CONTINUED FROM PAGE 43

always advancing, always changing, always reflecting the habits, manners, and art of the time.

Soon after…my return from Paris I was consulted by a prominent citizen of New York who intended to build a great mansion on Fifth Avenue, as to what French…architects he had best apply to for plans. I recommended my former master, Paul Blondel, than whom no architect in France stood higher, also Monsieur Daumet, architect of the Château of Chantilly for the Duc d'Aumale, and who was associated with Monsieur Girault, since architect of the Petit Palais of the Champs Elysées, of the royal palace for the King of Belgium, etc. My friend applied to Messrs. Daumet and Girault; the latter made the sketches which were altogether worthy of his great genius. They called for a work of art of the highest type. I saw the design and shall never forget its beauty, but it was not what was wanted. The drawings called for a work of architecture; the American taste demanded archaeology. They called for a building of the nineteenth century; my friend wanted one of the fifteenth.

…From an American architect he had no difficulty in obtaining a very beautiful archaeological study, which when constructed satisfied his taste and, it may be supposed, the taste of the community.

…During the last twenty-five or thirty years a great many young men have gone from here to Paris to study architecture; but except in a few instances they have brought home the shucks of the French…teaching and missed the kernel, which is the reasonableness of it all. They have failed, for the most part, to acquire that appreciation of the fitness of things upon which the whole structure of French taste is founded.

In my designs of these little houses the aim has been to begin at the foundation, so to speak, to use simple and primitive forms and methods, with the hope that they may commend themselves, and prove a new basis in house design, and so aid in establishing a more healthy environment for future growth. ❧

---

*This essay is excerpted from* SMALL HOUSES: THEIR ECONOMIC DESIGN AND CONSTRUCTION, *by Ernest Flagg, 1922.*

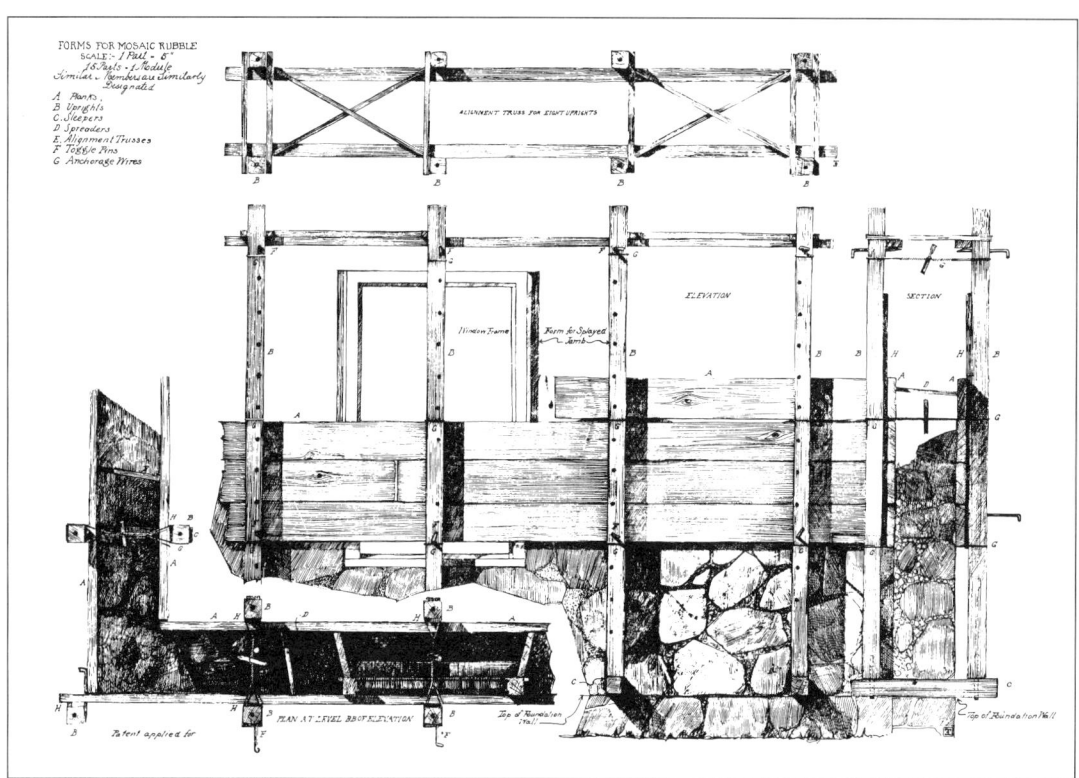

*Formwork device for constructing mosaic rubble. From* SMALL HOUSES: THEIR ECONOMIC DESIGN AND CONSTRUCTION, *by Ernest Flagg, 1922.*

THOMAS GORDON SMITH
CONTINUED FROM PAGE 42

lessons of archaeology to contemporary work. Beyond that, architects might even provide valuable insights to archaeologists out of their abilities in perception and inherent interest in how architectural pieces fit together in a building.

For at least a decade I have realized that recent archaeological discoveries can be as vital to our culture as other more obvious and highly touted technical developments, such as computers. The field of classical archaeology is particularly active today. Of especial interest to the architect is Lothar Haselberger's earth-shaking discovery of full-scale working drawings faintly engraved on the walls of the Temple of Apollo at Didyma in Turkey, built between 300 B.C. and 300 A.D. Haselberger's meticulous examination of this treasure will take years to publish, but the basic ideas are easily accessible in an article in the December 1985 issue of *Scientific American*. Here we see the only known image of the ancient method of creating entasis. Even Vitruvius did not bother to describe this subtle concept, but referred his readers to a perhaps similar image at the back of Book III—a figure which has been lost since late antiquity. What a resource to have this concept so clearly articulated for us at Didyma! Now we must learn to apply it.

Recently the assistant of a famous architect called me for advice on what method of entasis should be used for greatest accuracy. Should it be a (vaguely described) method given by Vignola or should the radius point be set a mile away? I sent faxes of Haselberger's discovery, but learned later that the pages were unfurled through the office with the protest that the method was far too complex to understand! This quick study approach does not lead to refined and rigorous architecture, nor does it provide the pleasing pain of grappling with innovative problems. It illustrates, instead, a far too common attitude taken by some architects who are taken seriously by the public as part-time classicists.

I believe that it is natural for a true classical architect to be involved with archaeology. The obvious first place to turn to is antiquity. While engaged in a project to provide illustrations for a new edition of Vitruvius I learned that Hellenistic and Roman sites along the Turkish coast and foothills offer a gold mine of ancient intellectual property—some of the best architectural paradigms on earth. On the other hand, I have re-

cently discovered that valuable sites need not be so far away. For instance, I have begun to research and do measured drawings of American Grecian houses of the mid-west, built 1825-60. Although some

of both geometric and figural type, and were highly colored. From the original position of the tiles we could deduce things about the overall roof configurations, for which I helped pro-pose some

of these buildings are well preserved, many are in a state of near ruin. One of the most interesting is the Swift house, once located near Vermilion, Ohio, but burned by vandals in 1923. Fortunately, it was pho-tographed, measured and published by Pro-fessor Thomas O'Donnel from the Univer-sity of Illinois before its destruction. The Historic American Buildings Survey even did a post-mortem in the 1930s.

The site of this house can still be visited in the now fallow alluvial valley that, judging from the nearly vanished structure, brought unexpected wealth to its builder in 1840. What is particularly interesting is how a visit to the overgrown foundations can prompt *déjà vu* sensations of ancient sites. For, thanks to the sage documentation of our forbears, we know that the wooden cap-itals of the American building revived the archaeological paradigm of the capitals from the likewise obliterated Temple on the Ilissus near Athens. Here in Ohio we thus pay homage to members of an earlier generation of documen-tors, James Stuart and Nicholas Revett, for con-veying this artifact through engravings. By so doing, they inspired new architecture all over the world, from the American West of the 1840s to the American midwest of the 1990s.

In following a variety of archaeological para-digms, all of the work in this journal carries on this same tradition. In one of my own projects, called the Vitruvian House, Vitruvian symmetries were employed throughout the building except where recent archaeological insights could be applied. For example, the central block follows Vitruvius' prescription for the "well-columned" (*eustylos*) temple, while the column bases and shafts derive from Haselberger's discoveries at Didyma. Similarly, the profile of the *epistylos* follows a discovery that I made on the site of the Temple of Artemis at Magnesia by Hermogenes. There, each fascia slopes at a different angle, creat-ing a bulging sensation. At another project, the re-cently completed Kulb House in Central Illinois, I employed the Swift House in Vermilion as the generating idea. Here, the wide Ionic portico with its detailed allusions to Illisus has been inte-

*ABOVE: Pediment of temple at Garitsa, Corcyra, restored by Dr. E. Buschor.*
*BELOW: Vitruvian House, South Bend, Indiana, 1989-91. Thomas Gordon Smith, architect.*

grated into a two-story format. Whether the sources are from ancient or modern archaeologi-cal sites, the information behind these two designs has been realized through "applied archaeology."

Far from easily imitating ancient formulae as implied twenty years ago in an anxious jibe, a rigorous classical architect inevitably involves him- or herself with serious study of archaeologi-cal material. It provides both challenge and reward and opens new avenues for architecture. Embracing archaeology and discovering its rele-vance leads to both academic and artistic devel-opments. Through understanding these remains of our forbears and seeking to re-integrate their physical and spiritual meaning, we better under-stand our own humanity and can better solve current architectural problems. ❧

---

**STEPHEN FALATKO**
CONTINUED FROM PAGE 42
hypothetical reconstruction of the buildings to which they belonged. Some of this took place in New Jersey, and some in Sicily.

My largest assignment involved architectural terracotta from the roofs of archaic period Greek structures. These all came from Morgantina, were

hypotheses. These buildings were evidently bizarre, not at all what you think of when you think of classical architecture. Yet for every building we of the twentieth century consider paradigmatically Greek—every Paestum, every Aegina—there were thousands of these little *naiskoi,* sanctuaries in the form of ceremonial granaries or treasuries with their big, brightly colored roofs, which have yet to enter into our version of the classical canon.

Although their makers must have intended them to arouse feelings of terror, I was very much moved to handle these beau-tifully wrought fragments. The Abbé Laugier had a philosophical point to make with his fiction of the rustic hut, but had he been there with me among the expedition scaf-folds, he too would have recognized in them the First Architecture.

Sometimes I am called upon to design buildings in rural New York State. When I see its wooden neoclassical architecture from the 1830s and 1840s I always travel back in my mind to my work in Morgantina. For there, in 1980, we also knew what the ancient Greeks knew. The same hot African wind blew up at precisely the same time each morning to disturb our surveying instruments. The same spring below the city gate—the Sicilian workmen called it "*Il bar cen-trale*"—gave us the same cold water, sometimes carried up in clay amphorae of the same shape. We trudged up the same ridge, sweated under the same sun, broke our backs moving the same stones, and at the same thresholds were greeted by the same motto as they: *EU EXEI*— "it's good here." And we would know the end of summer in exactly the same way they knew it, with the first clouds, the first cloudburst, after which the haze over the plain of Catania would vanish and we would have the year's first view of Mount Etna.

I think of all this when I build now because others need to know it, people whom I will never meet but through my work. Some archi-tects would say that just because we drive cars now and watch television, none of this matters; such a depressing, deprived, provincial outlook! I pity them for it. ❧

# FROM THE OFFICES

When architect Ken Tate traveled to Italy in 1993 to study Palladio's Villa Emo as a precedent for a new house, he entered into a tradition of the scholarly documentation of architecture beginning with Vitruvius in ancient Rome. Vitruvius's *Ten Books of Architecture*, rediscovered in the fifteenth century, led to a classical revival largely instigated by Leon Battista Alberti, whose 1485 *De re aedificatoria* was the first architectural treatise to appear since the fall of Rome. Alberti's work in turn influenced that of Donato Bramante, an architect especially favored by Palladio, who himself contributed to a new edition of Vitruvius published in 1556 and also produced his own *Four Books of Architecture* in 1570. The *Four Books*, along with buildings like Villa Emo, became important references in the next century for British Georgian architects who were taken by Palladio's austere facades masking ornate interiors. This Georgian practice can be seen in this portfolio in Appleton, Mechur & Associates' interpretation of two Edwin Lutyens houses in their design for a California estate, where spare masonry elevations give way to formally elegant living quarters.

In the United States, treatises and the pattern books derived from them, helped early American builders apply the European tradition to the beginnings of a native classical architecture. Books like Asher Benjamin's 1827 *An American Builder's Companion*, gave even the most untutored carpenter guides for proportion and use of the orders. Modern builders continue to consult pattern books, as did Geoffrey Carter when designing his new house, "Sneaker's Gap." Carter, a professional preservationist, used Benjamin's formulas to derive the proportions for his Doric order.

Professor William Ware originally composed his *American Vignola* (1906-1910) as a textbook, although the book eventually became a standard office reference. Appleton, Mechur & Associates looked to *The American Vignola* (as well as Vignola's original treatise of 1562) for instruction in interior detailing.

Of course, treatises are still being published to this day. One such compendium, *Classical Architecture,* was written by the British architect Robert Adam, who discusses in these pages his proposed addition to the Ashmolean Museum in Oxford. He explains not only his approach to the challenge of extending C.R. Cockerell's original building, but also his responses to the demands of function and fundraising imposed upon him by the university.

The scale and aspirations of the material presented here ranges from modest to imposing, yet all of the work owes a debt of gratitude to our architectural ancestors. The literature of architectural documentation has in no small part kept the classical tradition vibrant and accessible, and is perhaps even more important today than ever before. —C.C.

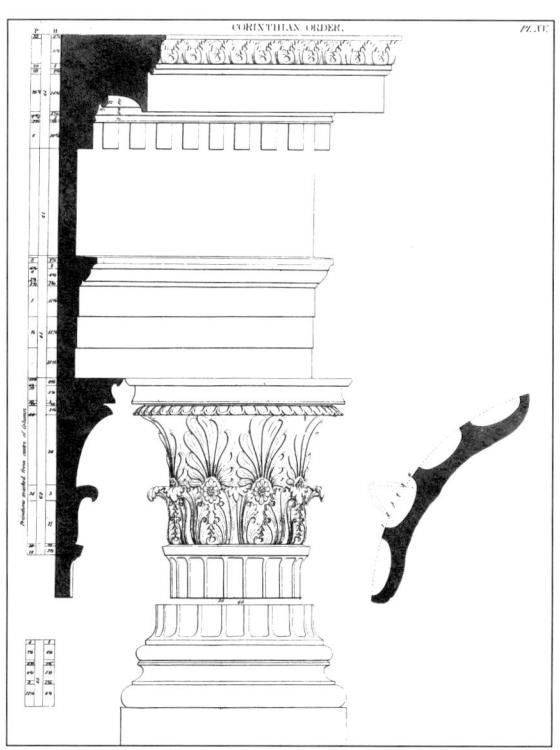

*ABOVE: Sections and elevation of a Corinthian column derived from an ancient structure. From Asher Benjamin's* THE ARCHITECT, OR COMPLETE BUILDER'S GUIDE, *1844.*

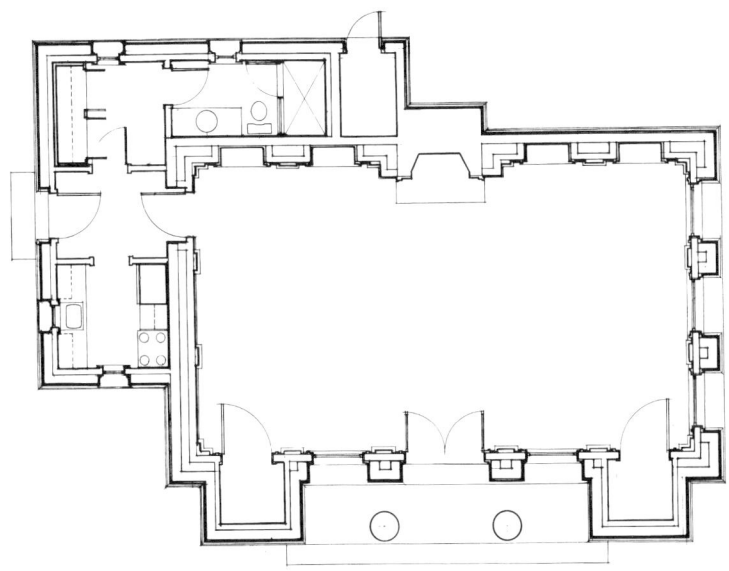

**ERNESTO BUCH, ARCHITECT**
**NEW HAVEN, CONNECTICUT**

This library, built for Picasso biographer John Richardson on the grounds of his country estate, serves as both workplace and retreat. Sited near the top of a craggy hillock some

distance behind the main house, the new building relates topographically to the site rather than orthogonally to the house. A path winds through the landscape, ending at a broad flight of stairs leading up to the Greek Doric portico. The library's main room opens onto the portico with its paired columns framing the view over a swimming pool to wooded hills beyond.

*ABOVE LEFT: Floor plan.*
*ABOVE: View of the library's interior.*
*LEFT: Entry facade with Doric portico.*

## ZANUCK RESIDENCE, LOS ANGELES, CALIFORNIA

APPLETON, MECHUR & ASSOCIATES, ARCHITECTS
VENICE, CALIFORNIA

PROJECT TEAM:
MARC APPLETON, THOMAS VREELAND, DONNA JOHNSON, DONNA D'ANASTASIO, ADOLPH ORTEGA, JOLIE WAH, STEVEN O'LEARY, SCOTT WALKER, ANGELA BROOKS

Two houses by the English architect Sir Edwin Lutyens provided inspiration for the design of this palatial Los Angeles estate. The massing of the house borrows from Lutyens's Heathcote, while the building materials are similar to those at The Salutation. As one approaches the California house, the site's

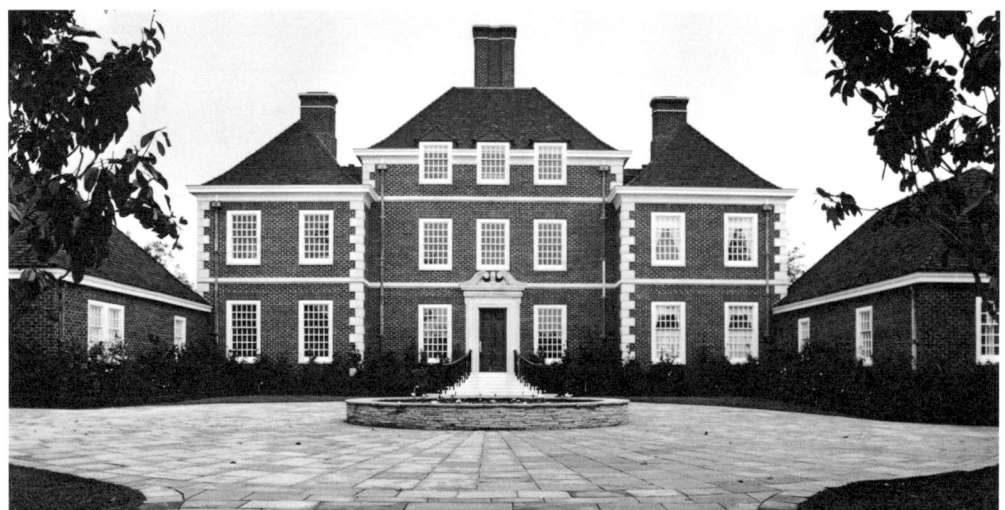

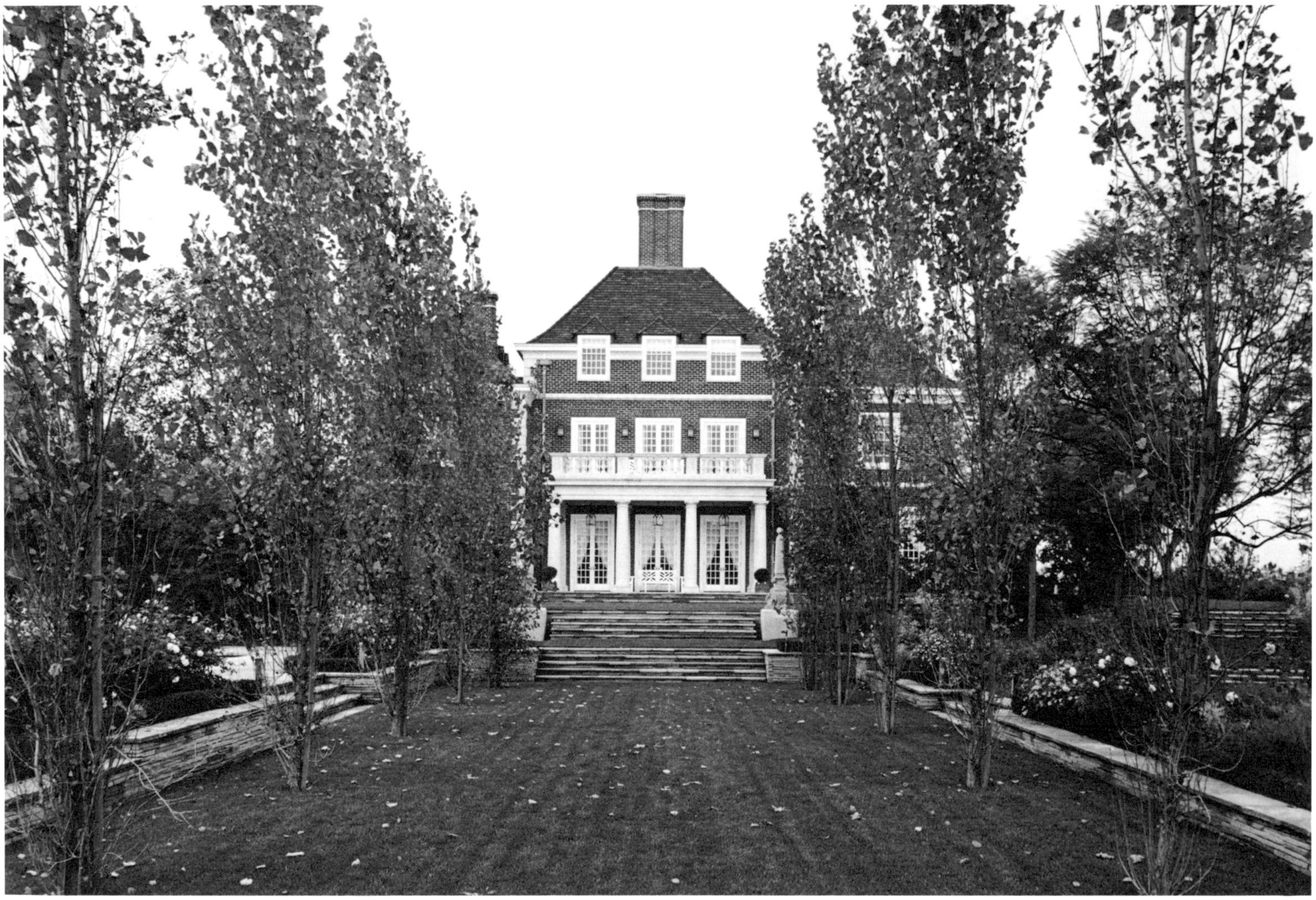

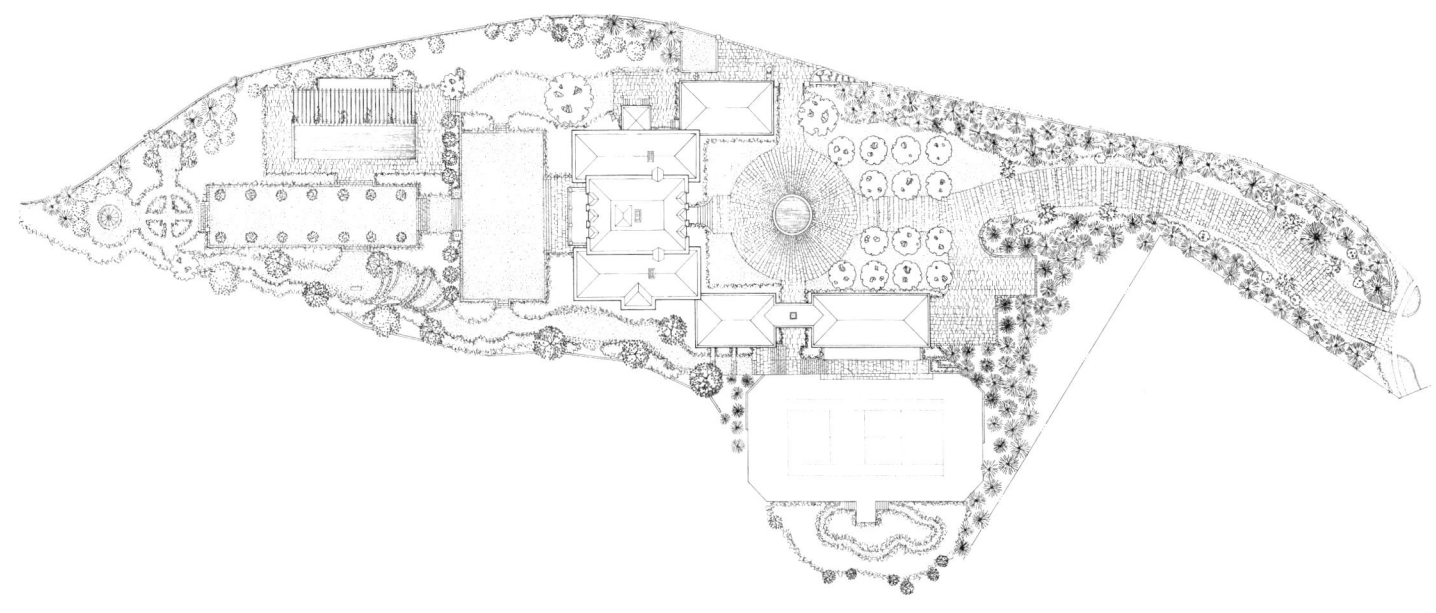

magnificent views remain artfully hidden by thickets of trees and flowering shrubs along the stone drive. The wings of the house—one containing guest apartments, the other a garage—enclose the circular motor court, whose entrance lies on axis with that of the limestone-pedimented front entrance to the house. A double-height stair hall leads from the entry to the living room, where the formal gardens and panoramic views of the city beyond first reveal themselves to the visitor. Flanking the living room are the dining and billiard rooms, which together form a large open space for entertaining.

*ABOVE LEFT: The entrance facade as seen from the motor court.*
*LEFT: The garden facade and lawn with poplar allée.*
*TOP RIGHT: Site plan.*
*MIDDLE RIGHT: East elevation.*
*LOWER RIGHT: Dining room with living room and billiard room beyond.*
*Photographs by Alex Vertikoff.*

IMAI/KELLER ARCHITECTS, INC.
WATERTOWN, MASSACHUSETTS

PROJECT TEAM:
RANDALL IMAI, JOHN KELLER, CHARLES
BARRETT, JULIE FERRARI, WILLIAM MELCHER

Constructed of Indiana limestone columns
with Chelmsford granite bases, brick walls,
standing seam copper roof, solid bar steel
gate, and cedar plank ceiling, this Greek
Doric design seeks to convey and to become
a timeless symbol of academia. Built as part
of a new campus quadrangle plan, the
entrance gate complements an adjacent
formal garden, serving as an outdoor
vestibule to the campus green beyond.

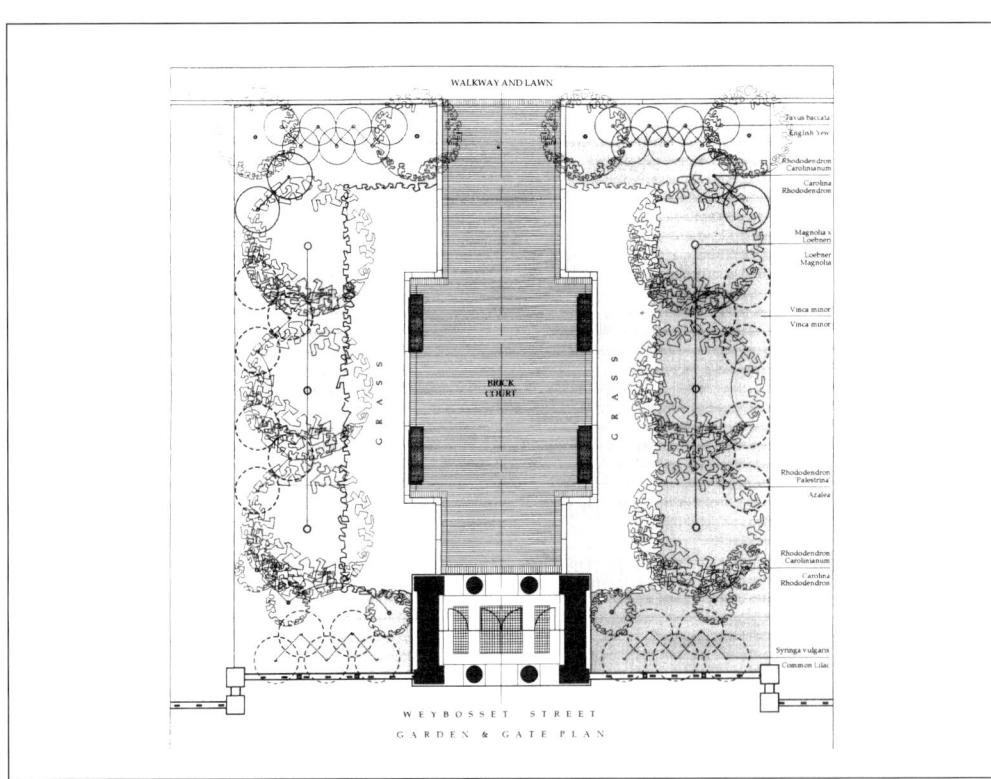

*ABOVE: Front elevation.*
*BELOW: Site plan.*
*Photograph by Elton Pope-Lance.*

KOHN PEDERSEN FOX P.C., ARCHITECTS
WITH ARTHUR MAY, DESIGN PARTNER
NEW YORK, NEW YORK

PROJECT TEAM:
ARTHUR MAY, JOHN LUCAS, PAUL KATZ

This competition entry proposes a Vermont granite colonnade and a grand arrival plaza on Washington's Columbus Circle. Along with companion buildings Union Station and the U.S. Post Office, the new building helps create a gateway to Capitol Hill beyond. The arched main entrance to the building is situated at one end of the giant order Ionic colonnade on Columbus Circle.

*LEFT: Entrance facade on Columbus Circle.*
*BELOW: Plan, section, and elevation details of entrance.*
*Renderings by Thomas Schaller.*

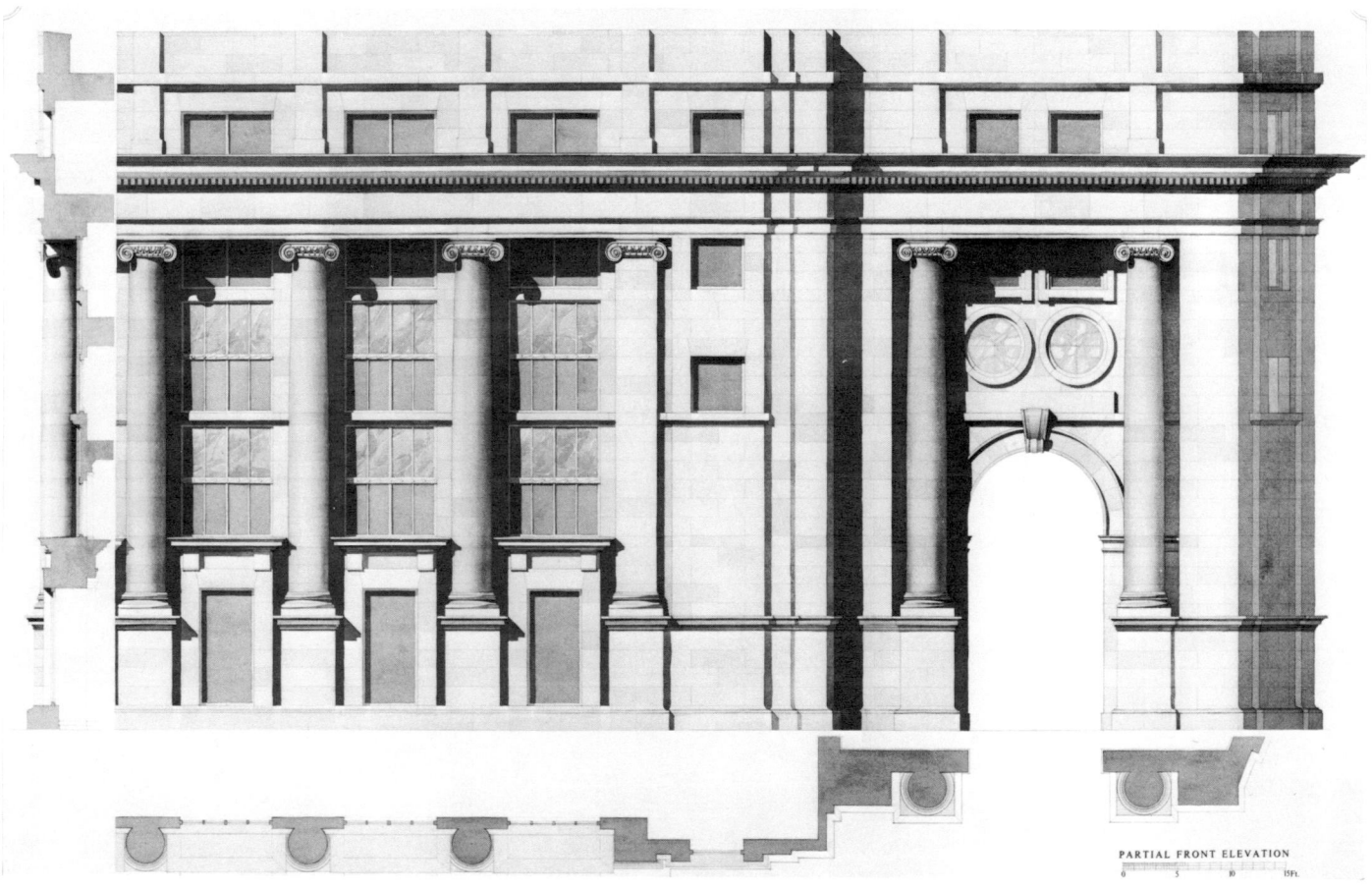

PARTIAL FRONT ELEVATION

**VICKY JAKOVLJEVIC CAMERON,
ARCHITECTURAL DESIGNER
BROOKLYN, NEW YORK**

The renovation of this 1838 brownstone townhouse earned the designer a New York Landmarks Conservancy Award in 1995. Executed work included such new features as a massive hand-carved cornice, a drafted masonry brownstone stucco base, a rusticated garden wall, and a front door and surround.

*ABOVE: Front elevation.*
*ABOVE RIGHT: Front entrance surround.*
*RIGHT: Rusticated garden wall and wrought iron gate.*
*OPPOSITE: Construction details for cornice.*

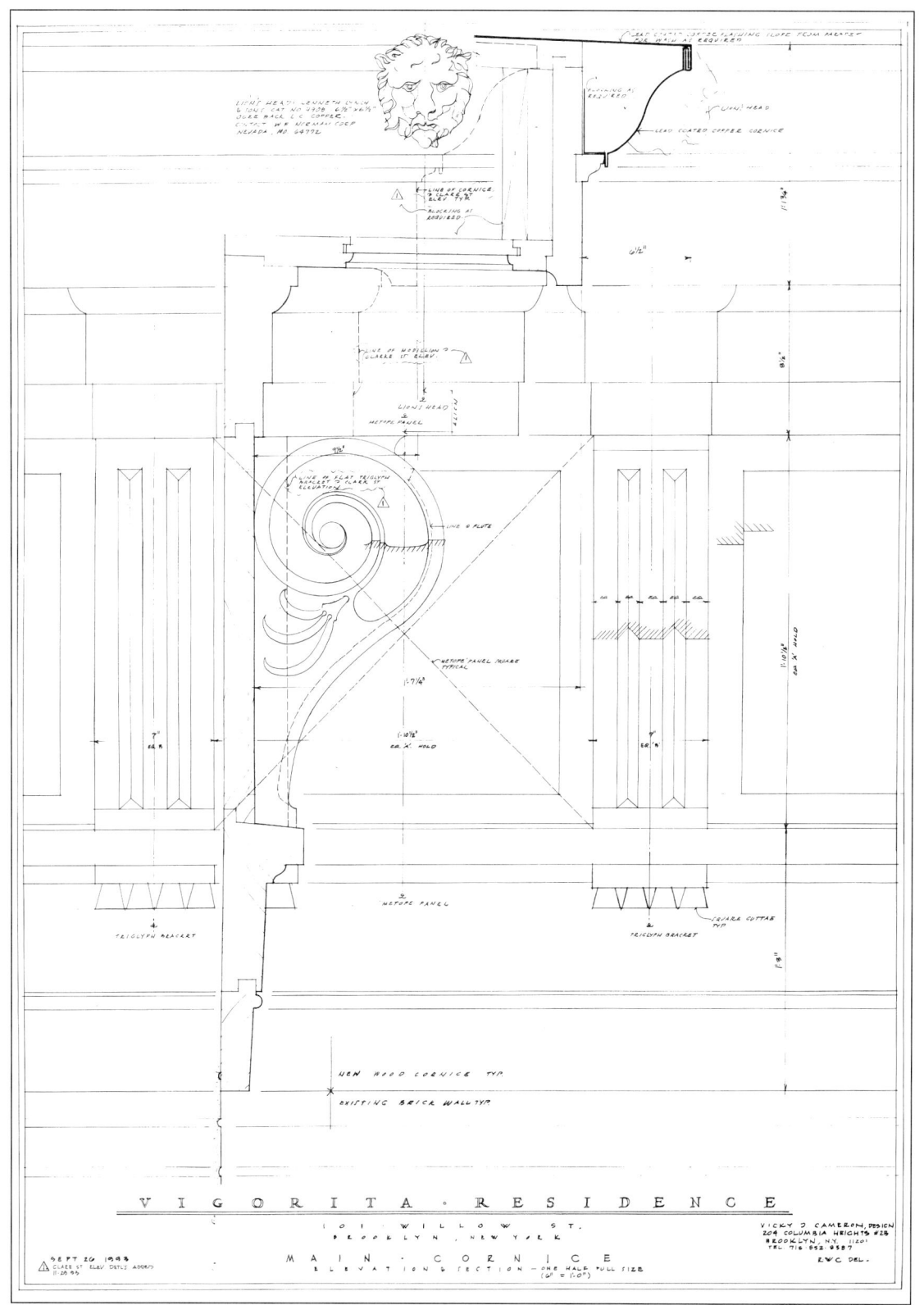

V I G O R I T A · R E S I D E N C E

101 · WILLOW · ST.
BROOKLYN , NEW YORK

MAIN · CORNICE
ELEVATION & SECTION — ONE HALF FULL SIZE
(6" = 1'.0")

VICKY J. CAMERON, DESIGN
204 COLUMBIA HEIGHTS #2B
BROOKLYN, N.Y. 11201
TEL 718 852 9587

R.W.C. DEL.

SEPT 20 1993
CLARK ST. ELEV. DETLS. ADDED
11.28.93

**KEN TATE, ARCHITECT**
**JACKSON, MISSISSIPPI**

**PROJECT TEAM:**
**KEN TATE, JOHN GAUDET, BRIAN O'KEEFE,**
**MIKE MCMAHEN, TOD MOSTERO, DAVID COLLIER**

After researching Northern Italian villas with interior designer Bruce Foreman, the owners engaged Mr. Tate to produce a villa with antecedents in Palladio's Villa Emo in Fanzolo, Italy. Upon completing on-site studies of the villa, the architect determined that the new structure should retain certain Palladian aspects, while scaling down the house to suit its suburban site. Thus the wings of the house extend forward to create an enclosed forecourt. The carvings of Emo's tympanum were likewise modified into a carved stone grille.

*RIGHT: Perspective of the front facade.*
*BELOW: Rear elevation and building details.*

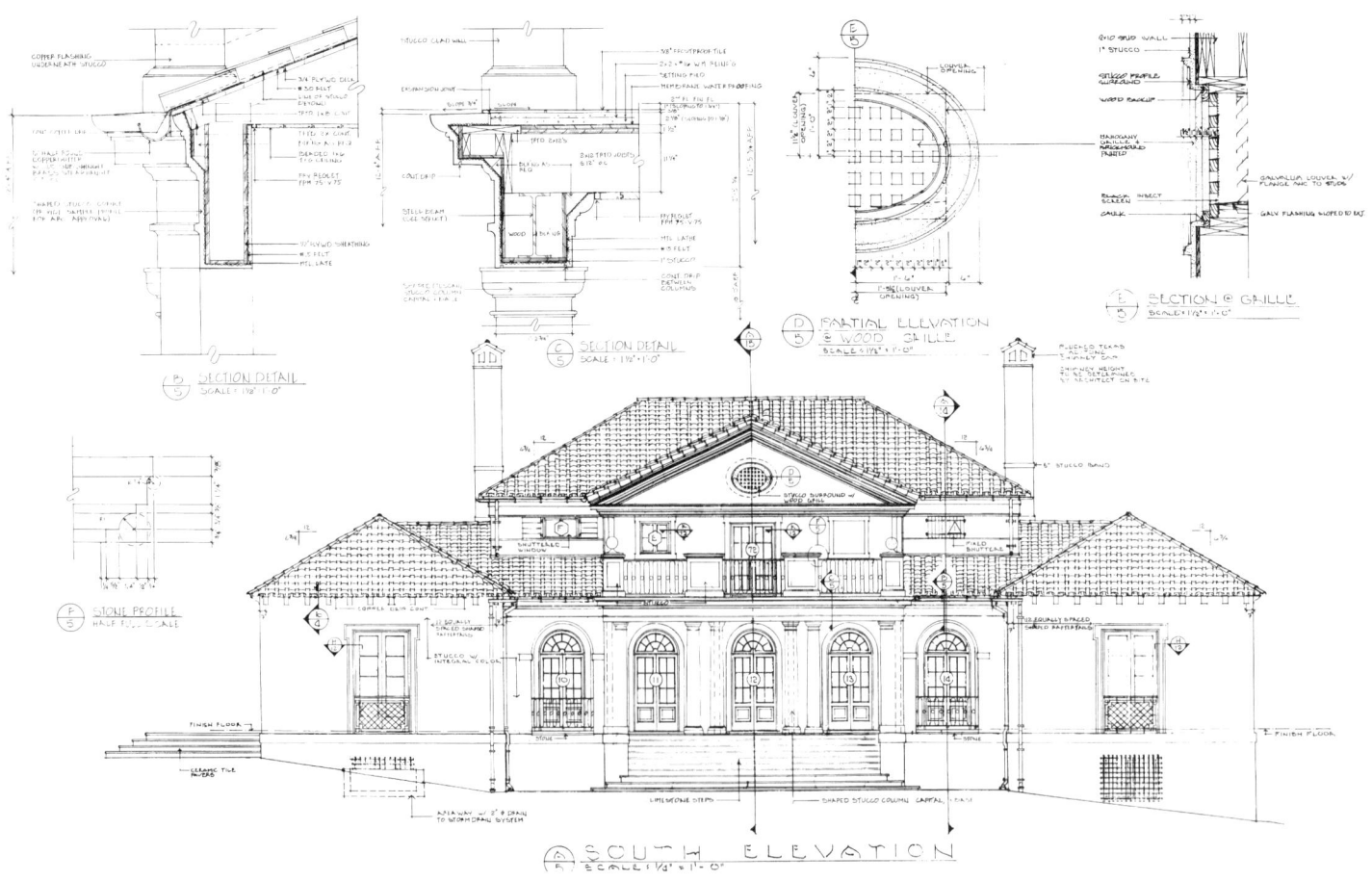

**LEON KRIER, ARCHITECT**
**CLAVIERS-VAR, FRANCE**

**PRODUCED BY GIORGETTI S.p.A.**
**MEDA, ITALY**

"Wondering why he was so meticulous with collecting beautiful objects and pieces of furniture, Massimo Scolari once told me that they were like the only friends who never betray you," says Krier in explanation of his solid and elegant new furniture line for Giorgetti. The table and chair shown here are crafted of the line's signature cherry with polished nickel accents. Adds Krier, "Pieces of furniture are not dead objects, because just like people you live with or deal with in a habitual fashion, they will shape you, influence you in subtle ways."

*RIGHT: Krier's sketch of the elevation and details of the Mensa table.*
*BELOW: Sketch of Sella chair.*
*BELOW CENTER: Sella chair.*
*BELOW RIGHT: Detail of Mensa table.*
*Photographs by Aldo Ballo.*

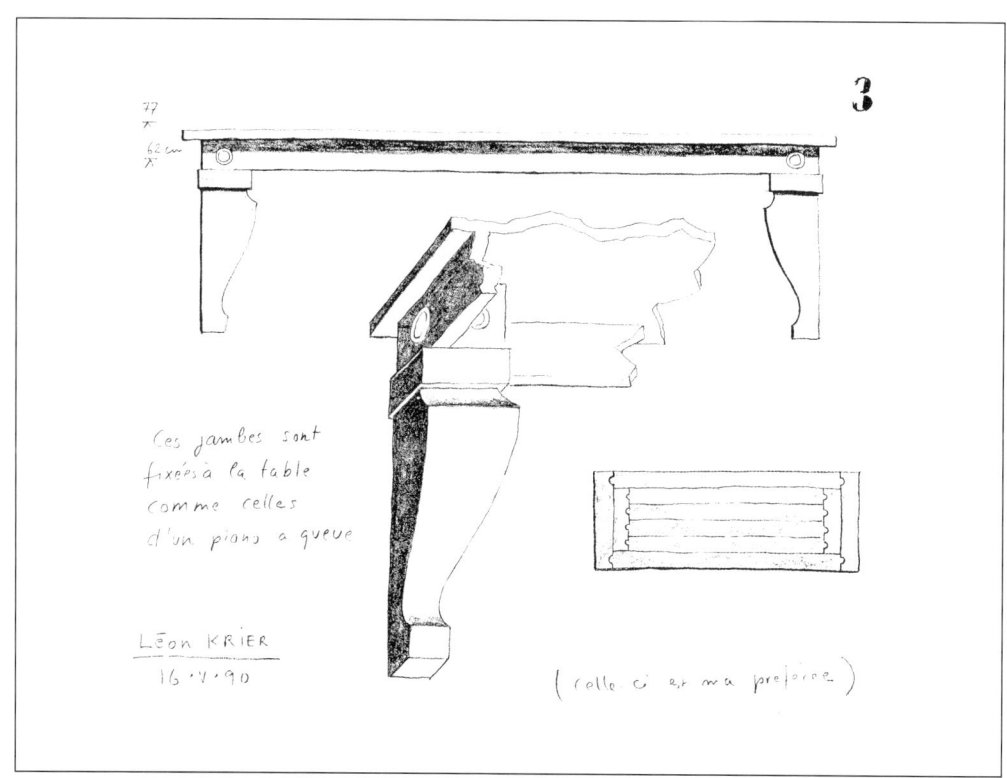

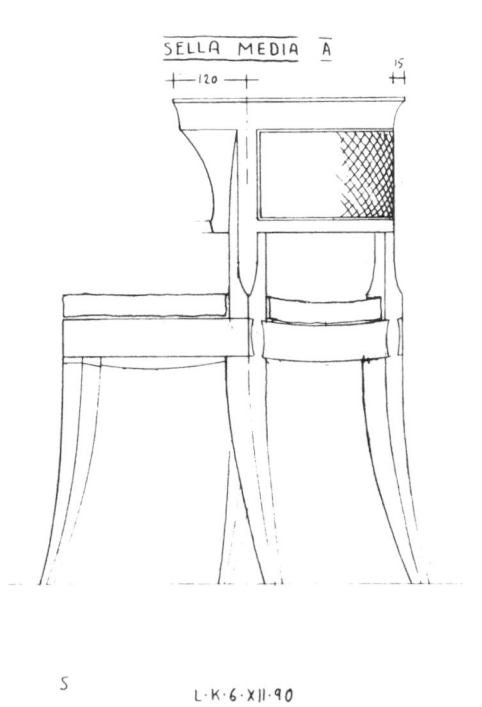

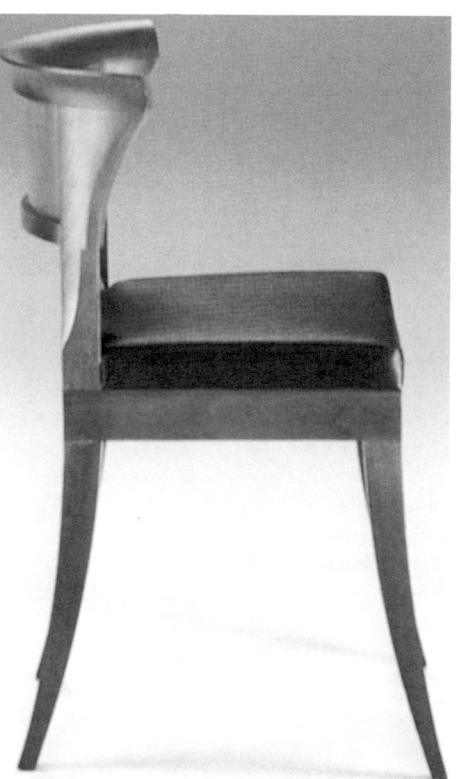

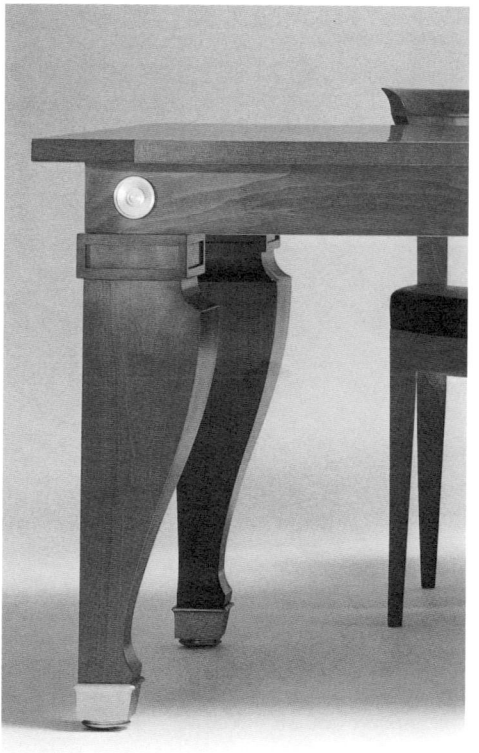

**GEOFFREY B. CARTER, BUILDER**
**BARRYTOWN, NEW YORK**
**STEPHEN FALATKO, AIA, CONSULTANT**
**SINGAPORE**

While researching material for a biography of his great-great-great grandfather Samuel Thompson, Geoffrey Carter first had the idea of building a house using construction techniques from the early 1800s. Thompson had been a prominent builder in early eighteenth century New York City, erecting such structures as the New York Custom House in lower Manhattan. But it was the search for information about Thompson's Greek Revival mansion on the Hudson River that inspired Carter to undertake construction of his own house in 1989. He determined that no synthetic building materials such as plywood, pressure treated wood, or plastics would be used. A crew of friends volunteered time on weekends for various chores, including hauling fieldstone and handmixing concrete for foundation walls.

Column shafts were formed of pie-shaped concrete bricks molded in an old steel drum. During bricklaying, a vertical length of conduit in the center of each column helped keep the work plumb. Entasis was achieved by varying the grout

joints between bricks. Molds for column capitals and bases were created by carefully rotating a template, or "knife" inside a box of wet plaster, leaving a negative image of the intended form.

The columns, portico, and some first floor framing had been completed by the time an intrigued Stephen Falatko wandered by and offered to help with the design of the floor plans. The two have since collaborated on the project, together designing much of the interior of the house, including trimwork, which Carter milled himself in his basement.

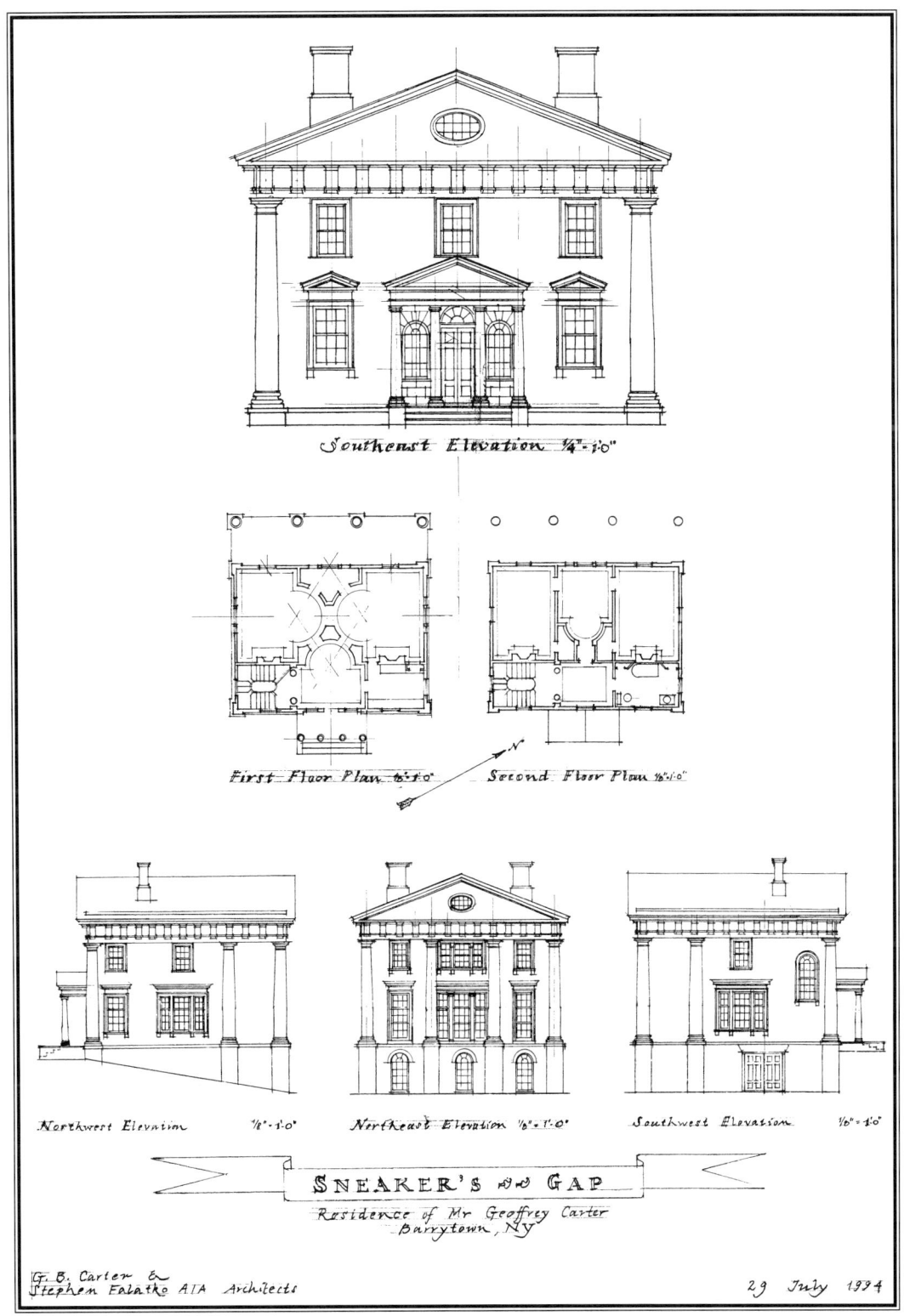

Southeast Elevation ¼"=1'0"

First Floor Plan ⅛"=1'0"    Second Floor Plan ⅛"=1'0"

Northwest Elevation ⅛"=1'0"    Northeast Elevation ⅛"=1'0"    Southwest Elevation ⅛"=1'0"

SNEAKER'S GAP
Residence of Mr Geoffrey Carter
Barrytown, NY

G. B. Carter &
Stephen Falatko AIA Architects                    29 July 1994

*FAR LEFT: Column shaft is constructed of pie-shaped concrete bricks. ABOVE LEFT: The nearly completed northwest facade. BELOW LEFT: Column capitals hoisted into place using a block and tackle. ABOVE: Stephen Falatko's rendering of floor plans and elevations. Photographs by David Funk.*

# A VIEW OF THE PROCESS:

---

## THE NEW
## LIBRARY, CLASSICS CENTER,
## AND CAST GALLERY
### AT THE
# ASHMOLEAN MUSEUM
### OXFORD, ENGLAND

*"There is perhaps no building in England on which the refined student of Architecture can dwell with so much pleasure. There is not a moulding or a chisel mark anywhere which is not the result of deep study, guided by refined feeling."* This high praise of the Ashmolean was published in 1873 in his HISTORY OF THE MODERN STYLES OF ARCHITECTURE by James Fergusson, perhaps the most popular architectural historian writing in the nineteenth century. Fergusson's judgement on a building, still generally known only for its contents and not for its architecture, was remarkable for its date at the height of the Gothic Revival, but is as challenging today as it was a century ago.
—David Watkin, "The Making of the Ashmolean," *Country Life*, February 7th, 1974

The Ashmolean Museum and Taylorian Institution stand today as the surviving masterpiece of the architectural career of Charles Robert Cockerell. From the outset the building was an unusual hybrid in housing two distinct and disparate institutions: the University Galleries and the Taylorian Institution for the study of the European languages (FIGURES 1-2). Cockerell's original design responded both to the exigencies of the site and the bifurcated program brief, leaving to Oxford the distinctive U–shaped building, with its porticoed entrance facing Beaumont Street, and its taller wings facing into St. Giles to the east and abutting the pre–existing eighteenth century terrace houses on Beaumont Street to the west (FIGURES 3-4).

*FIGURE 1, ABOVE: View of the entry portico to the Ashmolean Museum from the St. Giles passage to the Taylorian Institution. Photo by R. Cameron.*
*FIGURE 2, OPPOSITE: View of the courtyard of the Ashmolean, looking toward the Taylorian Institute and St. Giles. Photo by R. Cameron.*

Perhaps, due to its hybrid nature, the building was destined to receive additions. These have extended both along Beaumont Street to the west and St. Giles to the north, and have filled in much of the original site to the rear as well. The additions are from several periods, are in a broad range of architectural styles, and house both extensions to the museum's functions as well as a number of other institutions.

Robert Adam's project, which is presented here as part of THE CLASSICIST'S "View of the Process" series, is the first attempt to make a virtue of the proximity of the different institutions housed on the site, and to bring architectural order to the range of buildings. It achieves this by being both an intelligent infill project in the European urban tradition of the arcade and the French *hôtel particulier,* and by making elegant and erudite references to Cockerell's original building and its archaeological sources.

Because the project is still in the planning stages, it provides a rare opportunity to examine the early phases of the process of creating a large and complex group of public and institutional buildings. Thus the focus of the article—from the views of the model and drawings, to the statements by members of the universtiy involved in the planning, and the interview with the architect—contribute to a view of the challenge and opportunity of providing a worthy complement to Cockerell's masterpiece in Oxford. —R.W.C.

STATEMENTS ON THE PLANNING OF
## THE ASHMOLEAN HUMANITIES CENTER

### FERGUS MILLAR
#### CAMDEN PROFESSOR OF ANCIENT HISTORY

Behind the Ashmolean Museum in Oxford, with Cockerell's magnificent facade fronting on Beaumont Street, there now runs a dismal lane with the irregular brickwork of the back of the Museum on the one side, and a clutter of ill-coordinated modern buildings on the other: the Oriental Institute and Cast Gallery and the outhouses at the back of the Taylorian Institute Annexe, used by Modern Languages.

This is the area which will be transformed by the creation of an integrated architectural framework, and the insertion at its focal point of a newly created Classics Center. The lane will be roofed over, and the Classics Center, incorporating a restructured Cast Gallery, will open onto a semi-circular apse half way along the lane, now transformed into a covered arcade. Within Classics, the purpose is to bring together all the different disciplines which make up the subject, from Greek and Latin Literature to history, epigraphy, papyrology and linguistics, and provide meeting places and seminar rooms. More widely, the Ashmolean Humanities Center will link Oriental Studies to Classics, Byzantine Studies and Modern Languages, providing a modern lecture-theatre shared by them all, and relate all of these to the unique riches of the Ashmolean Museum. ❧

### SIR JOHN BOARDMAN
#### LINCOLN PROFESSOR OF
#### CLASSICAL ARCHAEOLOGY AND ART

A gallery of plaster casts of ancient statues sounds something of an anachronism in the 1990s. The perception is a false one, since in many respects such a collection can prove its worth as a major force in education in the most modern manner. The first cast acquired by Oxford is now some 250 years old, but the whole collection, of some 900 pieces, by now offers a very full selection of classical styles, since the casts come from museums of the world and there is no other way of making direct comparisons of such three-dimensional objects. Moreover, many are in a better condition in cast than they are by now in origi-

nal. Two hundred years ago galleries were explicitly designed to display such casts to their best advantage, while incomplete and battered original marbles were consigned to second place. Their prime use was for teaching, both scholars and academic artists. Both functions are still valid and active, and in Oxford there is even a weekly life class to supplement drawing from the cast. But the figures prove to have a direct appeal to the general public of all ages that seems timeless.

In recent years the Oxford Gallery has become much more than a parade of statuary in copies, and has added to its traditional function a role as a center for the study of all classical art in facsimile. It houses major collections of photographs, mainly of statuary and of decorated vases, now housed in many different museums of the world. With modern techniques of electronic recording and telecommunication it can become a center for the diffusion of information and pictures on all these subjects. This is already achieved with the recording of data and pictures of vases, which are 'on-line' to scholars worldwide, and it is becoming true of the statues too. The casts are recorded on video and programmes for instruction in museums, schools and as reference tools for scholars. What is still a delight for the visitor and source of instruction for the student becomes also the logical center for universal access to information which is to be the hallmark of intellectual and leisure activity for the next generation. In its new form the Gallery will be able to accommodate all its functions more generously both for the public, for whom there will now be direct access from the main museum, as well as for scholars. There will be provision for special displays of casts, photographs, and drawings. Its collections and research facilities are a natural adjunct to the Ashmolean's collections of original works and to the literary and historical studies of the Classics Center, which will be its close neighbors. ❧

### GILES BARBER
#### LIBRARIAN OF THE
#### TAYLORIAN INSTUTION

The project houses a number of elements but this is only one of the problems. The library element at least unites at present many separate subjects, not all identical in readership and nature of material. The site is one of great complexity and, in part, very hemmed-in; there are security problems arising from the proximity of the museum; surrounding buildings, often of notable architectural importance, are in differing styles, from Victorian stone classic to red brick gothic.

The initial designs by Robert Adam make notable headway with the more architectural side of these problems. On a practical level there is good provision for access, circulation, deliveries, and security. The library plans are not sufficiently detailed as yet to warrant much analysis although, it must be said, reaction has not been positive towards the concept, even in a university having such a well-known round library as the 1759 Radcliffe Camera. It could, however, be argued that Oxford is more likely to need reader seats than storage on this central site and that the proposed shape provides individual areas of character, often a high preference among users to the monotone reading room of mid-century.

Aesthetically the first designs match well with existing buildings, maintaining their august exterior appearance and indeed improving the interior atmosphere. Academics, even experts from many fields, continue to discuss their needs and to make the detailed planning evolve, but so far most of the suggestions put forward have significantly opened minds and taken this important development forward. Librarians, who need to provide a clearer strategic brief, also look forward to further detailed discussion on a highly desirable and so far excellent project. ❧

IN THE SPRING OF 1995, MEMBERS OF THE CLASSICIST'S EDITORIAL STAFF TALKED WITH ROBERT ADAM ABOUT HIS ONGOING WORK ON COCKERELL'S ASHMOLEAN MUSEUM AT OXFORD UNIVERSITY, A BUILDING WHICH EMBODIES MANY OF ITS CREATOR'S IDEAS ABOUT THE ROLE OF ARCHAEOLOGY IN MODERN CLASSICISM. ANOTHER TOPIC OF DISCUSSION WAS THE ROLE OF AN ARCHITECT IN PREPARING DESIGNS FOR UNFUNDED PROJECTS.

THE CLASSICIST: Perhaps the way to begin would be to ask you to explain the project and its history. Then perhaps you could talk about the plan of the buildings.

ROBERT ADAM: Basically, the university wanted to raise funds to create the vision that Fergus Millar refers to, and they couldn't do it just by saying "Look we've got this little garage around the back you know, we've actually tried to give it to somebody to shove some buildings in it." They had to produce something that people could identify with. So they came to me and said "Would you like to help us with this?"

This project unites a whole series of things which had not hitherto been drawn together(FIGURES 3-4). We're connecting different libraries for example; the Byzantine Library comes together within the Western Art Library, which would, under our plan now, be joined as "Libraries." There's also a Cast Gallery, which holds the Beazley Archive and the Bent Collection. The gallery contains its own holdings and has its own staff. Likewise, the Griffith Institute, which currently sits here, has independent interests.

TC: So this started out as an institutional master plan which pulled together all the parts?

RA: Yes. In fact, certain decisions had already been made as to who would be housed in this space.

TC: There are clear references to Cockerell both as an archaeologist and as an architect in your designs, but I was curious to know whether you were directly inspired by him or whether you saw this as a completely independent project, since this museum has obviously grown so much beyond its original designs.

RA: I've always admired the Ashmolean building. I think in many ways Cockerell is one of the most important nineteenth century neoclassical architects. But he's not neoclassical in the sense that he copies things precisely. He doesn't belong to the "it's got to look exactly like a Greek temple in order to be classical school." He was a neoclassicist creatively. He understood that the Greeks didn't build buildings as we do, and that you don't make our buildings look like buildings the Greeks built for other purposes. Instead, you absorb the principle of what they did and move it forward—something which I don't think is often recognized.

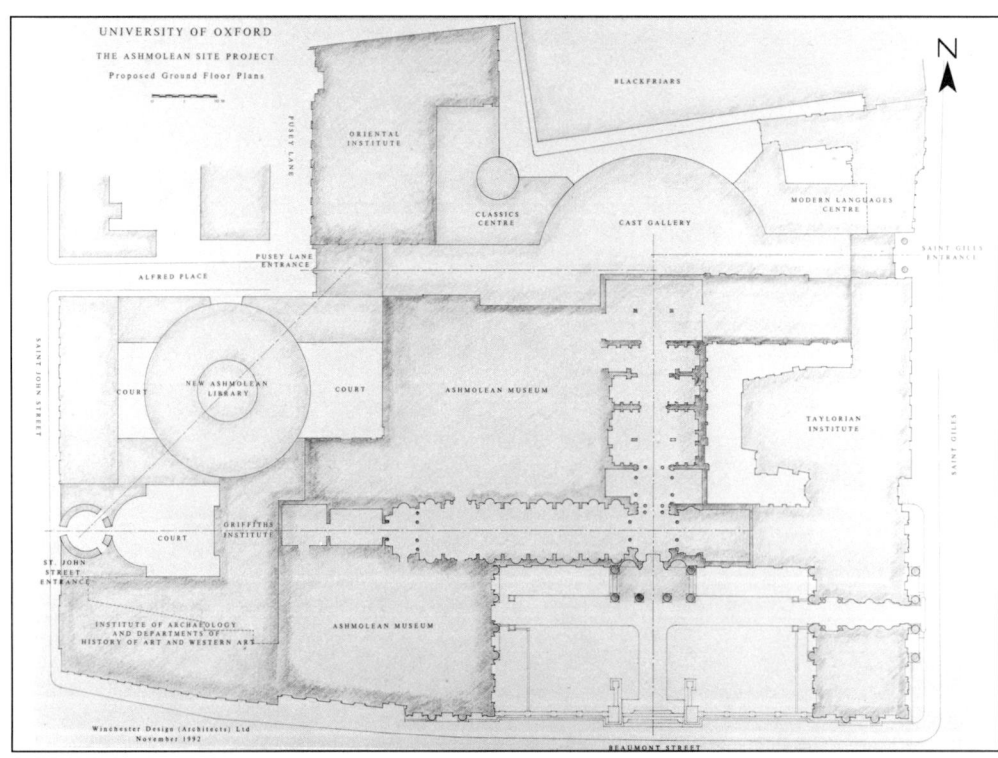

*FIGURE 3, ABOVE: Site plan of the existing buildings and proposed area of development.*

*FIGURE 4, BELOW: Ground plan of proposed new development.*

*Drawings by the office of Robert Adam.*

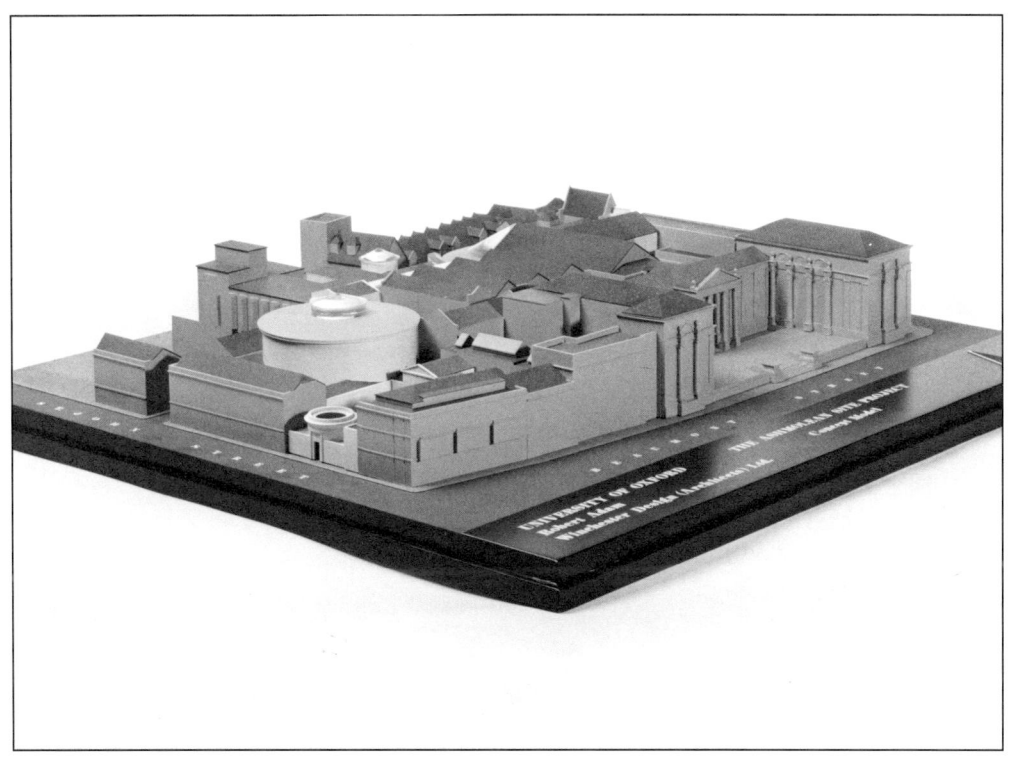

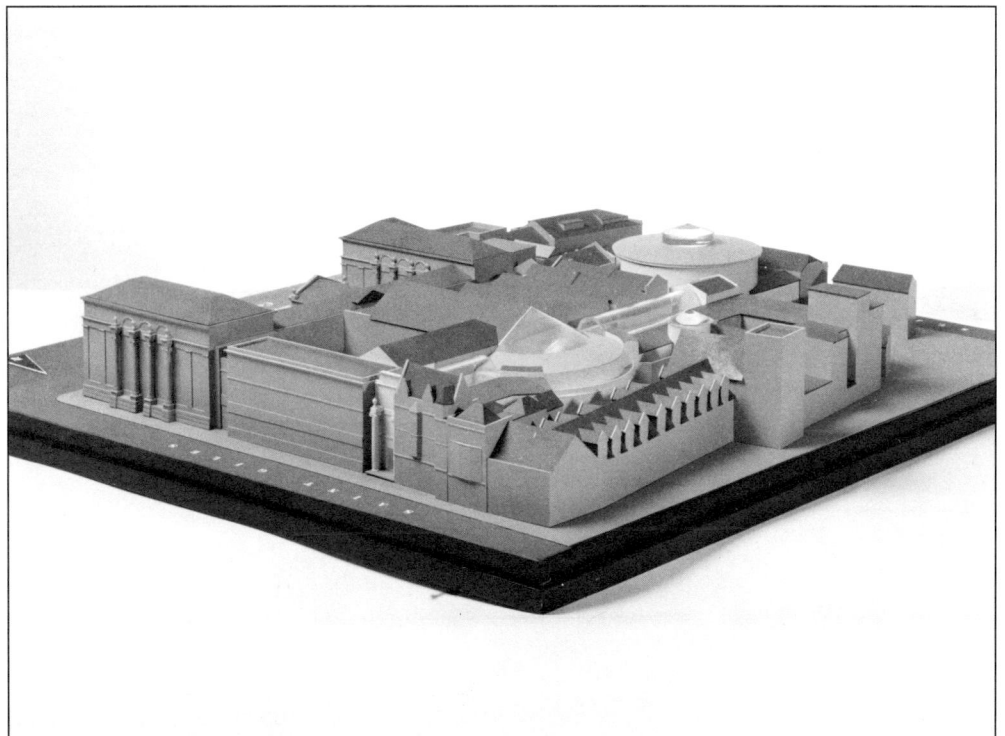

*FIGURE 5, ABOVE: Northeast view of the model, showing the existing buildings and proposed new development.*

*FIGURE 6, BELOW: Southwest view of the model.*

*Models by the office of Robert Adam.*

TC:     Cockerell has an interesting relationship to archaeology. David Watkin has an article in this issue of THE CLASSICIST in which he talks about Cockerell's critique of the Greek Revival . Although you might think him linked very directly to literal archaeological revivalism, in fact he was a great critic of it.

RA:     He didn't copy Greek architecture, because he understood that classicism was a flexible thing, that the Greeks themselves modified the language as time went on. In fact, this later phase is the great missing period of Hellenism. There still exists this historical fix, where you talk about Greece in the fifth century and suddenly you rush through history into the first century B.C. and Rome, and of course what's really important is that intervening period, because that is the period that turned the architecture of temples into the architecture of all sorts of other building types.

TC:     The line of continuity is very interesting. In fact, for Cockerell that's quite central—this idea of synthesizing all of the strands of classicism from the ancient Greek, and even as far back as the Egyptian, right up to contemporary practice. However, let's return to the project and your consideration of Cockerell in making your designs.

RA:     The whole history of the Ashmolean building is one of failed master projects. There have been an enormous number of additions, such that the museum has grown by little bits being tacked on.

TC:     For example where the Library is, or the drawing school?

RA:     That's right, that was part of a larger scheme. I think a whole series of bits and pieces were parts of larger schemes. So all we could really do was pick up on what Cockerell's drawing shows. And because of the difficulties of the site and the varied uses, the organization of the usage came first and Cockerell came second.

TC:     You have an axial connection to the Ashmolean. from the cast gallery. Is there going to be a physical one, too?

RA:     We did try to keep the main axis. You see, this is a late nineteenth century building that's been put in the back, a building clearly designed to be axial with the museum. In the meantime, the history of the museum is that it had great demands for space, but they've never had enough money, nor any faith in any great scheme. All sorts of things have happened here that make this connection probably not possible at the moment. But the architectural logic is so strong, not only in terms of the existing plan, but in all the possible ways of organizing this space, that we thought it was irresponsible not to try to make that relationship.

TC:     You've mentioned that you had a number of different entities competing for space within this program. Could you tell us about how that affected your designs?

RA:    There are a number of libraries inside the Ashmoleon, not all of which relate to one another—different curatorial departments, including the Griffith Institute, which is quite a separate institute situated in the northwest corner. So when you actually take a look at what could be kept and what couldn't, we really had several parts—what is now the Ashmoleon Library, with a series of very important eighteenth century buildings fronting Beaumont Street; and then behind the Ashmoleon, to the north, the Classics Center, which we knew was coming down; the Oriental Institute, which we knew was staying; and the buildings along St. Giles, which are protected. And the Taylorian Institution, a language institute, had a prior claim on this little eastern part. So we had a really awful site. We had to reconcile all of these things to make some relationship. In many ways the key to this is the left over spaces and their relationship with the buildings roundabout them.

TC:    Is that what led you to locate the Cast Gallery off St. Giles (FIGURE 7)?

RA:    Yes. I think it was the university surveyor department's suggestion, actually, that we should look at some sort of arcade. We picked that idea up and ran with it because it turned out to be probably the most sensible way of dealing with the  site.

TC:    There is, then, this urban arcade which is developed from St. Giles through the Cast Gallery and up Pewsey Lane on the back side.

RA:    Yes. At the same time we get this axis running from the St. John's Street entrance across to the museum entry. We realized that the Griffith Institute is an awful building and has no particular reason for being there. So we decided to move it to the St. John Street entrance, which actually was extremely convenient because the Ashmoleon also wanted a twentieth century gallery which it was agreed we ought to put on top of the Griffith Institute. Having done that and created an entrance from St. John Street—

TC:    Sorry to interrupt, but what is the Griffith Institute?

RC:    Basically, it's a library and a documentary resource of Egyptology and Near Eastern Studies. The Griffith Institute plays a big part in the library because it's largely a collection of books.

TC:    Why the choice of a rotunda for the library building?

RA:    This is a big question amongst the librarians who have a fairly negative response to being in a round library because they don't like round libraries. But the round building when seen from a distance actually pro-

duces a much less bulky profile than a rectangular building. The question I always pose is that you might not like round libraries from your experience of round libraries, but what diameter of library are you talking about? Of course, they've never answered the question and it's entirely relevant. There are some very famous round libraries—the British Library is one and Asplund's library as well, and of course the Radcliffe Camera in Oxford itself. Anyway, we put it on this cross axis, so we could tie in all of these lower buildings around the side with courtyards giving life and light into these areas here (FIGURES 5, 8).

TC:    Actually what interests me is this combination of what you might describe as the round library's neoclassical form within a Baroque plan arrangement—somewhat like LePautre's Hôtel de Beauvais in Paris.

RA:    The purpose of the rotunda is to bring together a series of things which previously had not been brought together and by doing so, great academic advantage is gained. For example, they'd never brought all the humanities together into a Classics Center, nor had they united the libraries despite the fact that they were related to one another. So we had to put a circular building here, because at the same time you are entering one

central location that unifies these disparate entities, you are still ultimately going to separate departments.

TC:    Now, what about the Cast Gallery?

RA:    The point is, you come in and see the casts. It's very important to remember that these casts are not arranged as decoration. The intention is that they serve a didactic function, in other words, that a logic is given to their arrangement. They may be decorative at the same time, but that's secondary.

TC:    So the notion is that there could be teaching and drawing and other things going on in the Cast Gallery?

RA:    Yes, absolutely.

TC:    Is there any worry that there will be some conflict between entry to the Classics Center and the kinds of activities that will be going on in the Cast Gallery?

RA:    Oh, I don't think so. I mean they're not talking about throngs of people, and we hope the design induces a very good use of space.

*FIGURE 7, OPPOSITE: View of the proposed Cast Gallery looking towards the entry to the new Classics Center.*

*FIGURE 8, ABOVE: Interior view of the proposed new library.*

*Renderings by the office of Robert Adam.*

TC:     I have a question about an aspect of the project which intrigued me when I saw it initially. First you established three entries, then you've played out a theme having to do with the Greek Temple of Apollo at Bassae [from the fifth century B.C.]. Could you elaborate?

RA:     To all intents and purposes you can enter the Institute in three different ways, though you can't see one entrance from the other. But they have a relationship to one another, so the principal entrance in the new scheme (FIGURE 10) uses the Ionic from the interior of Bassae, to pick up on what Cockerell has done in his elevations (cf. FIGURE 2). But we've used it with its archaeological, heavily splayed base.

TC:     And you've taken it off the pedestal, which is the opposite of the way Cockerell uses it.

RA:     Yes. And we've also made them project, to literally stand like sentinels on each side of the opening, and we put urns on top to represent receptacles of knowledge. Then, for the second entrance from St. John Street (FIGURE 9), we've used the Doric from Bassae's outer colonnade, again as a pair of columns, though these columns are engaged.

TC:     In this case they look as if they'd been used in a neoclassical fashion in that they're set over the walls.

RA:     Yes, this is going to be very simple and very geometrical because this is pretty much where the existing building sits. So this is a very low-key entrance, unlike here [the St. Giles entrance], where we had really quite dominant buildings on each side and we could do something very strong.

TC:     What's provocative is that you've dramatically changed the scale relationships between the three orders as they would literally be seen in the original temple where they're separated spatially and can't be seen together. It's been contextualized. Now, the third entry is perhaps the most intriguing (FIGURE 11).

RA:     Yes. Here we have a basic problem—the loading bay on one side and the staff entrance on the other. Whatever happens, this elevation is going to be split into two. It's quite nice, actually, because at Bassae, which has the first major use of the Corinthian order, the column sat on the center axis of the temple. Likewise, we used this column—the single freestanding prototypical Corinthian column sitting right in the

center—on the balcony of the common room so that it's in your view out the window.

That was the idea behind the three entrances: to give them each a separate identity, we used those three orders, and we used them in a way which is related to Bassae and therefore also related to Cockerell's building. In one sense it matters a lot and in another sense it doesn't matter at all and each entrance is quite an individual thing in relation to where it sits.

TC:     Another thing I find really quite fascinating in this pursuit of the theme of the orders is the fact that it would take you a bit of time to put it together going round this complex of buildings. It does give it this very engaging thematic pursuit from one entrance to the other, and one day it might all suddenly click in your mind, going in the various entries without it having to be explained—almost a three-dimensional puzzle.

Clearly, in its very origin, the hybrid nature of the program joining the Taylorian Institution and the Randolph Galleries was a difficult issue which Cockerell had to struggle with very much. In fact, there was a critique, as you probably know, of the Cockerell design—that it didn't properly satisfy the requirements of decorum because the wings were taller than the center but the site and the program made Cockerell's solution almost inevitable. In a way you continue the theme, making the best of it with this interesting combination of entries.

RA:     That's right, each entrance has to work on its own contextually. Any one of these should be capable of being judged on its own, but they do have a relationship and that relationship is to Cockerell.

T C:     To what level of detail do you take designs for a project like this?

RA: The tricky thing, as far as we're concerned, is that we had to go into much more depth than the documents show, because when all the conflicting and compatible interests were sorted out, we got quite a detailed program for the building. We then had to investigate it rather thoroughly. For instance, as anyone who's an architect will know, to be confident that you can draw something round and call it the Library, you've got to know you can fit all the books in it, so you've got to produce at least a rudimentary plan.

TC:     But you didn't want to reveal too many of the details.

RA:     Well no. We had to be confident that this would work. But remember, our appointment was really just to produce a sufficient concept to fund the project, to fire the imagination of people who might be interested in backing it. Obviously it is my great hope that it goes further. And in fact there is now a sub-committee which was set up to move the project forward and we're members of it. But primarily we were here to consolidate the idea, to develop an efficient concept, and to produce enough representation of it to attract funds. And we have to constantly bear that in mind.

TC: We are interested in the way you're going about pursuing the project from the point of view of trying to get it done, because you're also involved to some degree with trying to raise funds for realizing the building you're potentially designing.

RA: Well, inasmuch as I'll do anything I can to help it.

TC: It must be very complicated given the number of institutions involved.

RA: Not only the number of institutions, but also there's a certain amount of reticence, I think, until things move a bit further forward.

TC: Move forward in terms of raising money?

RA: Yes. And we'll try to sort out some of it. For example, we've looked into replacing the lecture theater and really developing that courtyard in order to help relieve some of the problems which would be created if we were to do this part of the building first. As I said earlier, we are there to provide the collation of all the information available. It's gone a slightly different tack now, in the sense that I think there are some funds available, but there's still a reticence in developing the scheme too much further forward, because there's so much work involved in doing that. And we shouldn't really be doing that work at this stage, because by the time we get the money, the ground rules may have changed completely. So there's a very difficult sort of balance between us saying, "Well look, we can actually take this further," and them saying "Well no, don't take it any further, we just want reassurance on certain points."

I know exactly why they're reining us back. I mean, I hope I know why they're reining us back. I hope it's a pragmatic point that we musn't take this too far because we'd be wasting money until fund raising and decisions abut space planning are both further along. ❧

*FIGURE 9, ABOVE: Elevation of the proposed new St. John's Street entrance, employing the exterior Doric order from the Temple of Apollo Epicurius at Bassae.*

*FIGURE 10, MIDDLE: Elevation of the proposed new St. Giles' entrance, employing the Bassae Ionic with its original flared bases.*

*FIGURE 11, BELOW: Elevation of the proposed new Pusey Lane entrance, employing the Bassae Corinthian order.*

*All renderings by the office of Robert Adam.*

# FROM THE SKETCHBOOKS
## OF
# DAVID
# ANTHONY
# EASTON

VIEW TOWARDS LIBRARY

*T*he process of design in architecture often begins with the sketchbook. Sketches offer insight into the architect's thinking, and can form an invaluable record of design development. They reveal not only their creator's facility with line drawing but also that person's ability to conceive architecture in the abstract. With this issue THE CLASSICIST introduces a new sketchbook section and chooses for its first subject the drawings of David Anthony Easton.

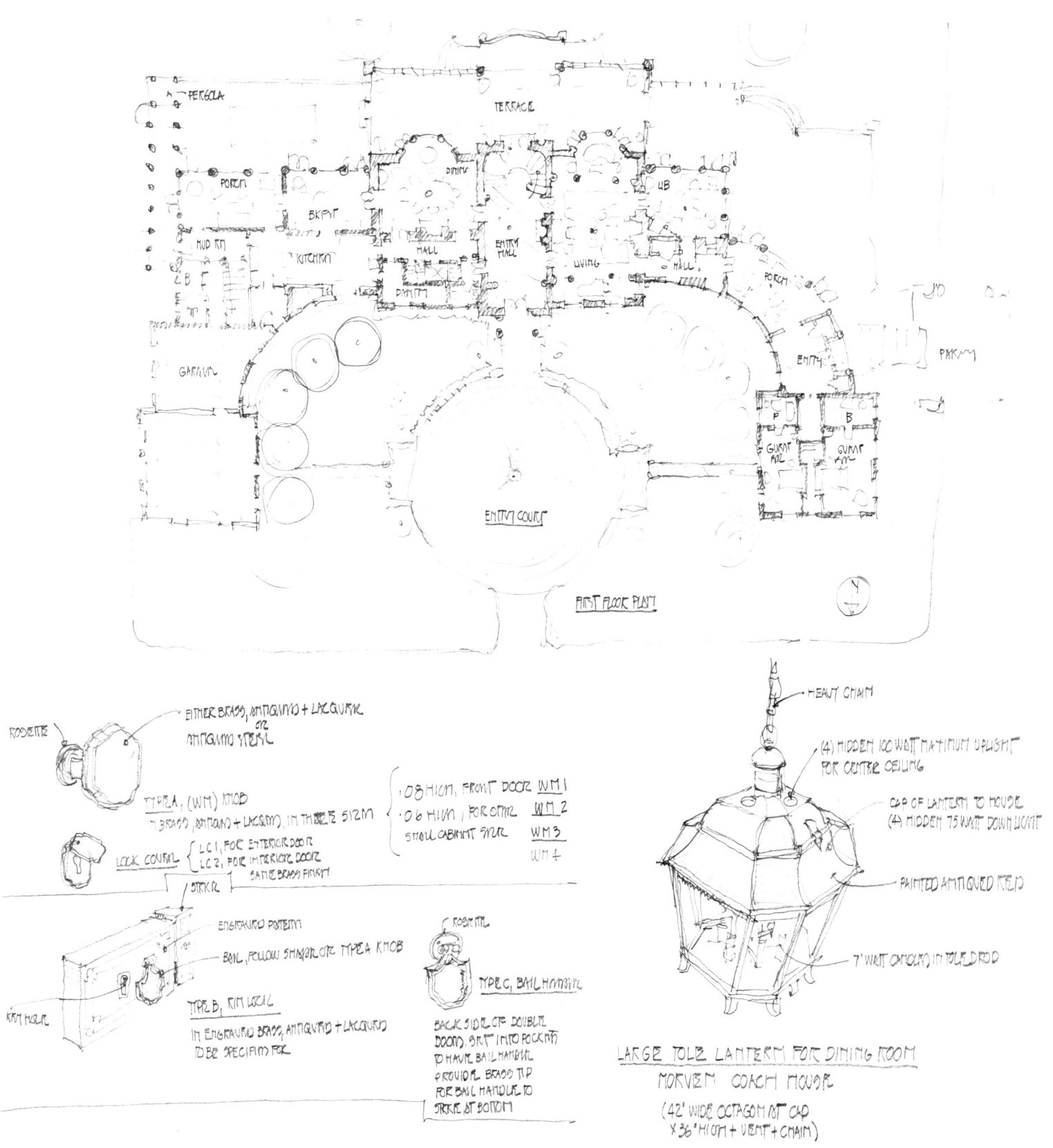

*Mr. Easton, a renowned designer, begins a project by sketching casually in a notebook assigned for that purpose. The very earliest images of the design are therefore captured, as in a childhood snapshot, and its evolution can be traced from page to page.* ⌐ *The scope of his work is extremely diverse, consisting of ground-up houses, apartment renovations, landscape architecture, and even yacht design. His commissions can be enormous in scope or relatively*

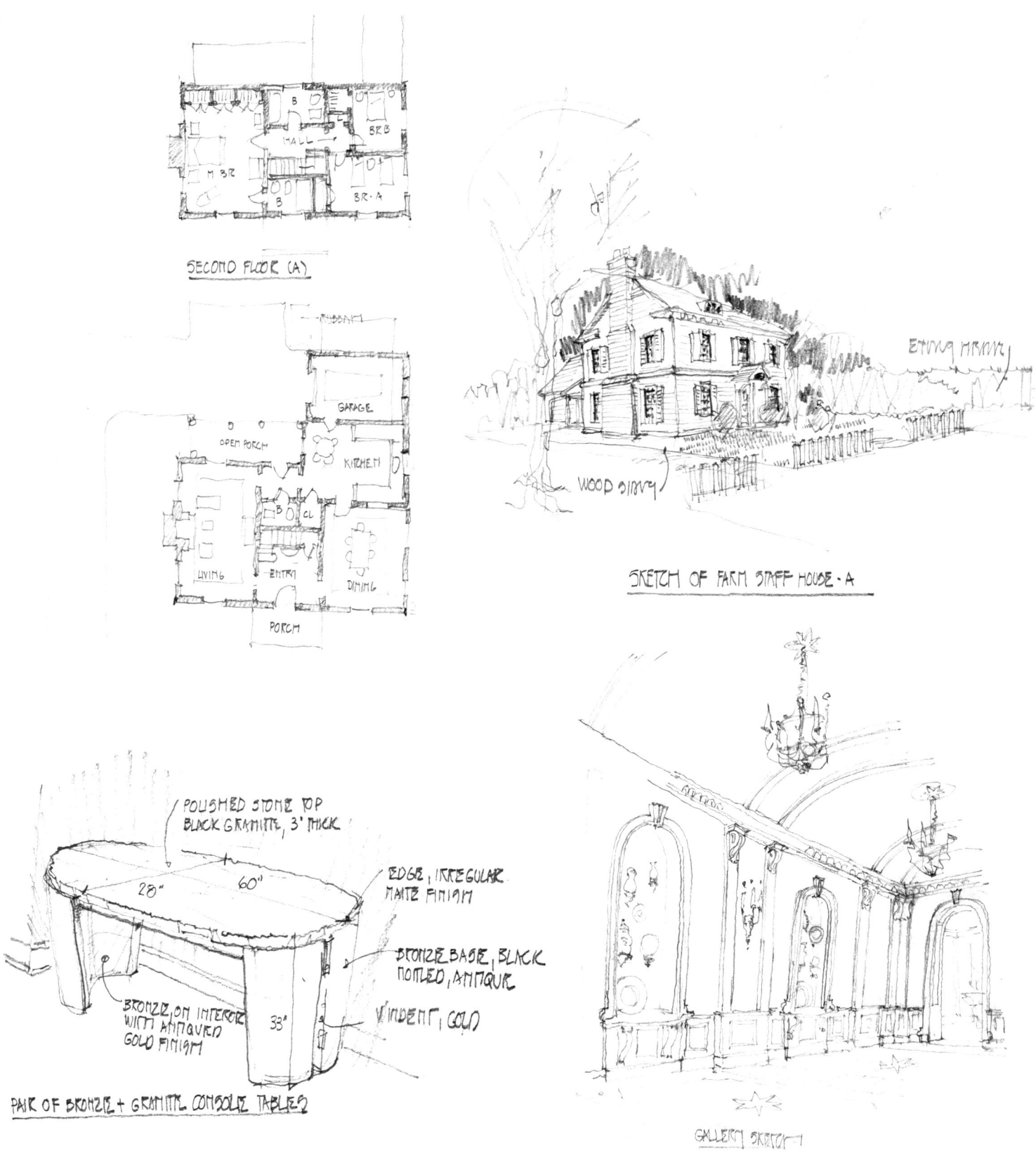

SECOND FLOOR (A)

SKETCH OF FARM STAFF HOUSE · A

PAIR OF BRONZE + GRANITE CONSOLE TABLES

GALLERY SKETCH

*modest, but what is shared from project to project is a sense of appropriateness and grace. The ability to resolve issues at all scales is particularly evident from the varied drawings found in the sketchbooks, which show him thinking as an architect in terms of volumes and massing, as well as a designer with a rigorous interest in details such as furniture and fittings. For those who enjoy the diversity of modern practice, his mastery of both realms is impressive. —D. T. N.*

# FROM THE ACADEMIES

It was on something of a whim that a young archaeologist named Lothar Haselberger decided one day to detour from his planned itinerary through coastal Turkey in order to see the remains of the colossal Temple of Apollo at nearby Didyma. Having arrived at the site, he was walking through what had once constituted the temple cella when he noticed on the masonry walls some lightly etched lines laid out in a seemingly regular pattern. Intrigued by what he saw, Haselberger returned the next day to make a closer examination of these lines, which were so faintly incised that they were only visible with concentrated examination and at those times that the sun shone on them at the proper angle.

It was not long before Haselberger realized that he had uncovered an extraordinary treasure, for these lines were determined by him to be full-size details and diagrams created by the masons engaged in the construction of the temple nearly 2,000 years ago. Had the building ever been finished in the five centuries it was under construction, the lines would have been erased by the final dressing of the ashlar walls, and so lost forever; instead, they provide the major portion of the physical body of evidence we currently possess regarding ancient working drawings (see "Good Practice" in this issue for more on construction documents).

Of the many images since uncovered at Didyma, one in particular speaks volumes about the very essence of classical architecture (CENTER). This drawing, which represents both the preliminary design of the profiles forming a column base (light line), and a secondary series of revisions imposed on the initial scheme (bold line), reveals two great truths. First, that the large thumb molding was originally constructed from a pair of

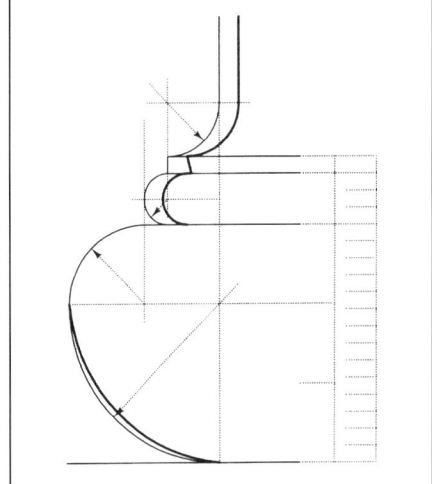

circular arcs of differing radii, and then altered by tautening its lower arc in a *freehand* curve, proves that the Greeks did not base their eccentric profiles on true conic sections, as is often portrayed in books from the nineteenth century on, but relied on intuitive methods to approximate these complex mathematical curves. More importantly still, in abandoning the rigid geometry of the first scheme in favor of a series of visual refinements in the second (for example, moving the upper bead back slightly to make more of the thumb molding visible to someone looking down on the base), the architect-mason validated the premise that in classical design abstract rule must be subordinated to the dynamics of subjective perception.

The value of the Didyma drawing to modern practitioners is therefore enormous, if for no other reason than that it prompts us to reconsider the validity of those pre-established rules for composing the orders which have guided classical architects in the 500 years since the Renaissance. Beyond this, however, looms an even larger lesson—that archaeological inquiry continues to be as much about reinforming the present as it is about distinterring the past. Thus, we need not construe archaeology solely as the investigation of the remains of Greco-Roman antiquity; such efforts as those by the students in this portfolio to recover a working knowledge of the classical system are themselves a form of cultural archaeology, insofar as they seek to restore access to a nearly forgotten aspect of their artistic inheritance. In doing so they have repudiated the contemporary clichés that we have nothing to learn from our predecessors, and that only the future lies ahead. Perhaps William Faulkner was trying to convey that same insight years ago when he observed: "The past is not dead, it's not even past." —D.R.

## THE INSTITUTE'S SUMMER PROGRAM IN CLASSICAL ARCHITECTURE

The summer program in classical architecture is a unique offering of the Institute. Open to practicing architects, preservationists, landscape designers, builders, craftspeople, educators, and students of the building arts, the six-week intensive course of study provides individuals with a foundation knowledge of classical design and technique.

In keeping with the Institute's policy that an effective knowledge of classical architecture goes beyond simply an acquaintance with its historical data, the courses conducted during the summer session explore classical building primarily from the vantage of the practitioner, with equal emphasis placed on past and present contexts. For that reason many of the instructors, lecturers, and critics in the summer program are drawn from the ranks of professionals and educators active in the fields of traditional design, construction, and decoration, in addition to scholars versed in historical disciplines. Similarly, classroom hours are balanced between time spent in a studio or workshop format, and time engaged in lecture or discussion, in order to attain that equilibrium between practice and theory sought by the informed professional.

The program has been devised to serve students currently enrolled in a degree program, as well as individuals further into their professional pursuits who wish to supplement previous training. A rich and varied student body representing all strata and aspects of the building professions is therefore characteristic of the program.

Participants uniformly enroll in courses on the elements of classical architecture, proportion,
*(continued on next page)*

STUDIO I: "Analytique of the Richard Morris Hunt Monument." Stephen Falatko, David Genther, instructors. Summer, 1994.

*ABOVE LEFT: James Bollinger, India ink on paper.*

*ABOVE RIGHT: William Brockschmidt, India ink on paper.*

*BOTTOM: John Burge, India ink on paper.*

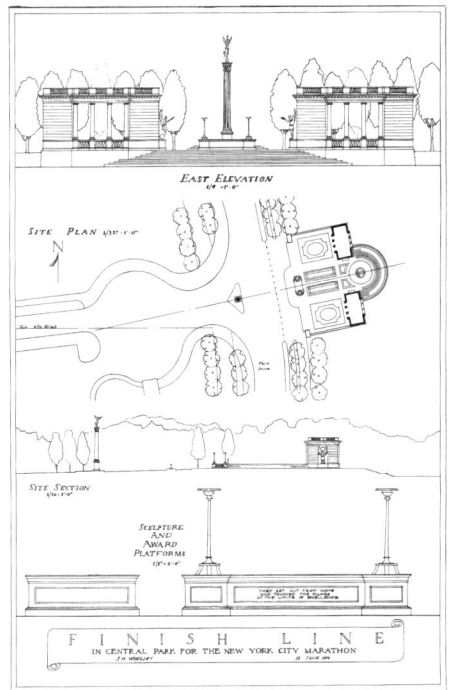

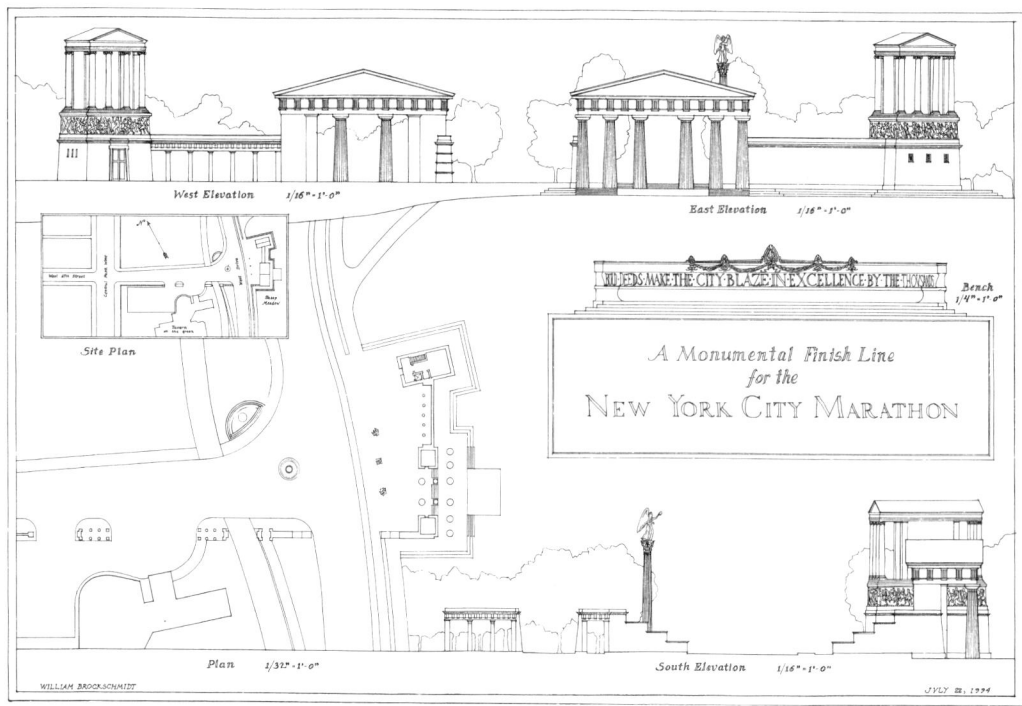

*(continued from previous page)* building technology and the crafts, theory and literature, rendering, figurative drawing, and studio. Augmenting these offerings are workshops on such topics as engineering the tall classical building, drafting the orders by computer, and monumental lettering, as well as field trips to the facilities of local artisans and to New York's pre-eminent cultural institutions. A guest lecture series features distinguished members of the Institute and affiliated organizations. Open to the public, these talks acquaint students with the latest developments in the scholarly and professional worlds of traditional building, and with such allied disciplines as archaeology, landscape architecture and furniture design.

At the core of the summer program is a two-part *atelier* where students apply their coursework and experiences. In the first segment of the studio, students work as a team to survey and create measured drawings of a small-scale monument in New York City. These drawings are then used to prepare an *analytique*—a drawing in which the important elements of the structure are placed in thematic relationship to one another. This drawing, in turn, is later transformed into a finished rendering in India ink wash (FIGURES PREVIOUS PAGE). In 1994, the monument selected was Bruce Price's Richard Morris Hunt Monument of 1896, with sculpture executed by Daniel Chester French.

In the second part of the studio, the students work individually on an original design for a project again sited in New York (ABOVE). By this stage the students are called upon to synthesize their earlier lessons not just in matters of form, but also in terms of adjusting the program to the typological and scalar conditions of an urban site and program. In addition, the program brief specifically required them to integrate the human figure and typographic inscriptions into an eloquent work of civic architecture. The public dimension of the undertaking is further underscored in the context of several other assignments executed in the satellite courses. Thus, not only did students in the 1994 program have to conceive a monumental finish line for the New York City Marathon, as called for in the studio, but they also had to design under the aegis of their figure drawing instructor a medal to celebrate the event (CENTER).

Perhaps one of the most powerful lessons that students take away from the summer program is this: just as classical architecture admits a tremendous formal and temperamental diversity within a unified outlook, so too can one's creative imagination be fulfilled while working within a conventionalized system of design. It is a lesson which they will no doubt apply throughout their professional lives. —Stephen Falatko

STUDIO II: "Monumental Finish Line for the New York City Marathon." Stephen Falatko and Mark Hewitt, instructors. Summer, 1994.

*ABOVE LEFT: John Woolsey, Plans and elevations. Pencil on vellum.*
*ABOVE RIGHT: William Brockschmidt, Plans and elevations. Pencil on vellum.*

FIGURATIVE DRAWING: "Medal for the Winner of the New York City Marathon." Leonard Petrillo, instructor. Summer, 1994.

*CENTER: John Barron Clancy, Design for a medal. Charcoal and conté pencil on Canson paper.*

CLASSICAL ARCHITECTURAL RENDERING:
THE TRADITIONAL METHODS.
Richard Wilson Cameron and Thomas Felton,
instructors. Spring, 1994.

Offered each spring and fall at the Institute, this
class introduces students to the traditional architectural rendering media of India ink and watercolor,
and the various ways in which they can be used to
create wash drawings of architectural subjects.
Among the topics covered are materials, India ink
wash, toned ink wash, watercolor, free wash rendering, understanding shades and shadows, simu-
lating texture, sheet composition and the production of the *analytique*.

Students are required to produce three thematically
and pictorially linked renderings in the class. The
scale as well as the subject matter progress in a
definitive sequence from a large-scale monochro-
matic drawing of an architectural element, to a
toned ink rendering of a building elevation, to a
full-color depiction of an urban setting.

An excerpt from the course textbook, H. Van
Buren Magonigle's *Architectural Rendering in Wash*,
originally published in 1926:

*The rigid discipline academic rendering enforces in
the judgment of value and tones, the training the eye
gets in discerning the difference between two whites
in which there is scarcely a breath of difference near
by but which at a distance count with a totally different force, the exercise the hand gets in perfecting a
technique, are all of inestimable value. Why so much
emphasis upon draughtsmanship, upon presentation? Because by means of drawings the eye is
trained to appreciate values in the distribution of
light and shade and color—and it is with light and
shade and color the architect deals all his life. And
how is he to effect the distribution of his light and
shade and color without making drawings which
accurately express it, first? How can he make drawings which accurately express it without learning
how to do so with his own hands? How is he to
train his own eye by the use of someone else's hands?*

*UPPER LEFT: Stephanie Murrill, Doric order from
the Temple of Hercules at Cori. India ink on paper.*

*UPPER RIGHT: Jeffery Langston, Elevation detail of
Earl Hall at Columbia University, New York. Toned
India ink on paper.*

*RIGHT: Charlotte Worthy, View of Earl Hall at
Columbia University, New York. Watercolor on paper.*

TEMPLE OF HERCULES AT CORI

EARL · HALL
COLUMBIA UNIVERSITY

THESIS PROJECT: "Expansion of the New Orleans Museum of Art." E. Eean McNaughton, advisor. Spring 1989.

MICHAEL ROUCHELL, STUDENT:

The New Orleans Museum of Art was built in 1910 to the designs of Lebenbaum & Marx Architects of Chicago. Unlike other museums situated at the edge of urban parks, the building is located well inside New Orleans' City Park, where it sits within a traffic circle that terminates the axis of Esplanade Avenue. The museum was therefore designed to be a classical island in a picturesque setting.

In the late 1960s, the museum embarked upon an expansion program that would more than double the amount of gallery space. The expansion was executed in a minimalist expression so as not to compete with the original building. The addition comprised two wings on opposite sides of the building and a larger gallery wing at the rear.

In 1983, the museum held a competition for a second expansion to double again the amount of gallery, administration and curatorial space. The program of my 1989 thesis project is loosely based upon this program. My intent was to design an addition that blended in with the original museum building. The *precis* was that any contemporary mode of expression, such as that utilized for the expansion of 1971, would further compromise the premise of the first building.

The two existing wings flanking each side of the existing building were retained, but were given new facades on the exterior and replanned on the interior. Most of the rear gallery was demolished.

The new rear addition repeats the two pavilions of the original structure, suggesting a square in plan. Within this square rises a new third level that would contain a restaurant, while increasing the monumentality of the original building. The height from the building's base to the third floor cornice is the same as the central pavilion's width and depth, forming a perfect cube in proportion.

The museum completed its second expansion in 1992. The winning scheme from the 1983 competition was abandoned and the existing building was enlarged with a modernist addition within the existing traffic circle. The vision of a unified, classical museum therefore remains unrealized.

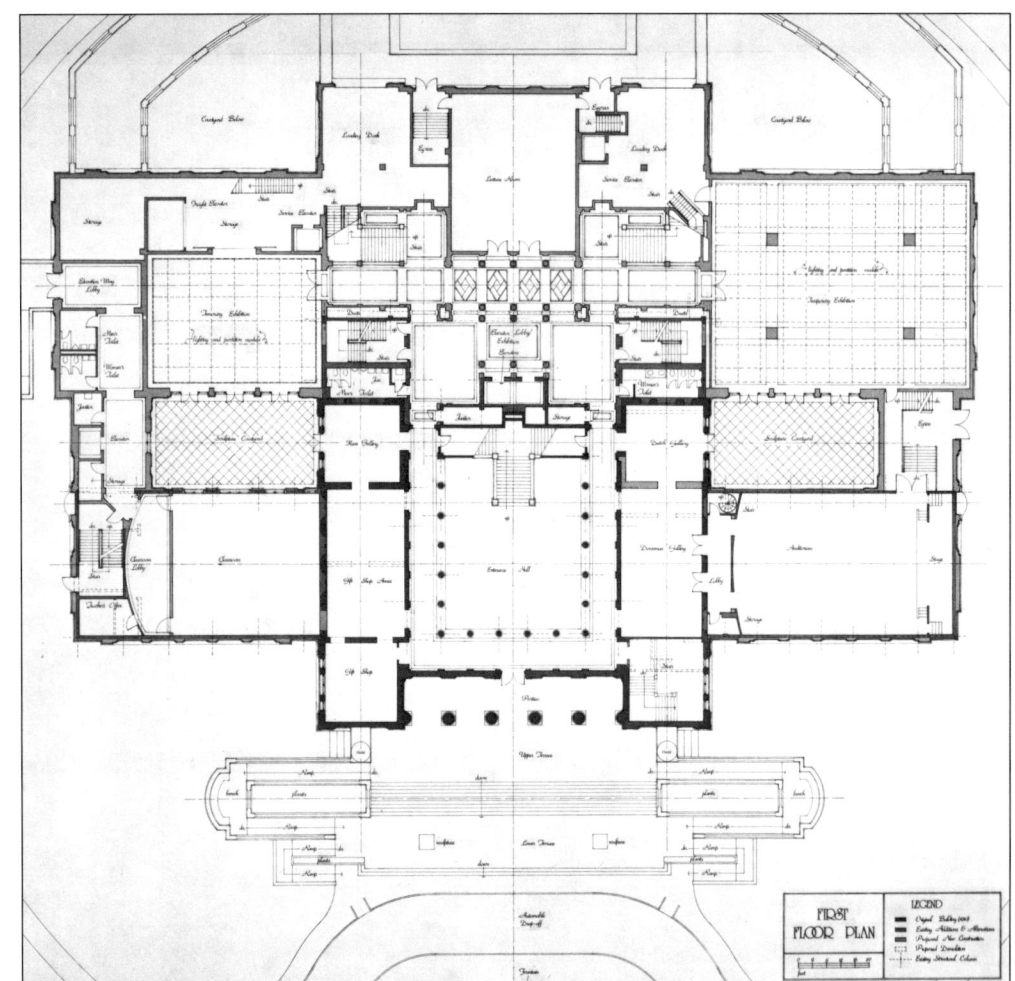

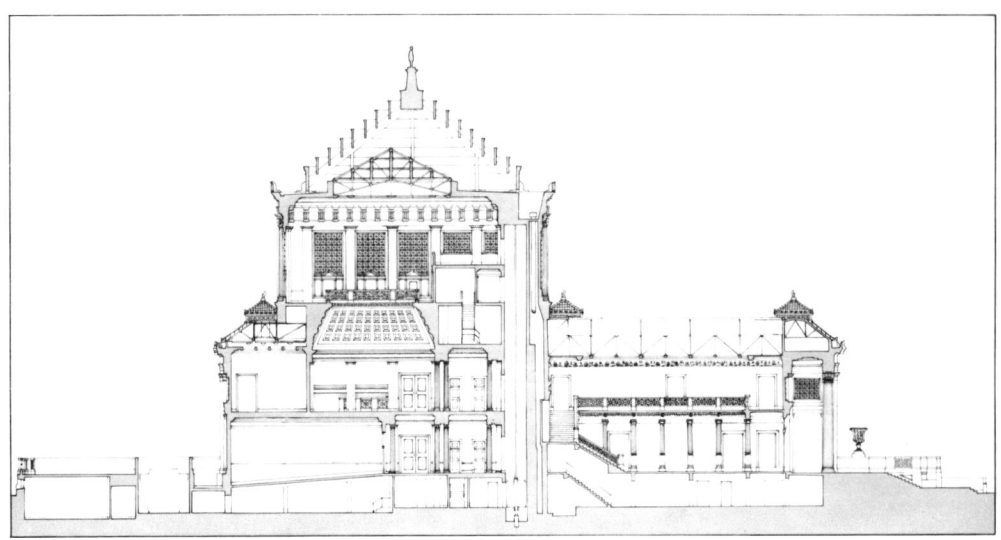

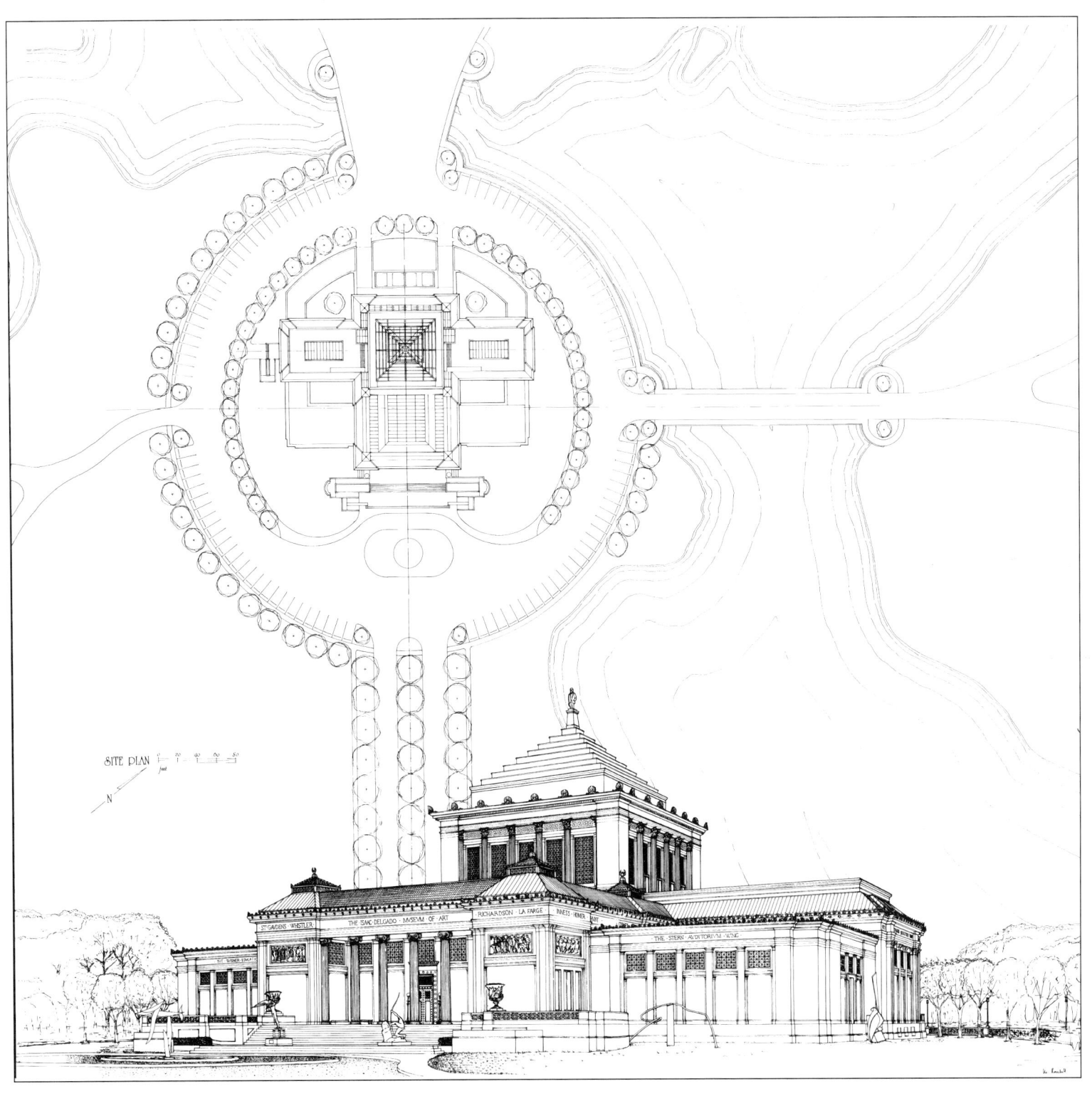

SITE PLAN

N

*ABOVE LEFT: Main floor plan. BELOW LEFT: Longitudinal section. ABOVE: Perspective view, with site plan. Pencil on vellum. Drawings by Michael Rouchell.*

ADVANCED INTERIOR ARCHITEC-
TURE STUDIO: "A Stair Hall and Library for
the Chicago Athenaeum." Linda Nelson Keane,
instructor; Thomas Norman Rajkovich,
Elissa Morgante, visiting architects. Spring, 1994.

EXCERPTS FROM PROFESSOR KEANE'S
PROGRAM BRIEF:

You are asked to use the following written
description as the interpretive basis for your

design for a stairhall and library for the
Chicago Athenaeum. There are virtually no
explicit dimensional requirements for this
project. Rather, you should imagine the
place described and determine dimensional
parameters individually.

*The Chicago Athenaeum building is remarkable
particularly for its grand stairhall entry and library.
Upon arriving from the city street, one enters a
foyer vestibule (a rather dark space) with piers supporting a coffered ceiling. At one end of the foyer is
situated a coat room, at the other a small office for
a reception desk.*

*Ahead the beautiful light of the stairhall draws one
forward, the stairs themselves seeming to spill
down from above. The room which contains the
stair is a model of decorum. The ground level is
enclosed and contained in character, while the
piano nobile is brilliantly transparent, its edges
defined by graceful Ionic columns and pilasters.
One is also impressed by the way in which the
Ionic order is used, most notably at the corner conditions. Scholarly discussions, muffled through the
distance, summon the visitor up the stair to the
library. The stair is generous in scale, easily accom-
modating three persons or more across its width.
Several landings provide opportunities to view the
splendid skylight and coffered ceiling and ease the
climb. The piano nobile has ceilings which exceed
twenty-two feet in height.*

*The library is found directly off the stairhall,
through a group of three doors. Its broadly vaulted
room is encircled by a pattern of bookshelves and
reading carrels which support a delicate mezzanine
level of additional bookshelves. The back wall of
the library provides a dramatic backdrop for the
librarians' desk, while light filters in from windows
along the side walls.*

*Throughout, there is evidence of the symbolic
theme, making clear to the visitor in an instructive,
legible manner many important aspects of the
history of architecture and the allied arts (especially
painting and sculpture). Truly the arts find mean-
ingful balance here. One leaves this place aware of
how architecture's tradition will affect its future.*

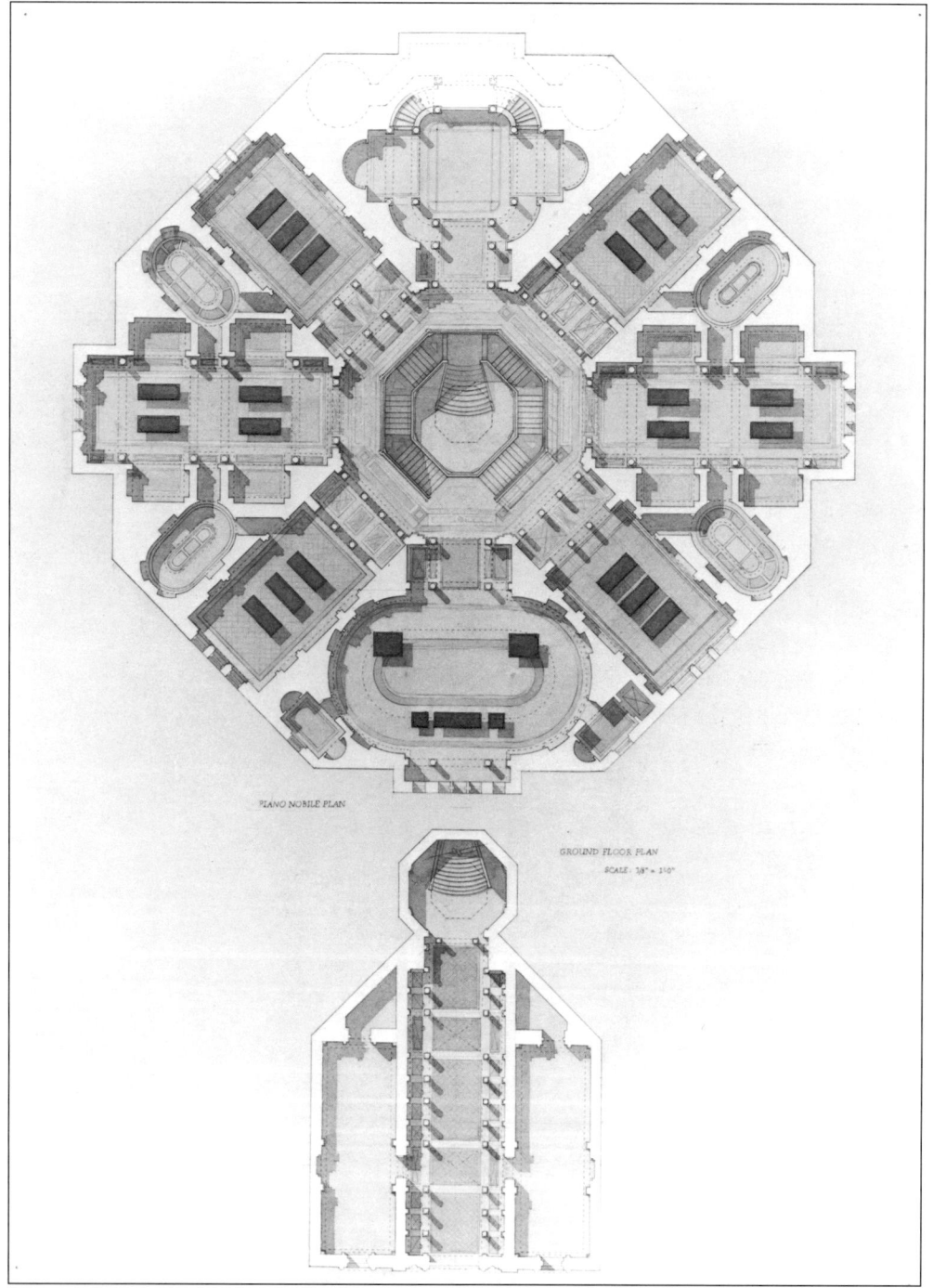

PIANO NOBILE PLAN

GROUND FLOOR PLAN
SCALE: 1/8" = 1'-0"

*LEFT: Marcia Thompson. Plan for the stair hall and library
at the Chicago Athenaeum. Pencil and watercolor on paper.*

INDEPENDENT PROJECT. John Blatteau, mentor. Spring, 1992.

RALPH MULDROW, STUDENT:

As with gnarled vines and well-barnacled fountains, buildings left to weather embody an undeniable pathos, yet they also are enriched by those actions of nature which are at once consistent and arbitrary. Thus, in this ornamented tympanum, forces such as gravity, thermal expansion, and the effects of moisture may be interpreted as agents of destruction as well as embellishment. Here paint peeling from wood both dematerializes its subject into an abstracted cornice profile, and enlivens the ornamented surface by endowing it with a rococo veil which becomes intensified in the late afternoon sun. Through the journey of time nature inveighs against the moment of construction, and the architect's eye and the builder's logic are made to face the future and her elements.

*LEFT: Ralph Muldrow, A West Philadelphia tympanum in decay. Charcoal on paper.*

SOPHOMORE STUDIO: Duncan Stroik, instructor. Fall, 1994. A studio formatted in four parts: canon, precedent, measurement, and design. In the precedent project *(left)* students study the composition of a facade and analyze its relationship to other buildings. The design project *(right)* calls for an elevation of a new building employing the Doric type.

*BELOW LEFT: Dana Gulling, Precedent study: Palazzo dei Conservatori. India ink on paper.*

*BELOW RIGHT: Joseph H. Cruz, Elevation and details for a Philosophy Building at the University of Notre Dame. India ink on paper.*

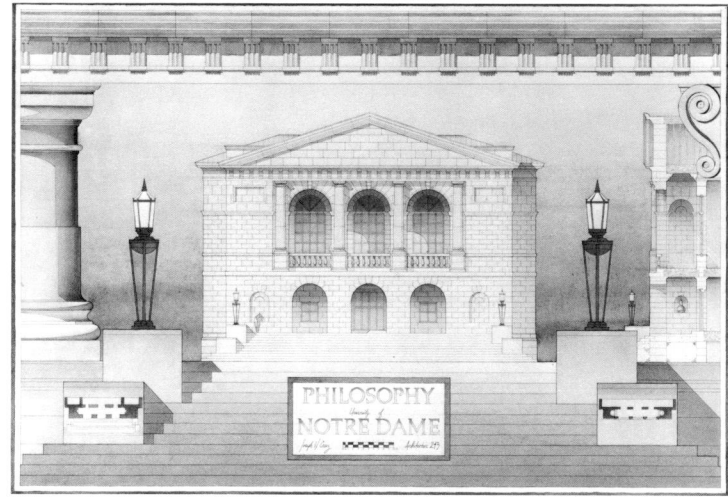

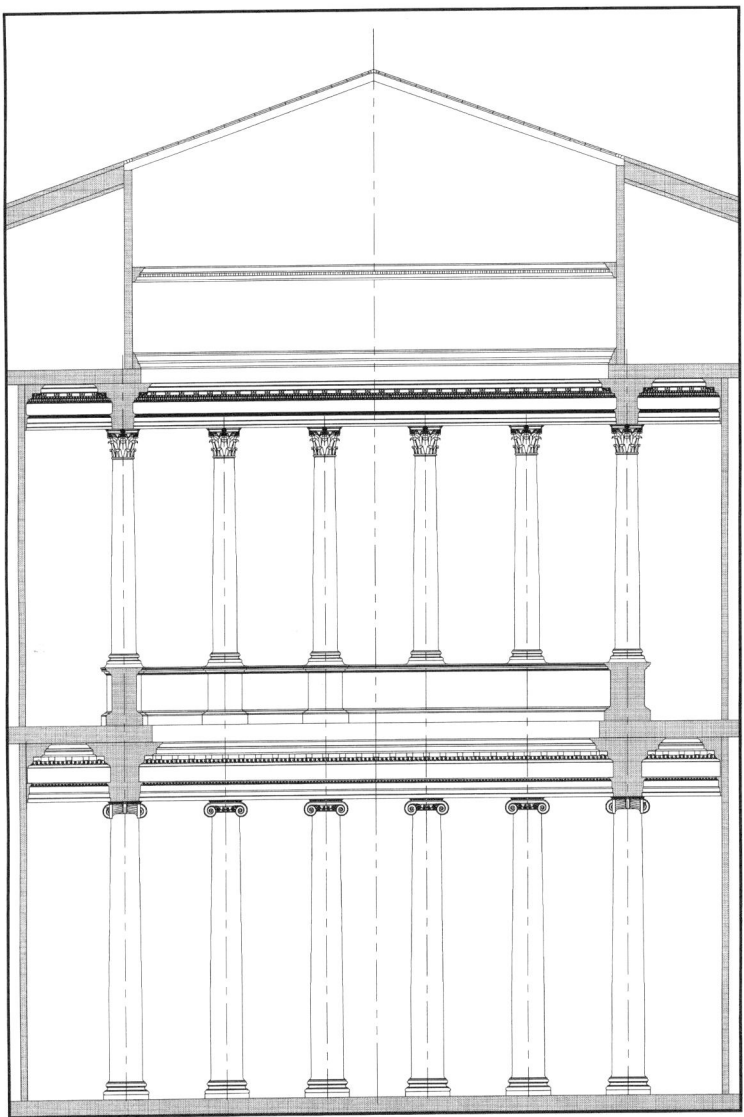

THOMAS JEFFERSON AND ARCHITECTURE: "Reconstruction of Jefferson's Rotunda in the Virginia Capitol." Charles E. Brownell, instructor. Spring, 1994.

BRIAN MCROBERTS, STUDENT:

The purpose of this exercise was to produce a conceptual drawing of the interior hall from Thomas Jefferson's final design for the Virginia State Capitol in Richmond. Since all that remains of this design are two floor plans drawn by Jefferson (K110, K111) and some very general specifications, there is much room for conjecture. What is certain, however, is that Jefferson intended a two-story peristyle hall, topped by a skylight.

Since the floor-to-floor dimensions Jefferson specified were of equal height, a pedestal would have been required for the second floor order to maintain proper classical proportions. This raised many questions, since Jefferson had never shown any interest in pedestals or even balustrades for his balconies or porticoes. The solution chosen here was to use two versions of a continuous pedestal scheme. The version shown on the left half of the section drawing (FIGURE LEFT) shows articulated pedestals, while a continuous pedestal is shown on the right half.

This drawing was produced using AutoCad version 12. It will be included with accompanying drawings of the Virginia Capitol in a forthcoming essay by Professor Brownell entitled "Thomas Jefferson's Architectural Models and the United States Capitol."

*LEFT: Brian McRoberts, Two conjectural elevations for the interior hall, Virginia Capitol. Ink on vellum.*

## SYRACUSE UNIVERSITY

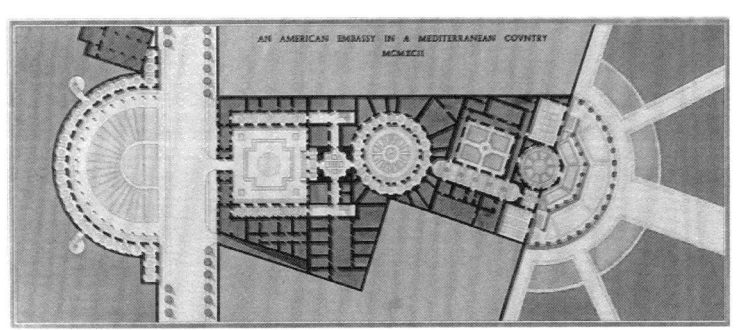

SECOND YEAR DESIGN STUDIO: "An American Embassy in a Friendly Mediterranean Country." J. François Gabriel, instructor. Spring, 1992.

*LEFT: Richard K. Colson, Plan. Pencil and watercolor on paper.*

# COMPETITIONS

The projects in this section are selected from recent architectural competitions. Continuing the theme of archaeology in this number of THE CLASSICIST, two of the projects are entries for a competition to design a new museum housing the state collection of antiquities in Athens. Others include a town monument in Augusta, Georgia and a design for a mass transit ventilator in New York City. Interestingly, only one of the five projects in this portfolio is residential, reflecting a renewed interest in classical design beyond this sector and into the civic realm.

## AUGUSTA MONUMENT

DAVID T. COLGAN
VERO BEACH, FLORIDA

The tradition of a freestanding monument as the focus of a square or piazza is vigorously interpreted by David Colgan in his winning entry for a competition held in Augusta, Georgia (FIGURE RIGHT). The competition was sponsored by a consortium of local business and civic interests, and called for a monument dedicated to the history of the city on a site originally occupied by a nineteenth century market building. The design features a group of four columns

*AUGUSTA MONUMENT, Georgia. David T. Colgan, architect.*

supporting a copper roof with projecting wood rafters, and successfully combines the rustic forms of the Tuscan order with the contextual materials of brick and granite. The project was under construction at the time of this writing.

## THE ACROPOLIS MUSEUM PROJECTS

In 1990 a competition took place for the siting and planning of a new Acropolis Museum in Athens. THE CLASSICIST presents two submissions to the competition, each of which shows differing approaches to contextual and urban issues. The designs are both classicizing in their reference to Hellenic precedent, but it is interesting to contrast the approaches to massing and the distribution of function.

OCTAVIAN CIUPITU
SKOGÅS, SWEDEN

Perhaps the most ambitious in scale of the competition entries, Ciupitu's design presents a descending series of colonnaded galleries which intersect to form a complex of interior courts (FIGURES NEXT PAGE). The architect defies the irregularities of the site by introducing a strong diagonal axis at a contrasting angle to the surrounding streets, along which the frequent level changes occur. The uniformity of the colon-

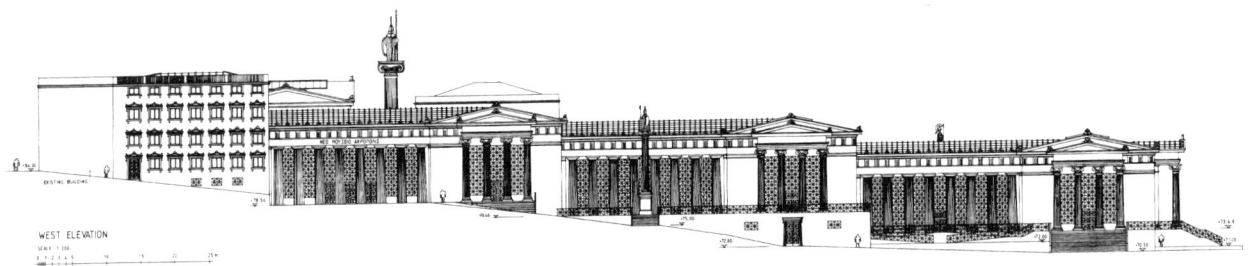

nades is effective in making a building of many separate components into a legible whole, with an Ionic portico concluding the axis of each longitudinal gallery.

MICHAEL LYKOUDIS
SOUTH BEND, INDIANA

Lykoudis takes an interpretive approach to the forms of Greek classical architecture as a European architect of the early nineteenth century might have seen them (FIGURES OPPOSITE). The project consists of three connected pavilions of similar proportions, two containing galleries and another the auditorium. The rigorous axial symmetry of the composition is artfully broken at the entrance to the auditorium, which pivots slightly to the west. A portico with a double stair makes the south elevation the most monumental, endowing the facade with the qualities of neoclassical English country house architecture. The well-disciplined elevations are marked by a continuous rusticated base, a tectonic feature which contrasts effectively with such architectural flourishes as the elaborate stairway.

## THE JANUS HOUSE

IAN FLEETWOOD
SAN FRANCISCO, CALIFORNIA

A villa for a writer and financier, this entry to the international competition "La Casa Piu' Bella Del Mondo" is a tightly articulated exercise in contemporary classicism (FIGURES PAGE 80, ABOVE). The deftness with which the house exploits a limited site, as well as the abstracted forms of its exterior, recall the residential work of Scott Merrill in the new town of Windsor, Florida (see the Portfolio "From the Offices" in THE CLASSICIST, No. 1). The Janus house seems to recompose itself when viewed from different angles, combining elements of picturesque massing with elevations of stark local brick. Pergolas are flung out from the

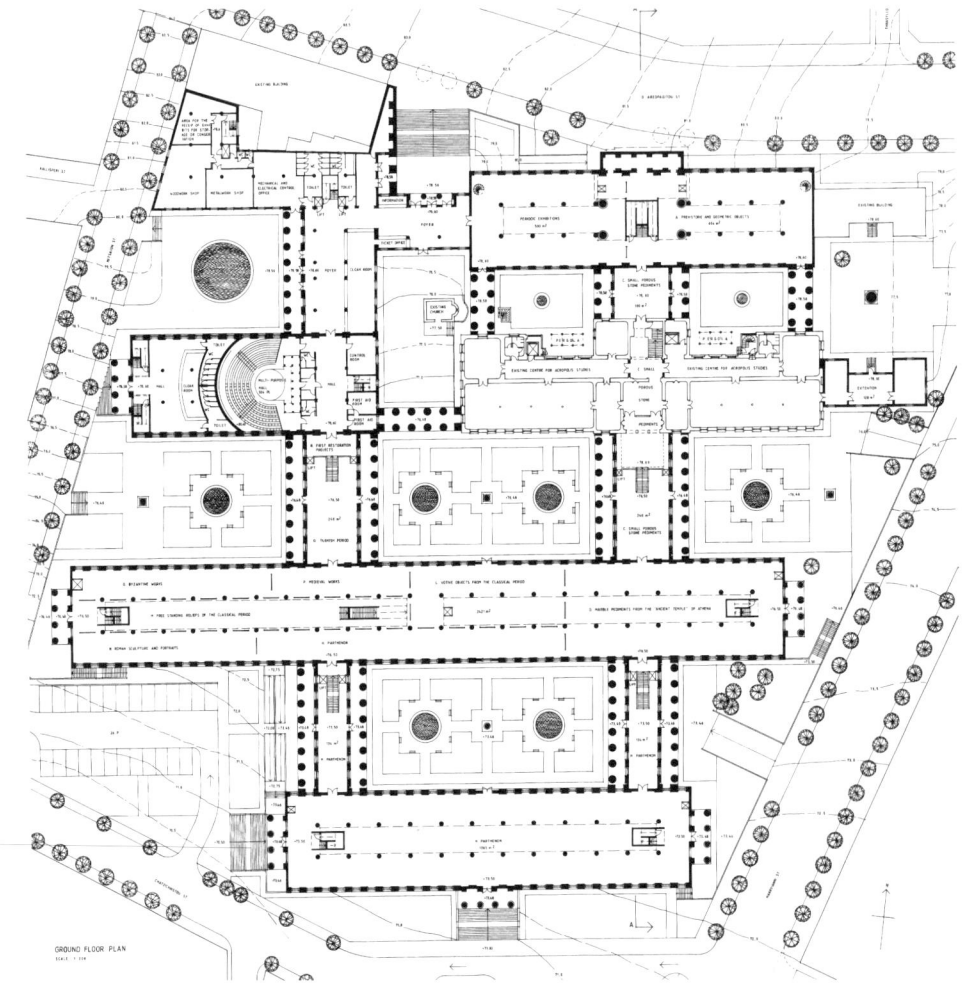

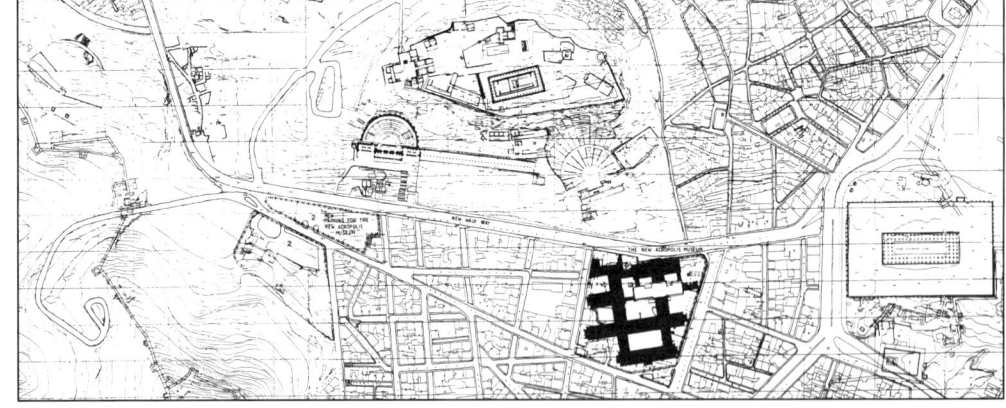

*ACROPOLIS MUSEUM COMPETITION. Entry by Octavian Ciupitu. TOP: West elevation. MIDDLE: Ground floor. BOTTOM: Detail of survey plan, showing relation of proposed museum to the Acropolis.*

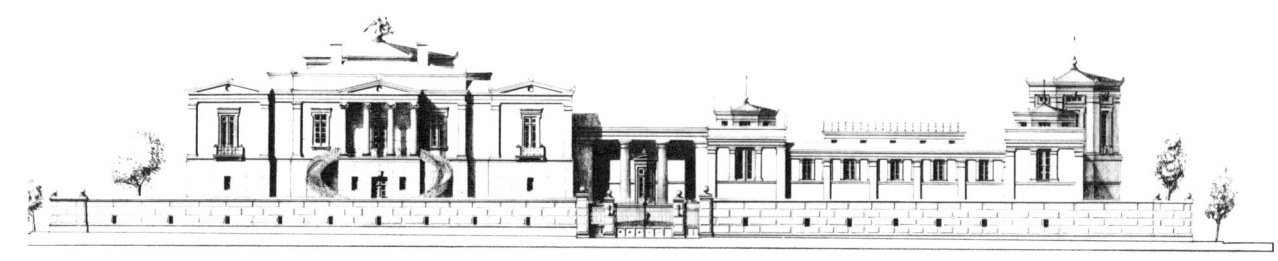

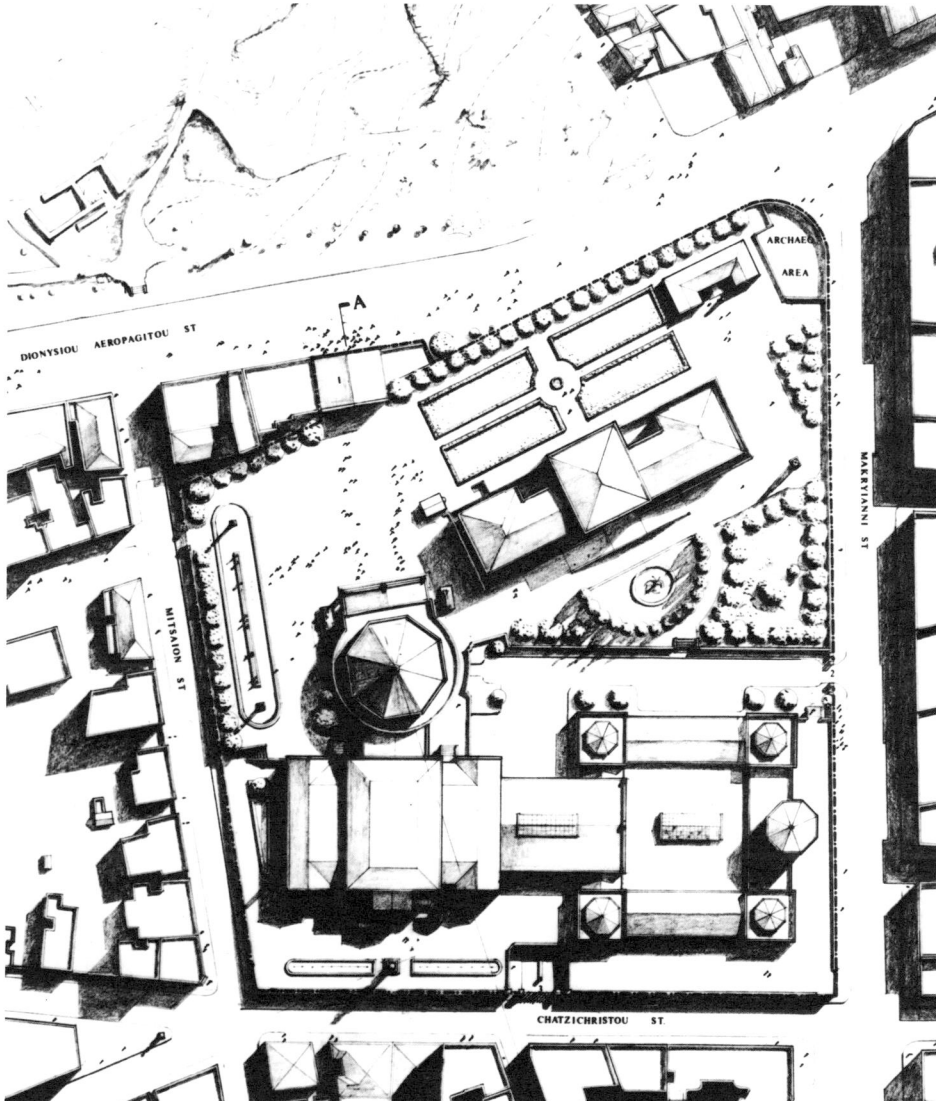

house to imply architecture where there is none, connecting the villa to its street entrance and incorporating the design harmoniously into a conjectural suburban community. The plan provides accommodation for the financier and writer on the first and second floors respectively, with the ground floor designated for communal use. The financier's central area contains a cylindrical volume that can be used as a conference room, while the writer's space evolves around a forced perspective library which functions both as a room and a circulatory space. The compression of spatial planning to provide diverse uses and room shapes within a limited exterior shell is characteristic of Fleetwood's design throughout the project.

## MORTON STREET VENTILATORS

ROBERT A.M. STERN
NEW YORK, NEW YORK

It is interesting to address a project whose program is both civic and industrial (FIGURE NEXT PAGE, BOTTOM). Monumental industrial architecture, like Sir Giles Gilbert Scott's Battersea Power Station in London (1931), demonstrated the ability of an abstract classicism to house technology; here Robert A.M. Stern uses a similar vocabulary for a structure to contain ventilation systems for the PATH train system at a site in New York City. The location of the project is rich in the history of traditional building modes, as much New York pier architecture is Beaux Arts in character and the neighboring residential areas consist principally of Greek Revival brick townhouses. Most importantly, the design combines industrial components with an esplanade for pedestrian traffic, creating much needed recreational space on New York's waterfront. The rationale for this program is compelling: as New York's commercial harbor traffic has declined, the possibilities for civic and leisure use of the waterfront remain sadly underexplored. Robert A.M. Stern's project for the Morton Street ventilators makes a welcome gesture toward the reinstatement of these priorities in architecture and urban planning. —D.T.N.

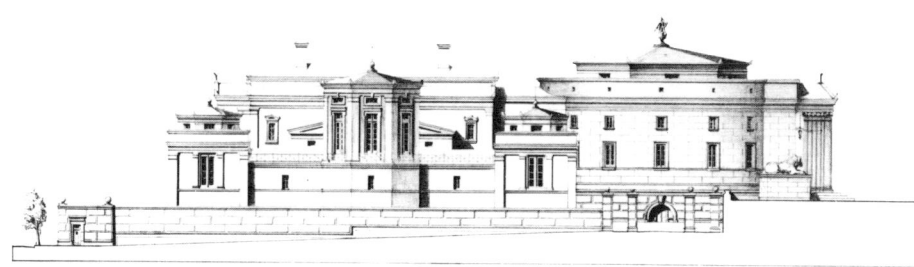

*ACROPOLIS MUSEUM COMPETITION. Entry by Michael Lykoudis. TOP: South elevation. MIDDLE: Site plan. BOTTOM: East elevation.*

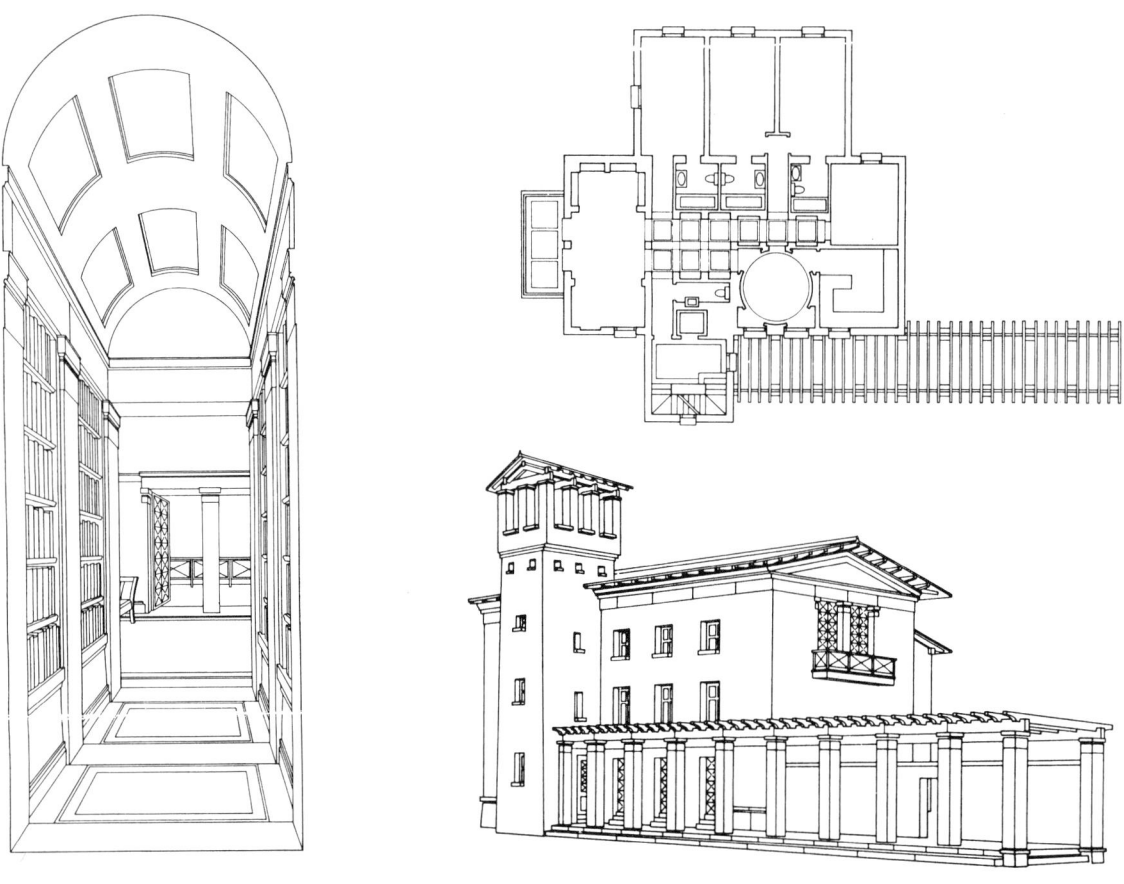

TOP: THE JANUS HOUSE. *Ian Fleetwood, architect. Clockwise from left: Interior perspective of the writer's library; first floor plan showing financier's accommodation; exterior perspective from the south.*
BOTTOM: MORTON STREET VENTILATORS, *New York City. Robert A.M. Stern, architect. Photograph of model.*

# WORKING DRAWINGS

## CLARITY FOR CONSTRUCTION

**THE WORKING DRAWING IN HISTORY:** There is ongoing scholarly debate as to the nature and character of ancient working drawings. Though it is difficult to imagine that some graphic format did not precede the construction of the outstanding monuments of ancient times, the fact remains that with the notable exception of descriptive stone carvings found at various sites, little evidence has come down to us of how these documents might have appeared or how they were utilized in the process of constructing a building.

The absence of such evidence should be judged against what is known of the architect's role in ancient building practice. J. J. Coulton, in his book *Ancient Greek Architects at Work,* notes that several *syngraphai,* or specifications, which list in detail the sizes and use of building materials, are still extant. He further observes that within the *syngraphai* the architect in charge of construction was called on to supply a *paradeigma,* which was a three-dimensional template or sample that would serve to direct the builders.

The recent discovery of a large hoard of ancient working drawings at the Temple of Apollo at Didyma, in present-day Turkey, sheds new light on the subject of ancient construction documents (see pages 44 and 68 of this issue for more on this finding). The location of these drawings on the actual masonry walls of the temple indicates that a certain level of design and documentation took place on site. The endurance of the Didyma model is demonstrated by the discovery of detailed drawings uncovered during the restoration of an eighteenth century structure in Williamsburg, Virginia. Discovered on the backsides of boards used for interior wood paneling were moderately detailed sketches of a mantle and archway, which correspond fairly closely with the items as they were actually executed elsewhere in the structure.

Now, the relationship of design and building where the architect is on site, and directing the operation of the building, raises a wealth of issues. Of these the most significant concerns the architect as master-builder—that is, the person responsible for both directing and designing during the building process. Today, the option of the architect being continually present on site may not be practical, although it should serve as a reminder of the level of integration and coordination of design and building that existed in antiquity and colonial times.

This ought to encourage us to redevelop more fully that link and to amplify our knowledge of such practices in an effort to facilitate the process of building today. The implication of a shared background, an acknowledgment of the priority of convention and of a unified and coherent building system, should remain the foundation of any discussion regarding the detailing, or working drawings of traditional and classical architecture.

**SCOPE OF WORKING DRAWINGS:** Several issues come up in the context of the working drawing. First, what is the nature of this type of drawing, and how does it differ from a design drawing? Second, what information does this type of drawing intend to convey?

The principal consideration of the working drawing is to communicate, through a graphic format, the methods of erecting a building which will achieve the design intent. Implicit in this statement is the architect's familiarity with the following:

1. A KNOWLEDGE OF MATERIALS AND THE BUILDING PROCESS
2. AN ABILITY TO DIRECT THAT PROCESS THROUGH DRAWINGS
3. A MASTERING OF THE GRAPHIC METHOD, FORMS AND TOOLS
   THAT ARE REQUIRED TO ACHIEVE THE INTENDED RESULT

Let us begin by discussing the graphic method. In the design process, it is appropriate to be relatively loose and free regarding dimensions in the initial stages. At a certain point, however, a tightening of dimensioning begins to take place, thereby providing the foundation for the working drawing. The restrictions inherent in a scaled drawing ought not to be looked upon as a detriment to the design process; rather, one must consider the discipline analogous to the poet working within the sonnet format. Thus, one distinction between the working and design drawing is that the first constitutes an accurately scaled document illustrating the actual conditions within which the building will be realized.

At the same time, there remains a reciprocity between the design drawing and the working drawing. Later in the article we will look at examples

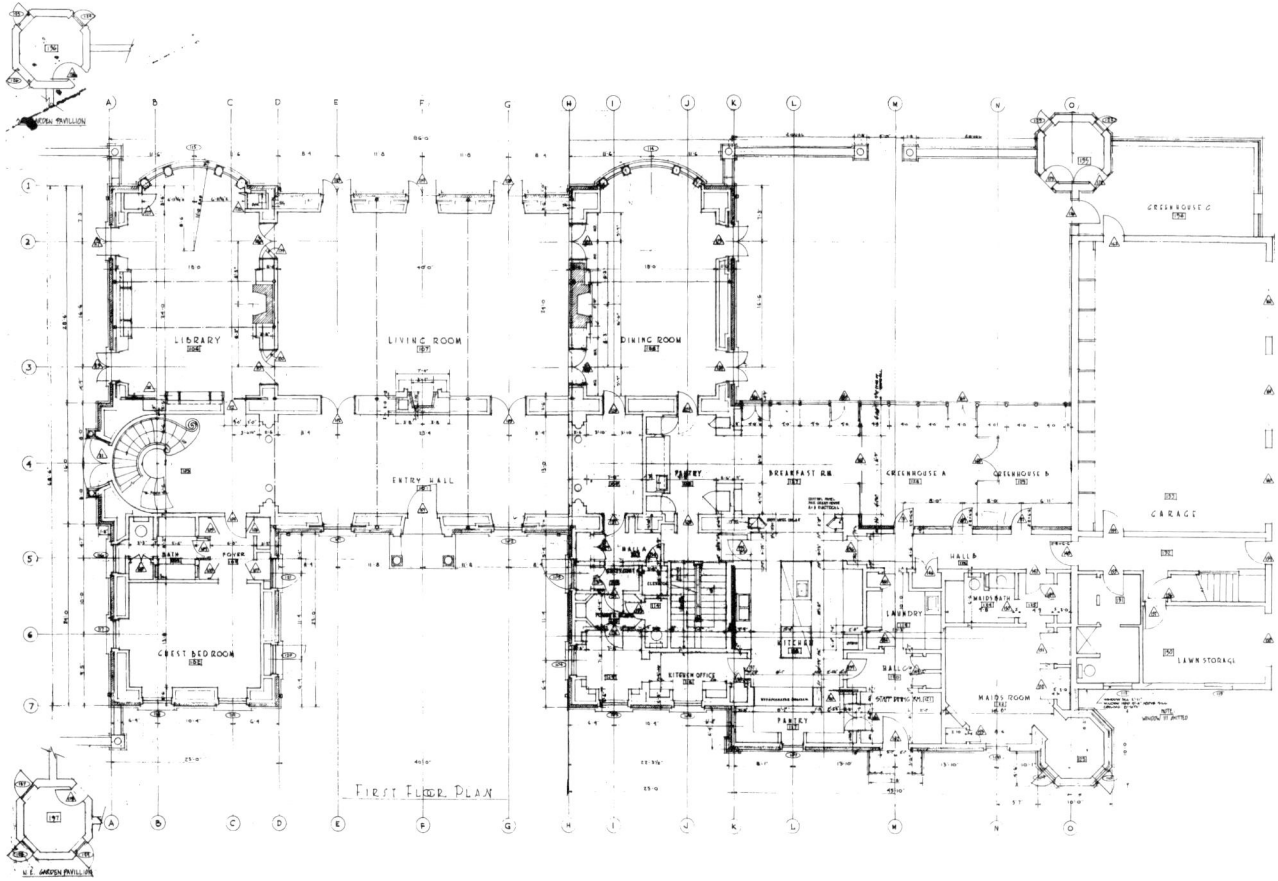

*FIGURE 1, ABOVE: Easton & La Rocca, New York, New York. A residence in Lake Forest, Illinois.*
*FIGURE 2, RIGHT: Ken Tate Architect, Jackson, Mississippi. A residence in Baton Rouge, Louisiana.*

of working drawings which reinforce this relationship. Too often, we slight the one for the sake of the other, leading either to a designer who does not deign to be limited by the conventions of the working drawing, or a detailer who thinks only about the practical aspects of the design element. It is between those extremes of a designer and detailer that architects find their place, and it is the coalescing of each which can return us, conceptually, to the ancient model of the architect as master builder.

**MODERN WORKING DRAWINGS:**    The three principal forms of architectural drawing today are:

1. GENERAL DRAWING—scale 1/8" or 1/4" = 1' - 0"
2. SCALE DRAWING—scale 3/4" or 3" = 1' - 0"
3. FULL SIZE DRAWING

The tools for presenting information in all scales of drawing are the same; they are the conventional means of conveying two-dimensional information for a three-dimensional object. They include:

1. THE PLAN
2. THE ELEVATION
3. THE SECTION

THE PLAN:  Information to be conveyed is horizontal dimensioning, and the relationship between some known point of reference, or datum. Depending upon the scale of the drawing that reference may be a survey bench mark, the known corner of the building, or the finished jamb of the door. The reference must be immediately apparent to an informed eye, and if it is an abstract reference, e.g., a surveyed bench mark noted above sea level, it should be reconciled to the building proper, such as to the finish first floor.

THE ELEVATION:  Information to be conveyed is vertical dimensioning, requiring some known point of reference. Again, depending upon the scale, that reference may be the floor levels of the building, finished ceiling condition, or the door head height. Identification and coordination of material is important, and depending upon scale, delineation of the material may be essential. The elevation is the view, the visual reference of the building.

THE SECTION:  Information to be conveyed is both horizontal and vertical dimensioning. Typically, the section is considered in a vertical format; the plan section, however, is a specific drawing used to coordinate vertical and horizontal conditions. Regarding the building process, the section is the drawing that most completely identifies the specific requirements of the materials of the building. Once more, this is applicable in both the horizontal and vertical planes. Whereas no single drawing is self-sufficient, the section does coordinate the plan and elevation, and grounds the two by revealing the specifics of the building.

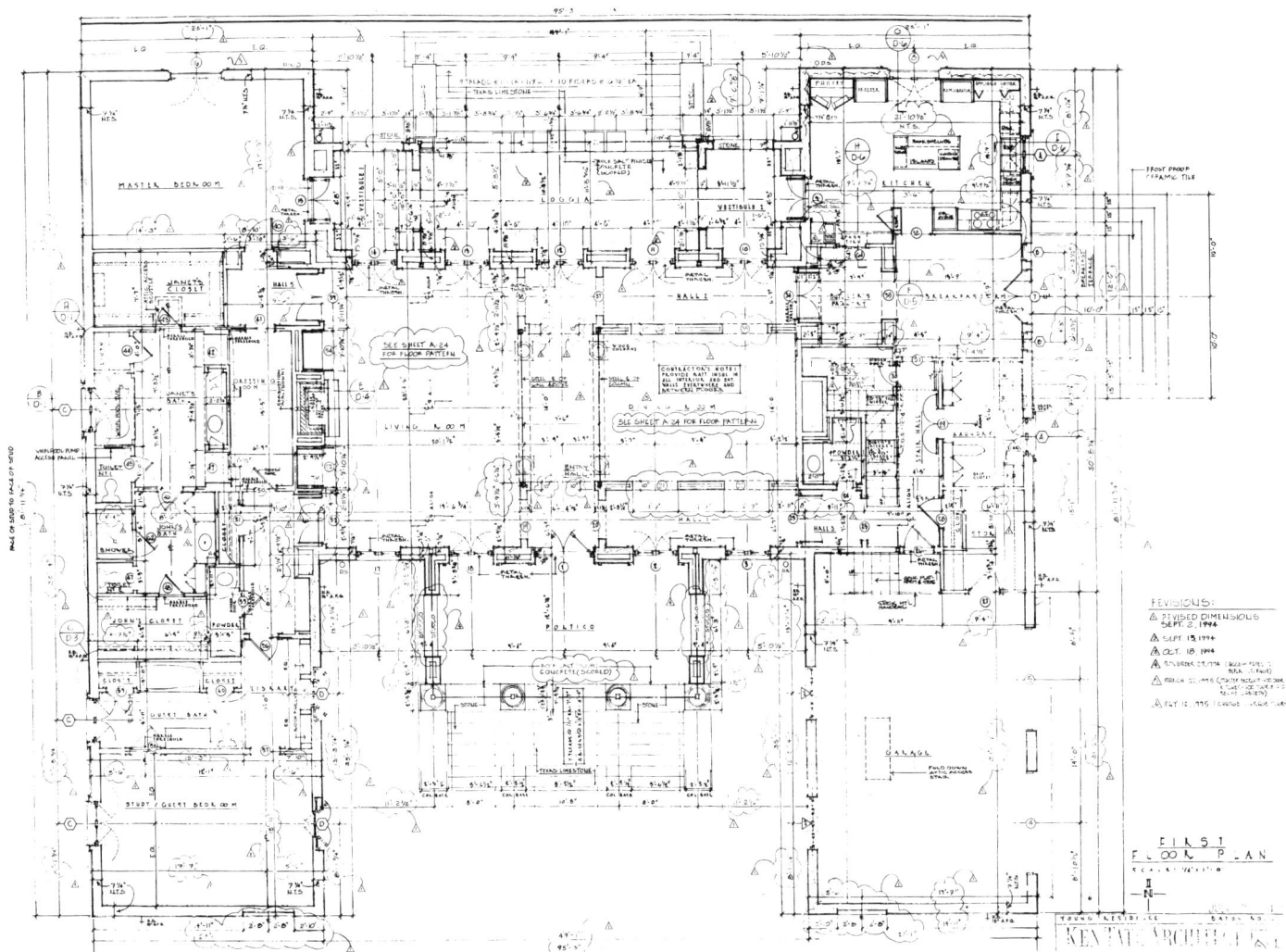

It is the task of the architect to coordinate these graphic tools. The method in which these are presented underscores both the working drawing's origins in the design document and reflects the architect's understanding of the integrated nature of the building process. Just as the discipline of drawing simultaneously in plan, elevation and section is fundamental to good design, so too can the presentation of information in a multiple format working drawing reveal all the anticipated conditions that might occur in the building process. A coherent logic between design and execution is now established, and the potential for a well-constructed project may be realized.

We will now review examples of the three forms of drawing, and what kind of information is conveyed in each instance.

**GENERAL DRAWING:** FIGURE 1 is the first floor plan from a residence in Lake Forest, Illinois. A technique employed in this drawing, and one which deserves attention, is the implementation of a grid system which overlays the floor plan. This grid system, driven by governing, or axis lines, such as centers of doors, windows or columns, becomes the operative tool for measurement. As such, the grid serves as a datum to both the designer and builder by establishing consistent reference points. Further, as one develops drawings at larger scales, the grid can coordinate those details to the general drawing. This benefits both the designer and builder.

Overall dimensions are found in the outer string. As the string moves closer to the building, more specific dimensions appear. There is a tendency by many designers to dimension excessively; using a grid system mitigates the problem somewhat by encouraging the designer to focus on reconciling or measuring to the grid. In any event, one should avoid providing complex information prematurely, and in so doing run the risk of encumbering the drawing with too much information.

It is important to remind oneself to what trade a drawing is speaking. In the case of the section, the primary audience would be perhaps the foundation contractor, or more likely the carpentry framing contractor. FIGURE 1 is an excellent example of the amount of data appropriate to this scale and type of drawing, thereby preserving the clarity of the sheet. An accompanying wall section or detail, however, would have allowed one to understand the building condition that exists at the wall, thereby reconciling the floor dimensioning to the larger scale without confusing the document with too many dimensions.

FIGURE 2 graphically suffers from revised dimensions having occurred after the issuing of the drawing. At the same time, it highlights the convention for adjusting a document of record after it has been issued so as to identify new information. This point is worth emphasizing.

Once a construction drawing is issued, any alteration must always be in reference to the previously released document. Thus all parties have access to

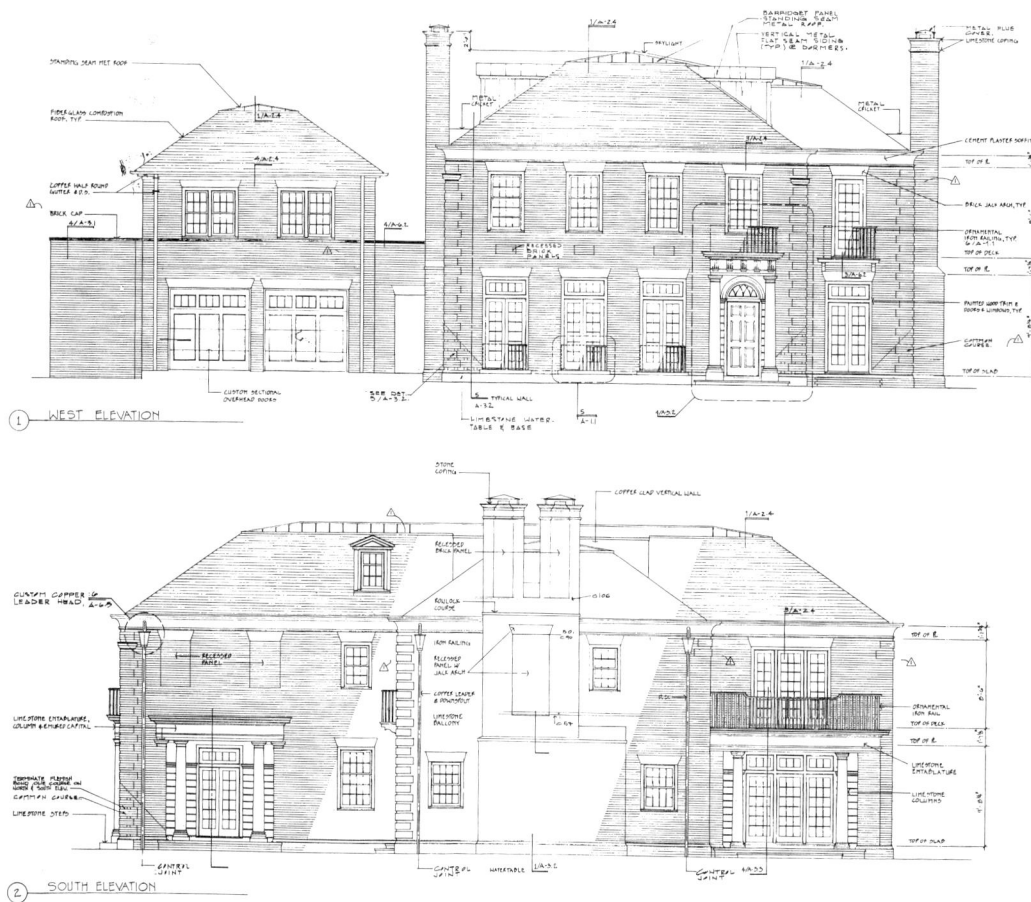

FIGURE 3, ABOVE; FIGURE 4, TOP RIGHT: *Curtis & Windham Architects, Houston, Texas. A residence in Houston, Texas.*
FIGURE 5, BOTTOM RIGHT: *Easton & La Rocca, New York, New York. A residence in Lake Forest, Illinois.*

the same information. There is no greater fear in the field than to suddenly be informed that the drawing you have been using "is not current"—second only to discovering that some known dimension has been altered but not highlighted in a document in hand.

FIGURE 3 underscores the kind of concerns that arise when drawing an elevation at this scale. First, the elevation provides the vertical dimension string; in our figure, the dimensioning begins with a datum set at the top of slab and from that benchmark dimensions are taken to limestone details. Nevertheless, the reader may be puzzled as to whom this dimensional information is directed. Perhaps it is of interest to the finish mason; however, what direction does this provide regarding floor levels or heights of windows and doors? Additional information is therefore required.

The second concern of the elevation should be the identification of material, and its graphic representation in a way that is appropriate to the scale. In that regard FIGURE 3 constitutes a successful representation. The indication from right to left regarding brick detailing, for instance, indicates an appropriate economy of drawing as the intensity of the drawing diminishes.

**SCALE DRAWING:** FIGURE 4 is a detail drawing of the front entrance shown in FIGURE 3. It serves as an example of the extent and type of information that occurs at a larger scale, as well as how the scale drawing can be reconciled to the general drawing.

From a material standpoint, the relationship and dimension of the brick veneer to the structural framing is clarified here in both the typical brick ledge detail and the wall section. The plan detail of the entrance portico, moreover, is elaborated and dimensioned, while the unified composition of plan section and elevation convey coherently the relationships of the various dimensions of this building feature. And, as in the previous figure, from both a design and building sensibility the document informs the viewer graphically of what to expect to encounter in the course of the building process.

Nonetheless, there is lacking a dimensional reference to a particular datum. This is especially evident in the case of the wall section, where dimensioning begins at the brick ledge. One can only presume that the missing datum is clarified on another drawing. Similarly, head and perhaps sill heights of the window and door conditions should have been identified; otherwise one must look for that supplemental information on another sheet.

With the noted exception of these dimensional issues, FIGURE 4 is graphically accomplished and indicates a direction that drawings ought to follow in order to reconcile the components of plan, section and elevation.

FIGURE 5 reconciles all of the previous critiques. First, by indicating at the same scale the plan, section, and elevation of the building, all principal building details are described. While the presentation is of a typical condition, additional details serve to clarify other circumstances found in the building.

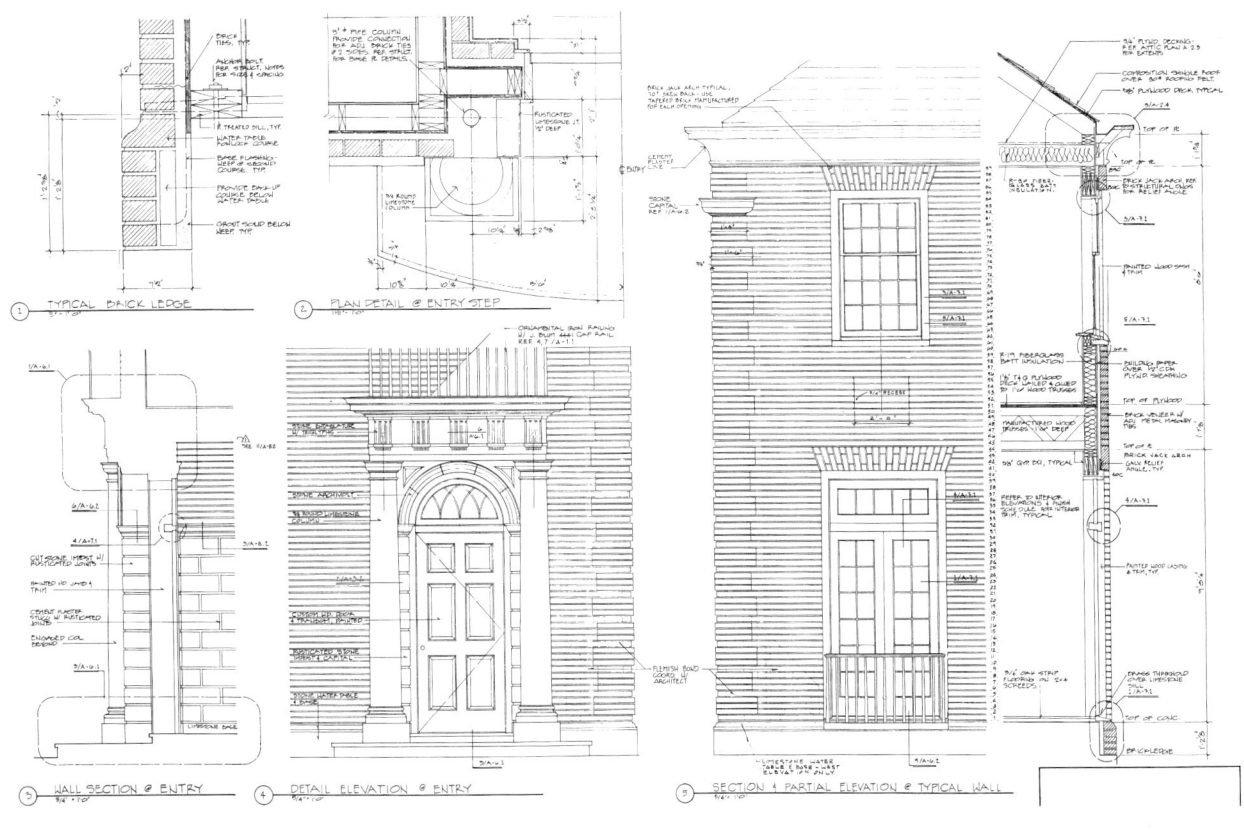

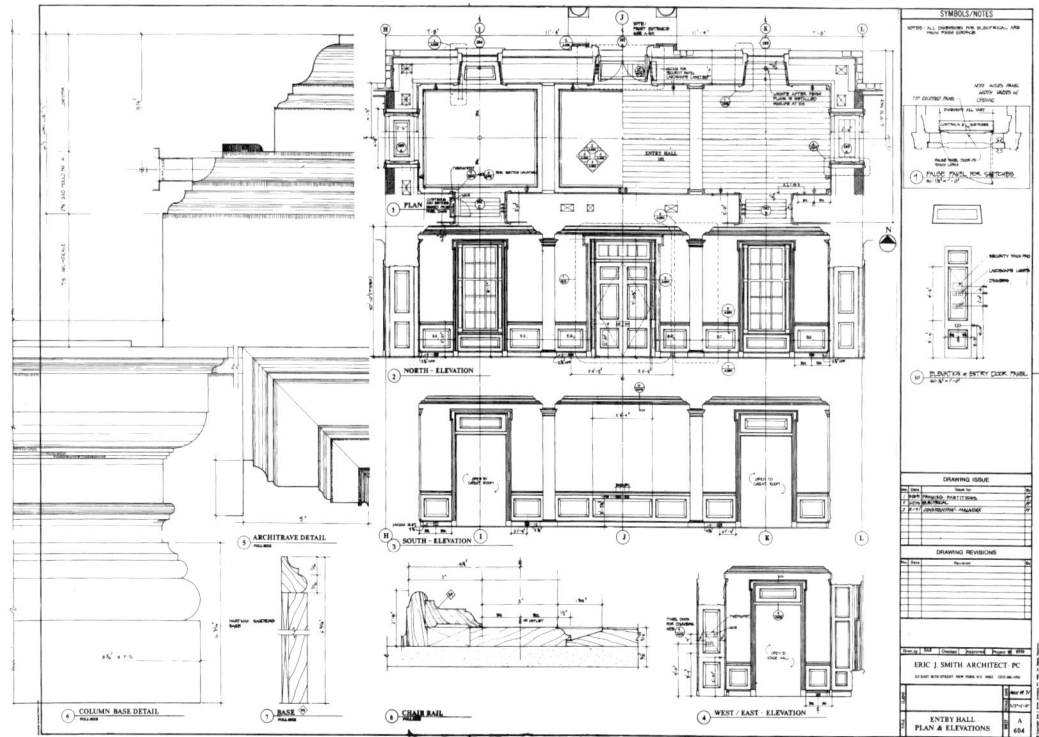

*FIGURE 6: Eric J. Smith, Architect, New York, New York. A residence in Bedminster, New Jersey.*

Dimensionally, the information is supplied in a clear and coherent fashion, particularly in the wall section. Here a datum is established at the finish first floor, from which all the dimensions are generated. The exterior string dimensions answer questions regarding overall height and brick and masonry coursing; the interior string provides head height, floor to ceiling, and floor framing dimensions.

FIGURE 5, while seemingly spare in information, reveals a well-studied composition. Clear and precise information is provided in a format which allows the designer and builder to reference the consequences of a detail in plan, elevation and section.

FIGURE 6 represents this same format applied to the interior. Again, a dimensioned grid implies the reconciliation of this scale drawing to the general drawing. The plan provides both floor and ceiling information in the same drawing. The elevations are referenced to the specific millwork details that are to be applied, thus insuring coordination among the trades. Lastly, the full scale details of the cornice and pilasters are immediately referenced.

One could easily imagine this drawing stapled to the framed walls of the room during construction—as in fact did happen! As such, it provides the specific information required by the carpenter, millworker, electrician, floor installer and other tradesmen. It is a true working drawing in that it graphically directs the resolution of all trades to the design intent.

**FULL SCALE DRAWING:** The full scale drawing is an enlargement of the scale drawing in which absolute detail information is shown. Specific dimensioning is resolved insofar as the finalized product is identified and all accompanied relationships are specified. The full scale details resolve the relationship of parts, as well as the use and specific requirements of the material. While distinct from a shop drawing, i.e.: a manufacturer's or fabricator's production drawing, full scale drawings imply a thorough comprehension of the materials with respect to strength of material, jointing and methods of securing the material to the structure. In this regard, the full scale drawing brings all of the concerns and abilities of the designer previously noted to the fore.

FIGURE 7, a detail drawing of an entablature for a restored brownstone (illustrated on page 53), provides a reference between the full scale drawing and the scale drawing. Here detailed components of an entablature are highlighted and rendered in elevation and section. The projection of the bracket, and its relationship to the entablature are idenitified. At full scale, the compositional format of the drawing and the delineation in shade and shadow of the projecting elements serve to reinforce the relationship of the parts to each other. The specific requirements of joinery are also clearly indicated and nicely resolved, facilitating the millwork fabrication as well as the eventual installation.

**CONCLUSION:** To return to a question posed at the beginning of the article: what is the relationship between the design process and the built form, and to what degree can one as an architect affect that relationship? Clearly, for the architect the principal means of communication remains the drawing—the studied graphic presentation of what constitutes the building condition.

Now, to be successful a drawing must be precise in presentation and accurate in dimensioning; yet to fully amplify the relationship between design and building, one must also be aware of the tools that are necessary to accurately describe a structure. A central thesis of this article has been that the thought required for developing a working drawing corresponds to that required for a design drawing. The primary concerns for each are to communicate in plan, section, and elevation and to present, where possible, those drawings in unison. The multiple-presentation format is therefore a model for understanding a building's composition or detail, and the specific elements of which they are formed. As such, the drawings serve to reconnect the architect to the construction process, and back toward the role of the master builder. —P.T.

# THE ART OF
# SCAGLIOLA

## By Michelle Portman

The earliest known examples of scagliola, decorative plaster work which replicates marble, were created in northern Italy during the early sixteenth century. Knowledge and use of the scagliola technique spread through Italy, into France. and on to England by the middle of the eighteenth century. In America, the golden age of scagliola began in the late nineteenth century and continued through the 1920s.

In the earliest examples moist plaster was imbedded with *scaglie*, or marble chips, to both decorate and harden the surface. This process was similar to terrazzo, but the chips of stone were smaller and placed to imitate the pattern, veining and clouding pattern of cut marble, rather than to create an abstract pattern. The art of scagliola therefore lay in how closely the plaster matched a specific marble. Knowledge of this technique was traditionally passed from generation to generation with the same secrecy as a treasured family recipe.

There are two methods of scagliola: the solid and the liquid. In the solid method, batches of fine-grade plaster the consistency of bread dough are mixed with a range of pigments. Small loaves of differently pigmented plasters may be flattened and layered one atop another on a hard, smooth work surface and then rolled or folded to create one larger loaf. A slurry, meaning plaster with a high water content, may be painted over a flattened loaf and similarly rolled or folded. Loaves of different pigments may be chopped and kneaded together. A loaf can be put through any number of these processes any number of times to achieve the desired result, which is the creation of a pattern as defined or as ambiguous as the veins and clouds of the selected marble. If the scagliola is to be executed on site, the surface to receive this pattern is first covered with a layer of scratch plaster—a coarse-grade material which is scratched before completely dry—to provide a host surface for the later application of face plaster. One-inch thick slices, known as coils, cut from the final loaves of pigmented plaster, are then pressed onto the scratch plaster surface, resulting in a 3/4" overall thickness.

Marezzo, which is scagliola fabricated face down, is generally produced at the artist's workshop and brought to the site ready for installation. In this process, the plaster pats are pressed tightly abutting onto a greased base or mold and dried in place. Modern marezzo molds consist of a rigid form and a flexible liner which can be reused many times. Before the finishing process may commence, both solid method scagliola and marezzo must be allowed to dry for 6-8 hours.

The liquid method of scagliola production is an on-site process used primarily for round or complex surfaces (a version of the fabrication sequence for liquid method scagliola is shown in the photographs accompanying this article). Here the pattern is created face down on a base of heavy fabric, such as oil cloth, and transferred to the surface to be decorated while still damp. To make the face pattern, plaster batches of fine-grade slurry are mixed with a range of pigments. These slurries are applied to the dampened base with skeins of raw silk or linen, knotted at both ends, known as drop threads. The first skein is saturated with vein-colored slurry and laid onto the base in a manner intended to replicate the veining pattern of a specific marble. A second skein is repeatedly saturated with slurry and placed on and removed from the base, creating layer upon layer of clouding. Additional slurry may be splashed on at intervals to produce a less veined face pattern.

When the plaster is 1/2" thick, the first set of skeins is removed and the resulting voids are filled with vein-colored slurry. A scrim of porous cloth, like cheese cloth, is laid over the wet plaster and covered with a layer of dry coarse-grade plaster to absorb excess moisture. The scrim is removed and the coarse-grade plaster is reserved to be mixed with additional water, producing a backing plaster. This backing plaster is troweled over the face plaster 1/4" thick. The base and both layers of plaster are lifted and smoothed into place with a wood block or trowel. The smoothing removes wrinkles and air pockets and forces the backing plaster to bond with the scratch plaster. After the base is peeled away, the scagliola artist manipulates the face plaster to disguise the seam between this and previous scagliola applications. Before the finishing process may commence, liquid method scagliola must dry for 6-8 hours.

The finishing of all types of scagliola involves rough sanding (known as stoning), stopping, and sealing. Solid method scagliola must also be planed to remove irregularities prior to stoning. Planing removes approximately 1/4", and stoning 1/8", of the face plaster surface. In stoning, water and a sedimentary stone, or more commonly wet/dry sandpaper, are used to bring the scagliola to a uniform surface. Pumice, or any other soft stone which will quickly conform to the harder plaster surface, is utilized for certain profiles. Once the scagliola has dried, the surface is stopped by daubing and brushing slurry over the surface to fill any cracks or air pockets. When the stopping is almost dry, the excess is scraped away. After the stopping has fully dried, the process of stoning, with increasingly fine grades of abrasive, and stopping, are repeated twice more. The finished face plaster is 3/8" thick for solid and liquid method scagliola, and 5/8" for marezzo. All scagliola must dry for 2-3 weeks before being sealed. Three applications of linseed oil are then rubbed into the scagliola surface, each time being fully absorbed by the plaster. After the third application of oil, a coat of wax is applied and buffed to a high polish.

Finished scagliola is at times so convincing that only touching its surface will reveal its identity, plaster not being as cool to the touch as real stone. It is generally used in place of cut marble for at least one of three reasons—weight, cost, or availability. Being far lighter in weight than equivalent areas of stone, scagliola is used where excessive dead loads would overly stress the structure of a building. Scagliola is less costly than rare marbles or complex fabrications in common marbles. It is less expensive, however, to use common marble for simple forms than it is to create these designs in scagliola. Scagliola is also used when a desired marble is no longer being quarried, a common problem in restoration projects. Finally, if no natural marble suits your aesthetic requirements, you can always commission your own geologic masterpiece. ໄ

*Michelle Portman works in historic preservation with the firm of Phillips & Oppermann in Winston-Salem, North Carolina.*

*The author would like to thank Ahmad Suleiman for his direction and editing, and for staging the liquid method scagliola process for this article. Mr. Suleiman can be contacted at: Sleiman Studios, 423 Horsham Road, Horsham, Pennsylvania, 19044. Telephone (215) 441-5767.*

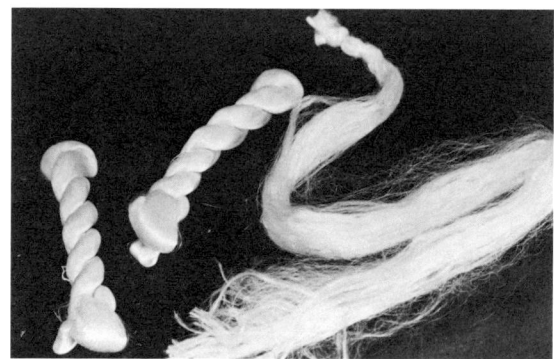

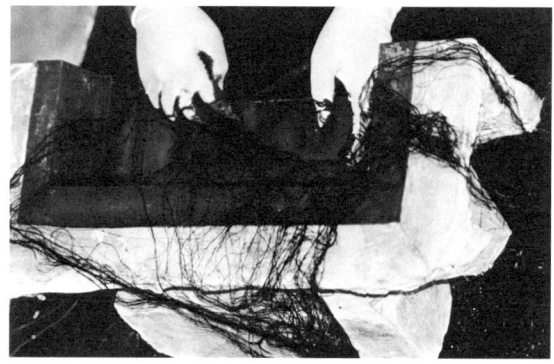

# LIQUID METHOD SCAGLIOLA

—

## PRODUCED IN CONJUNCTION WITH A MOLD, SIMILAR TO MAREZZO

—

FIGURE 1: *Skeins of raw silk are used as drop threads.*

FIGURE 2: *Drop threads saturated in vein-colored slurry are arranged in the dampened mold.*

FIGURE 3: *Slurry of a contrasting color is drizzled over the vein-colored drop threads.*

FIGURE 4: *The layer of contrasting slurry is allowed to dry slightly.*

FIGURE 5: *The vein-colored drop threads are removed from the mold.*

FIGURE 6: *The face plaster appears marbleized after the drop threads have been removed.*

FIGURE 7: *Additional plaster is applied to fill the voids left by the drop threads. After this plaster has dried slightly, the coarser backing plaster is applied. When the backing plaster has fully dried, the scagliola is removed from the mold and the liner is peeled away.*

FIGURE 8: *The scagliola is rinsed in preparation for the finishing process.*

FIGURE 9: *The scagliola is wet sanded, a process known as stoning, and then fully sealed to create the finished product.*

FIGURE 10: *At the end of the process, the finished product is fully sealed.*

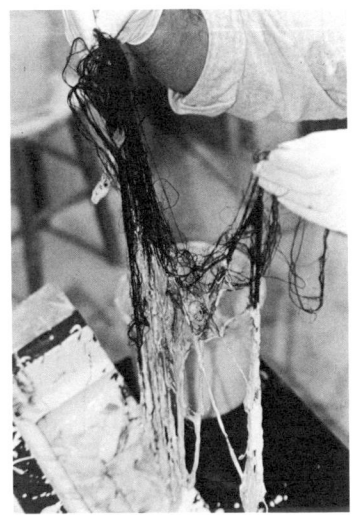

5

8

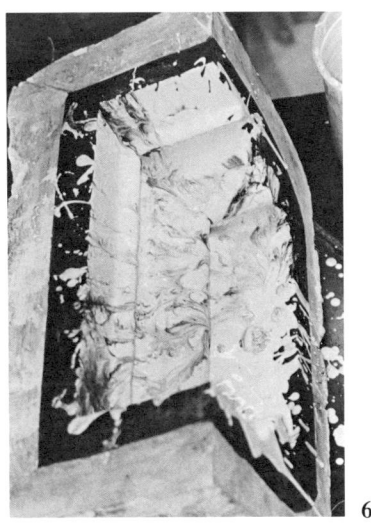

6

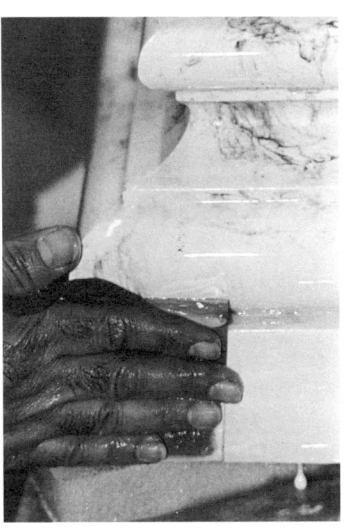

9

7

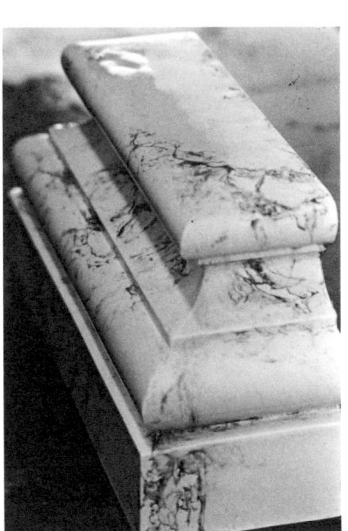

10

# DRAWING FROM THE ANTIQUE

## A FOLIO OF DRAWINGS BY FACULTY AND STUDENTS OF THE NEW YORK ACADEMY OF ART

### BY PIERCE RICE

*Goethe, when he was about to write his* IPHIGENIA, *wished to fill himself with the Greek spirit and did it not by reading Greek tragedies, but by taking a course of drawing from the Antique.* —Kenyon Cox

Originally, there was no such thing as art instruction. The nearest approach to it was what we would call on-the-job-training which, judging by results, was clearly best. It was so for two reasons: First, it enabled the master to multiply his output; second, the novice participated in actual creation. What better way to learn?

So much for big ideas. We know very well what art school amounts to today. Or do we? To some (many) people, art schooling itself is an anomaly. The art student should be left unguided, with no path pointed out. With a premium on novelty, what, in fact, can an instructor contribute?

In recent years some students and teachers have begun to reconsider aspects of the older ways of learning. We have before us as evidence of this in drawings from the antique by students and faculty of the New York Academy of Art. Of more consequence even than the talent these drawings represent is the very fact that they were made.

The traditional premise is that artistic promise is indicated by youthful mimicry, which is simply copying or imitation, and that this should be followed by direction in drawing from three-dimensional plaster casts as the surest path to command of the pencil.

This is a stage many students might fail to appreciate. In that light, it is not unreasonable to make the rendering of classical sculpture a required step in an artist's training. (In fact, it also has benefits for the practicing artist and teacher who continues it as a lifetime exercise.) There are two reasons for this. First is the mechanical consideration. The plaster cast can be approached closely and studied singly, that is, one student to one statue, and it doesn't move. Second, the antique cast is of far more breadth and grace than any human model. It might almost be said that study from it insidiously imposes a standard of beauty.

While exact rendering is an important objective, it is not in itself aesthetically satisfying. The instrument to insure that is close study of the work of the great artists before us who likewise learned their art by drawing the classical figure. ❧

---

*Pierce Rice is a painter and author living in Virginia. His latest book is* MAN AS HERO.

*STUDENT WORK, NEW YORK ACADEMY OF ART:*
*LEFT: Richard Combes, cast drawing.*
*ABOVE: Richard Combes, female torso.*

FACULTY WORK, NEW YORK ACADEMY OF ART:
TOP LEFT: *Jon de Martin, drawing after Michelangelo.*
BOTTOM LEFT: *Jon de Martin, head study.*
BOTTOM RIGHT: *Randy Melick, figure study.*
ABOVE: *Randy Melick, antique head.*

# NEW VOLUMES OF INTEREST

# THE CLASSICIST'S BOOKSHELF

ACROPOLIS RESTORATION: THE CCAM INTERVENTIONS. *Edited by Richard Economakis. Academy Editions, 1994. 224 pp.*

HADRIAN'S VILLA AND ITS LEGACY *by William L. MacDonald and John A. Pinto. Yale University Press, 1995. 508 pp.*

What have architecture and archaeology to say to each other? To begin with, when we ask "What has architecture to say to archaeology?" we may find an unexpected answer. With respect to the excavation, preservation, interpretation and potential restoration of classical architectural monuments, the methodological principles of the archaeologist are to a large extent shaped by the architectural theory operative at the time. It makes a difference whether current architectural thinking is in sympathy with, indifferent to, or in opposition to the principles apparently governing the work under study. Changes in archaeological practice have in fact mirrored the evolution of architectural theories in the last century or so, including the rise and fall of modernism.

As recently as the 1930s the restorers of Williamsburg, Virginia saw their work as recovering antecedents of a tradition to which they themselves belonged and which they wished to promote. It was their commitment to the aesthetic values of the eighteenth century as they understood them which prompted them to recreate the colonial town, including the restoration or reconstruction of pre-Revolutionary structures and, significantly, structures from subsequent periods which exemplified the classical tradition. The essential purpose of the enterprise was to give the visitor as complete a picture as possible of the broad design intentions of the original builders, not to present an exclusive document of the site as it existed at any one point in time.

The modernist rejection of the classical changed the archaeologists' focus by directing attention away from aesthetic considerations toward a "scientific" examination of the material remains in order to determine the monument's place in the history of technology and means of production. From this perspective, the architecture of the past had little or nothing to say to us about aesthetic issues. The value of the monuments lay in the age of the surviving material itself and what it revealed about historical conditions or obsolescent building traditions. The cultural aims of the original builders were considered alien to our own and any attempt to reconstruct their handiwork would be "falsification" of the historical record, a kind of architectural forgery.

Post-war restoration architects, all schooled in modernist theory and anxious to avoid charges of falsification, narrowed their role to the documentation and preservation of remains, substituting the ideal of the "stabilized ruin" for the earlier concept of the "museum restoration." In the 1970s Venturi and Rauch exemplified this alienation of the historical material by refusing to reconstruct Benjamin Franklin's vanished Philadelphia house and workshop, electing instead to erect an abstract steel framework outlining the presumed silhouettes of the missing buildings. The observer's attention was directed to the remaining fragments of original foundations preserved below; above loomed a ghostly symbol of the irretrievability of the past.

But what if architecture moves beyond the modernist view and reconsiders the relevancy of the classical tradition? How might archaeological attitudes respond to a conception of architecture that is once again understanding of, and sympathetic to, the artistic aims of the builders of Williamsburg or, for that matter, Periclean Athens? This is the question addressed by *Acropolis Restoration,* edited by Richard Economakis with contributions from the team responsible for the preservation and restoration of the Propylaea, Erectheion and Parthenon. Their work illustrates a shift away from the modernist preoccupation with the "historical." The aim of the restorers is once again to present the most complete possible picture of the original design of the monuments consistent with available knowledge and without relying on conjecture.

Of course, we are today the beneficiaries of modern scientific archaeology, which has given us an unprecedented level of detailed knowledge about the monuments and their construction. As the authors show, the current state of archaeological knowledge about these buildings makes it possible to restore nearly all the ancient stonework to its original configuration and detail. Equipped with this knowledge, why should the restorer not intervene to reintegrate the new understanding with the historical remains? Why would new or newly reconfigured material be any more false than leaving the site as it happens to appear after generations of fires, wars and decay have defaced the original design? Following this reasoning, the Committee for the Conservation of the Acropolis Monuments (CCAM) has elected to restore the monuments *in situ* and in three dimensions rather than presenting merely a two-dimensional graphic reconstruction, which might have been the preferred option a couple of decades ago.

For example, at the Erectheion, where original material in the exterior walls is absent (whether due to loss, physical deterioration or damage from fire or atmospheric pollution), and where the original appearance of the missing piece is known, replacement material is inserted, carved from the same Pentelikon marble used by the original builders. Material displaced from its original position by previous flawed restorations is returned to its rightful place. Decorative elements, especially sculptures removed for preservation, have been (temporarily, it is hoped) replaced by casts. A new image of the ancient building emerges: we now see a work of architecture that speaks to us, rather than a puzzling, fragmented artifact of a vanished civilization.

Two factors have contributed to the success of the CCAM program. First, command of the volumes of information needed to re-establish the original positions of thousands of displaced fragments of building material requires the aid of the computer, among other tools. (A high-tech crane with advanced controls helps, too.) This is not a return to nineteenth century archaeological practice, but an integration of current technology with humanistic scholarship. Second, understanding the building as a work of art, rather than an exotic artifact, requires knowledge of the formal logic of classical architecture and a commitment to making the building whole according to its own aesthetic principles. While there should be no less diligence in the research by which our knowledge of the monuments is gained, the goal of the research is now not simply documentation, but retrieval of the monument as a work of art.

Not surprisingly, these operations have been criticized; accusations of falsification are heard once again. Economakis has printed some of these critical views along with statements by supporters in a round-table at the end of the book. One hopes that readers will be convinced by the argument that the restorations are justified by the available documentation, the urgent need to preserve the dispersed fragments by reincorporation into an integrated building fabric, and the fundamental importance of these monuments as works of art.

The book includes essays on the transformations and depredations of the Acropolis monuments over time and detailed descriptions of the procedures and findings of the archaeologists. Students of the antique will find much material on the original configurations of the buildings, their materials and construction methods. But the primary purpose of the volume is less to document the buildings than to defend the process of restoration itself. This advocacy position may annoy some readers and one would prefer to see more measured drawings and fewer photographs of scaffolding and the Athenian smog. In

*CCAM proposals for restoring the Parthenon pronaos. TOP: Actual state. MIDDLE: restored with existing material only. BOTTOM: restored with existing and supplemental new material. Illustrations from* ACROPOLIS RESTORATION: THE CCAM INTERVENTIONS.

particular, the specific proposals for the Parthenon restoration are incompletely documented, though they are central to the concluding debate. Still, as presented by Economakis, the CCAM restorations deserve thoughtful consideration and continuing support. They promise to restore not only the unparalleled aesthetic achievements of the antique builders, but the fundamental dialogue between archaeology and architecture on which the entire classical tradition rests.

When we come to consider what archaeology has to say to architecture we reflect that so much of classical design since the Renaissance has been guided less by actual archaeological knowledge of antique precedent than by theoretical treatises preoccupied with the orders and their proportional systems in the tradition of Vitruvius. The Renaissance bias toward orthogonal geometry, simple shapes (square, rectangular and circular) and straightforward axial planning tended to outweigh fidelity to the actual remains in the widely circulated drawings of Sangallo, Palladio and others. Consequently, not only was the frequent irregularity and formal experimentation of mature Roman architecture "cleaned up" by the treatises, but the entire orthodox conception of classical architecture which they collectively represent was progressively skewed toward a more abstract, rationalistic view in many respects contrary to the apparent aims of the ancient Roman designers as revealed in their surviving built works.

The Roman buildings most frequently seen in the books of Palladio and other treatises, such as the Pantheon or the temples of the Roman Forum, are presented as hierarchically coherent, freestanding typologies suitable for adaptation in new buildings governed by simple geometric formality. Others were harder to assimilate. Hadrian's Villa, the second century imperial residence near Tivoli, possibly designed in part by the Emperor himself, is a model of a different kind of classical architecture. The rambling, mysterious, seemingly disorganized ruins of the Villa, with their subtle relations to landscape and views, their geometrical complexity and astonishing variety of volume and shape, were unsuitable precedents from which to derive principles of "classical" (i.e. Vitruvian) architecture. Perhaps for this reason it received little attention from the Renaissance compilers of the classical canon.

Modern archaeology has had limited success in bringing the Villa's remains to light due to the isolation of the site, its extensive despoliation and burial and the widespread dispersion of the original construction over a large territory. Today most of the site remains unexcavated, much evidence has been lost and, unlike the Parthenon, there is little hope that a complete understanding of its original construction will ever be possible.

Within this context, William L. MacDonald, an authority on Roman architecture, and John A. Pinto, a scholar of the Renaissance and Baroque, have collaborated on *Hadrian's Villa and Its Legacy*, a summary of what we know now of the villa and a history of its rediscovery and interpretation over the last four centuries. The bulk of the book contains a fascinating, detailed description of the Villa's architectural components and their possible original functions. The authors show us such transcendent set pieces as the Island Enclosure (also known as the Maritime Theater), the Smaller Baths, and the Scenic Canal and Triclinium (formerly known as the Canopus). Throughout the Villa we find examples of spatial composition regulated not by grids or orthogonal axiality but by diagonal views or circular geometries. There is no primary center or axis. Symmetry is relative, not absolute, and playful experimentation with space and structure is everywhere.

The Villa represents at its fullest the Roman synthesis of intellectual order and sensual delight, shown clearly in its wealth of ornament and decorative art, which was fully integrated into the architectural setting. MacDonald and Pinto discuss in detail the painting, stucco decoration, sculpture, and mosaic pavements which remain at the site or have been identified in various collections. Much of the artwork and the architectural character of several of the site's component parts seem to have been shaped by an elaborate narrative program, aspects of which survive tantalizingly in contemporary literary sources. Unfortunately, no "key" has been discovered, prompting commentators to assign poetic names to various features of the Villa site, such as "Hades," "Canopus" or the "Vale of Tempe." (The authors sidestep this issue by using neutral, architecturally descriptive names for these same features.) Particularly intriguing is the authors' discussion of evidence linking numerous sites at the Villa with the Eleusinian mystery cult, into which Hadrian had been initiated.

In their multi-layered, multi-disciplinary study, the authors invite us to adjust our concept of the classical in response to what archaeology tells us of the ancient architects' own aesthetic intentions as revealed by study of the monuments. The baroque qualities of the Villa constitute, alongside the orthodox Vitruvian tradition, another, heterodox tradition which we can rightly call the Hadrianic.

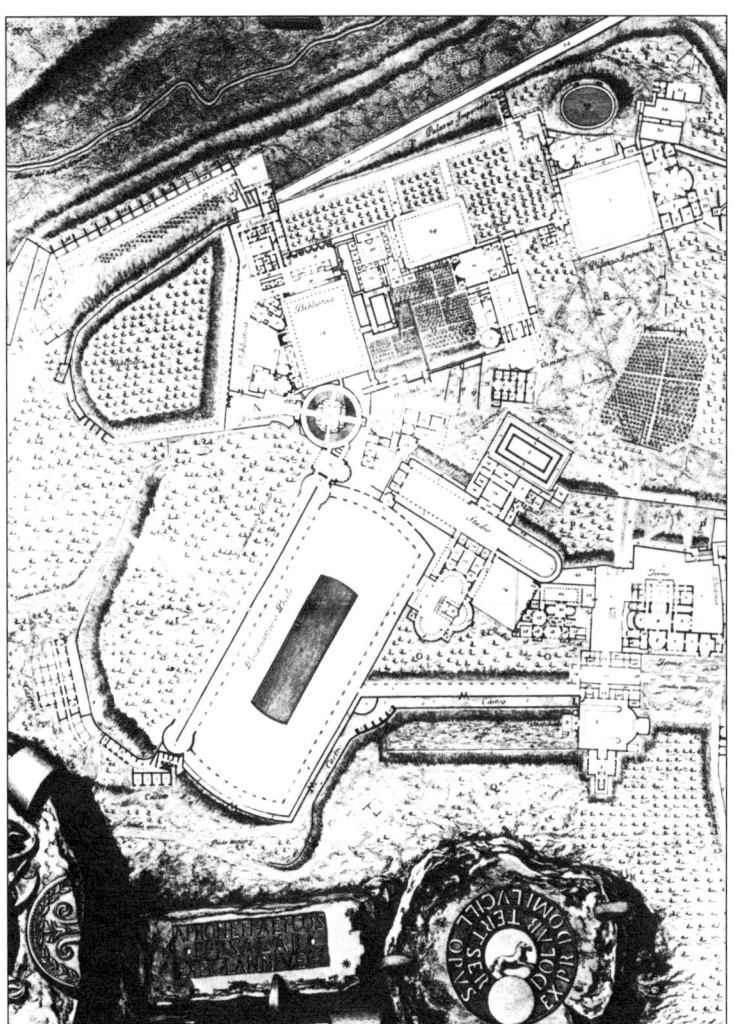

*Detail of Giovanni Battista Piranesi's plan of Hadrian's Villa, showing the central residential area. From* HADRIAN'S VILLA AND ITS LEGACY.

What, MacDonald and Pinto ask, might have been the effect on classical architecture since the Renaissance if a contemporary account of Hadrian's Villa (perhaps on the order of Pliny's description of his lost villa) had survived from antiquity alongside Vitruvius' *Ten Books*?

The outlines of this Hadrianic tradition are suggested by MacDonald and Pinto. Despite the official orthodoxy of the treatises, aspects of the Villa's ornamental designs, circular planning, and landscape integration were highly influential for Raphael (at the unfinished Villa Madama) and Pirro Ligorio (at the Villa d'Este and the Casino Pio in the Vatican Gardens), among others. The Villa's complex vaulting and sinuous wall treatments were essential precedents for Francesco Borromini (in his Oratory of St. Filippo Neri and the church of Sant'

Ivo). Such influence was exceptional, however, until Giambattista Piranesi's plan, published in the 1780s, made a comprehensive view of the Emperor's masterwork available for the first time. By the end of the eighteenth century the Villa began to attract greater attention, particularly among those who sought to synthesize the classical with incipient Romanticism.

The authors trace this widening influence of the Villa in what they call the "pastoral allusions" of William Kent's gardens at Stowe and the "pavilioned landscape" of Jefferson's Monticello. Robert Adam and John Soane undoubtedly found inspiration for their shaped rooms and ornamental styles in their studies of Hadrian's work. The Villa attracted the attention also of the *Prix de Rome* winners of the Ecole des Beaux Arts, whose graphic reconstructions, beginning with that of Daumet in 1859, presage the interest in spatial, structural and decorative extravagance we find in much late nineteenth century and early twentieth century classicism. Among Americans, Philip Trammell Schutze joined the French in their study of the site and brought back a fine Roman sensibility to his native Atlanta. Louis Kahn was apparently more interested in the decayed state of the Villa than in its original appearance, a reversal of values reflecting the modernist confusion of the authentic with the primitive or ruinous. Not mentioned by the authors but also Hadrianic in conception are the Central European baroque works of Fischer von Erlach and his followers, as well as the romantic classicism of Bernard Maybeck in twentieth century California. Ironically, the interest in the Villa as a paradigm for a new, more adventurous classicism intensified precisely at the moment that modernism swept all of the classical tradition away (Le Corbusier's sketches of the Villa reproduced here notwithstanding).

The attraction of the Villa for us today can be read in its principal themes: the cultural and literary associations which may be embodied in buildings; the possibilities of classical planning schemes not dependent on gridded or axial regularity; the complete integration of architecture, painting, sculpture, and decorative arts; and the intimate relationship between buildings and landscape. Not the least important is the model of the Villa as a laboratory for formal experimentation. If our current revival of classical architecture seems at times in danger of falling into rigid formulas and sterile antiquarianism, the example of the Villa points to the other tradition of the classical, beyond the constraints of the Vitruvian conception. Archaeology has much to say to architecture, not only about Hadrian's Villa, but about the roots of the classical tradition throughout the ancient world. Architecture can only benefit by listening carefully. —S.W.S.

# THE CLASSICIST'S BOOKSHELF : ARCHAEOLOGY AND THE ANTIQUE

*With this issue of* THE CLASSICIST *we inaugurate a new department for those readers with an interest in the literature of the classical tradition. Over the course of this and coming issues, we will present an annotated list of titles which one might expect to find in the well-stocked library of a student or practitioner of the classical. The list will be offered in sections, each organized according to a particular theme. In this first installment we continue the theme of archaeology and the antique by offering works relevant to that subject.*

*The list is not intended as an exhaustive bibliography. Rather, the titles have been chosen for their importance and usefulness. We have tried to select books available in English, although some are not. Similarly, while some editions are listed which are either in print or were so in recent years, some, sadly, have not been reprinted in our time and will be available only to those having access to specialized libraries, collections, or antiquarian book dealers. In some cases, even these materials will be found reproduced in secondary source material, since many of the seventeenth and eighteenth century plates are still relied upon by scholars in search of measured drawings of ancient sites.*

*The list is based on readings selected for a course on the literature of classical architecture taught by Richard Cameron during the Institute's Summer Program, with additional suggestions from Institute faculty and Fellows. —S.W.S.*

## I. ANCIENT TEXTS

*Pausanias.* GUIDE TO GREECE. *2 vols. Translated by Peter Levi. Harmondsworth, 1971.*
Pausanias was a Greek physician who visited many of the sites in mainland Greece during the second century A.D. His travel log is an ancient version of the Baedeker guide and an invaluable resource, not only for first hand descriptions of the still intact sites, but also for relevant mythological and historical information.

*Pliny the Younger.* THE LETTERS OF THE YOUNGER PLINY. *Translated by Betty Radice. Harmondsworth, 1969.*
See Pliny's Book II, Letter 17 for the description of the Laurentine Villa and Book V, Letter 6 for the Tuscan Villa. Both Villas are lost, but the detailed descriptions have inspired many imaginative reconstructions. See also Ruffiniére du Prey, below.

*Vitruvius Pollio, Marcus.* THE TEN BOOKS ON ARCHITECTURE. *Translated by M.H. Morgan. New York, 1960.*
The only architectural treatise to survive from Roman times has had incalculable influence on Western architecture since the Renaissance. Unfortunately, no illustrations survived and many passages remain obscure, leading to continuing debate among scholars. Although other translations may be found, this is the most widely available in English. A new English translation is in preparation as of this writing.

## II. ARCHAEOLOGICAL SURVEYS

*Adam, Robert.* RUINS OF THE PALACE OF THE EMPEROR DIOCLETIAN AT SPALATO IN DALMATIA. *London, 1764.*
A primary source not only for this late Roman site, but also for the architectural and ornamental designs of Adam himself.

*Bacon, Francis, ed.* INVESTIGATIONS AT ASSOS. *2 vols. London, Cambridge (MA), Leipzig, 1902-21.*
Beautifully illustrated volumes describing excavations and proposing graphic reconstructions at this Greek site by the archaeologist brother of Henry Bacon, architect of the Lincoln Memorial in Washington, D.C.

*Cockerell, Charles R.* THE TEMPLES OF JUPITER PANHELLENIUS AT AEGINA AND OF APOLLO EPICURIUS AT BASSAE NEAR PHIGALEIA IN ARCADIA. *London, 1860.*
For information about this important modern architect-archaeologist, see the article by David Watkin, and Richard Cameron's introduction to a lecture by Cockerell, both published in this issue.

*Cooper, Frederick A.* THE TEMPLE OF APOLLO BASSITAS, *VOL. IV. Princeton, 1992.*
Founded in 1881, the American School of Classical Studies at Athens has become the largest foreign archaeological institute in the Greek city today. In addition to offering educational programs and conducting archaeological excavations, the school publishes numerous books and periodicals containing work produced under its auspices. The second of a projected four volume set, this large folio reflects the latest research on an important site first examined systematically by Charles Cockerell and Haller von Hallerstein (see above).

*Desgodetz, Antoine.* LES EDIFICES ANTIQUES DE ROME. *2 vols. Paris, 1682. Published in England as* THE ANCIENT BUILDINGS OF ROME, *London, 1795. Reprinted London, 1969.*
Like many of the older volumes listed here, Desgodetz is hard to find in its original published form or in its reprinted version, but individual plates have been widely reproduced in secondary sources. His plates remain among the most reliable and most beautifully drawn modern documents of ancient Roman work.

*d'Espouy, Hector.* FRAGMENTS D'ARCHITECTURE ANTIQUE. *Paris, 1905; New York, 1923. Reprinted in the Classical America Series on Art and Architecture, New York, 1981.*
Selections from the *envois* of *Prix de Rome* winners at the French Academy, the beautiful reproductions of ink-wash renderings are especially useful as a resource for ornamental designs, as well as models of draftsmanship and rendering technique. An excellent complement to Desgodetz.

*Piranesi, Giambattista.* VEDUTE DI ROMA. *Rome, 1758; Paris, 1800-07.*
Piranesi may be best known for his fantastical views and dramatic presentations of baroque scenes, but he also made accurate recordings of Roman sites as they appeared in the late eighteenth century. His engravings are a valuable resource and a superb model of graphic representation. Various plates have been widely published in many places and several recent monographs about Piranesi are available which reproduce some of the best views.

*Society of Dilettanti.* ANTIQUITIES OF IONIA. *5 vols. London, 1769-1915.*
*Society of Dilettanti.* UNEDITED ANTIQUITIES OF ATTICA. *London, 1817.*
These and other volumes produced by the Society in the eighteenth and nineteenth centuries form a valuable record of the archaeological explorations undertaken by Western Europeans after the reopening of Greece, the Levant and other previously inaccessible areas of the world.

*Stuart, James and Nicholas Revett.* THE ANTIQUITIES OF ATHENS. *3 vols. London, 1762-1830. Reprinted in New York 1968, 1980.*
The first accurate documentation of the Greek sites following the country's reopening profoundly influenced classical design throughout the Western world. The engravings, incomparably beautiful, are still a primary resource for understanding these monuments.

*Wood, Robert.* THE RUINS OF BAALBEC. *London, 1757.*
> A visually stunning folio of engraved views and reconstructions of the great Roman religious complex at Baalbek in present-day Lebanon. Wood's companion volume on the Syrian site of Palmyra is also recommended.

# III. HISTORIES, REFERENCES, AND MONOGRAPHS

*Adam, Jean-Pierre.* ROMAN BUILDING: MATERIALS & TECHNIQUES. *Translated by Anthony Mathews. Bloomington and Indianapolis, 1994.*
> An excellent source for information on the constructive methods of the ancient Romans, with extensive photographs and drawings depicting both extant and lost structures.

*Brown, Frank E.* ROMAN ARCHITECTURE. *New York, 1961.*
> A compact introduction to the subject, well-illustrated, by the preeminent American archaeologist in Italy in the early post-war period.

*Boëthius, Axel, and J.B. Ward-Perkins.* ETRUSCAN AND ROMAN ARCHITECTURE. *London, 1970.*
> Considered the best compact handbook to the early Roman work and published as part of the useful Penguin series. Like all the recent books listed here, it relies heavily on photographs rather than drawn documentation, but can be a valuable supplement to the drawings appearing in the earlier surveys. The text is also very informative.

*Coulton, J.J.* ANCIENT GREEK ARCHITECTS AT WORK. *Ithaca, 1977.*
> The author takes a unique and fresh approach to Greek architecture by looking at it from the practitioner's point of view. What, Coulton asks, were an ancient designer or builder's design methods, goals, problems, and available technologies? What were ancient contract documents or bidding processes like, and how were architects paid? A vital work for anyone seeking insight into the dynamics of practice in Greek antiquity.

*Dinsmoor, William Bell.* THE ARCHITECTURE OF ANCIENT GREECE. *London, 1902, 1950; New York, 1950, 1975.*
> Perhaps the most complete general guide to the subject, still considered a standard reference in the field.

*Lawrence, A.W.* GREEK ARCHITECTURE. *Harmondsworth, 1983.*
> While a somewhat less detailed examination of the subject than the Dinsmoor tract (see above), a nonetheless up-to-date textbook in the Penguin series format.

*MacDonald, William L.* THE ARCHITECTURE OF THE ROMAN EMPIRE. *2 vols. New Haven and London, 1965-1986.*
> The standard reference on this topic, covering buildings throughout the Roman world with detailed descriptions, drawings and photographs.

*MacDonald, William L.* THE PANTHEON. *Cambridge (MA), 1976.*
> The history, design and construction of this essential monument, followed by the history of its interpretation and influence.

*Nash, Ernest.* PICTORIAL DICTIONARY OF ANCIENT ROME. *2 vols. New York, 1962.*
> An extraordinarily comprehensive reference guide to the physical form of the ancient city, including architecture, art, technology, inscriptions, and artifacts. Well illustrated.

PARIS-ROME-ATHENS. *Exhibition catalogue. Paris, Houston, 1982.*
> In the 1980s the Ecole des Beaux Arts mounted several important exhibitions of drawings produced by students at the school between 1793 and 1968, when the institution jettisoned its classical methodology. Most stunning was the exhibit featuring drawings made by *Prix de Rome* winners at Greek sites during this period. Documented in a lavish catalogue, the book has become an invaluable tool for demonstrating to modern classicists how archaeological information can become the stuff of imaginative interpretation today. Other titles in this series are *Roma Antiqua* (1985) and *Pompéi* (1981).

*Robertson,* D.S. A HANDBOOK OF GREEK AND ROMAN ARCHITECTURE. *Cambridge (U.K.), 1929, first paperback edition 1969.*
> A wonderfully compact but extensive treatment of both halves of the antique world, particularly valuable because of its detailed descriptions of buildings and architectural ornament. Whereas other titles on this list emphasize larger-scaled composition and historical development, Robertson discusses such topics as the fine points of molding profiles and their ornament, and the evolution of the Doric echinus. Engraved illustrations are similarly well-detailed and informative.

*Ruffiniére du Prey, Pierre.* THE VILLAS OF PLINY. *Cambridge (MA), 1994.*
> Reprints the famous letters in which Pliny describes his two now lost villas, followed by an illustrated history of the conjectural reconstructions undertaken by architects from the eighteenth century to the present. The drawings reveal more about the modern interpretations of Roman design than about the original villas, but are nonetheless useful indications of the suggestibility of the Roman villa type.

*Travlos, John.* PICTORIAL DICTIONARY OF ATHENS. *London and New York, 1971.*
> Does for Athens what Nash does for Rome. Comprehensive reference on the ancient city with valuable illustrations.

*Ward-Perkins, J.B.* ROMAN IMPERIAL ARCHITECTURE. *London, 1981.*
> Companion volume in the Penguin series to Boëthius and Ward-Perkins' earlier volume on Etruscan and early Roman work. Another compact survey with helpful illustrations.

*Wiebenson, Dora.* SOURCES OF GREEK REVIVAL ARCHITECTURE. *London, 1969.*
> A comprehensive study of the archaeological publications which gave rise to much of the architectural practice and theory of the late eighteenth and nineteenth centuries.

*Wycherley, R.E.* THE STONES OF ATHENS. *Princeton, 1978.*
> Synthesizing archaeological, historical, and literary remains, this book examines the development and growth of the ancient city on a broadly urbanistic level.

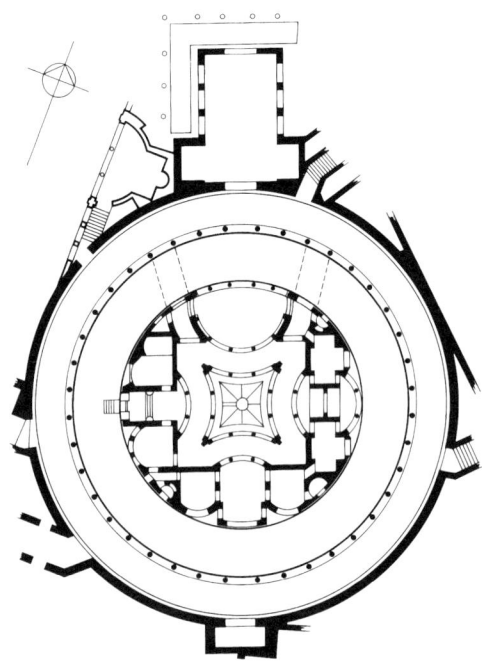

*Plan of the Island Enclosure, an example of "Hadrianic composition." From MacDonald and Pinto's* HADRIAN'S VILLA AND ITS LEGACY.

## SYMPOSIA & CONFERENCES

A symposium on architectural classicism was held on March 11, 1995 at Boston University during the Annual Meeting of the Institute for the Classical Tradition (ICT). Founded in 1983, the ICT examines diverse aspects of the classical heritage and related fields of human creativity, such as literature, the arts, architecture, philosophy, the sciences, medicine, law, the historical disciplines, education, and popular culture. The ICT undertakes research and educational projects, hosts conferences, symposia, and lectures, accommodates visiting scholars, provides informational services, and houses the editorial offices of the *International Journal of the Classical Tradition*, published since 1994 by Transaction Publishers, New Brunswick, NJ, and of the multi-volume works *Rise and Decline of the Roman World I (Aufstieg und Niedergang der Römischen Welt)*, and *The Classical Tradition and the Americas*, published since 1972 and 1994 respectively by Walter de Oruyter & Co., Berlin and New York. Wolfgang Haase and Meyer Reinhold are co-directors of the Institute for the Classical Tradition.

In the late 1980s the ICT took the initiative for the foundation, in 1990, of the International Society for the Classical Tradition (ISCT). It now serves as the primary home of the ISCT, which also has a European base at the University of Tübingen in Germany.

The symposium, which was jointly sponsored and programmed by the ICT and the Institute for the Study of Classical Architecture, comprised the following presentations:

- Donald M. Rattner, *Session Chair,* Institute for the Study of Classical Architecture
  Opening Remarks:"From Survival to Revival: American Architectural Classicism into the Twenty-first Century"
- Egon Verheyen, Robinson Professor, George Mason University
  "*Unenlightened by a Single Ray from Antiquity: The Meaning of the Pediment of the United States Capitol*"
- Jean D'Amato, Louisiana Scholars College, Northwestern State University
  "*The United States Supreme Court: The Propaganda of Democracy*"
- Christopher Thomas, Dept. of History in Art, University of Victoria
  "*Francis H. Bacon, American Archaeologist, Architect, Interior Designer, Classicist*"
- Richard Cameron, Institute for the Study of Classical Architecture
  "*Foundations: Building on American Classicism*"

- Stephen Falatko, Institute for the Study of Classical Architecture
  "*Modernism and American Neoclassical Practice: 1800-1850*"
- Mark Hewitt, New Jersey Institute of Technology, School of Architecture
  "*Beaux Arts Educational Paradigms for the Classical Architect Today*"
- Branko Mitrovic, School of Architecture, University of Notre Dame
  "*Contemporary Classicism and a Philosophy of Proportion*"
- Mark Ferguson, Ferguson Murray & Shamamian Architects
  "*The Architect at Work: Recent Projects by Ferguson Murray & Shamamian*"
- Robert Adam, Winchester Design Ltd. & Robert Adam Architects
  "*The Development of Modern Classical Architecture Through the Mechanism of Tradition*"
- Donald M. Rattner, Institute for the Study of Classical Architecture
  Closing Remarks: "*Architects, Historians, and the Quest for Continuity*"

On October 29-30, 1994, the Institute held its second annual seminar, entitled HOUSE, GARDEN, INTERIOR: CREATING THE CLASSICAL RESIDENCE TODAY. The program for the first day consisted of a series of 30-minute presentations on a variety of related topics, and was held in the Tisch Auditorium at the New York University School of Law:

- Witold Rybczynski, Author of *Home: A Short History of an Idea*
  "*House and Home: The Idea of the Dwelling*"
- Rocco Leonardis, Rocco Leonardis Architect
  "*Proportional Techniques for Residential Projects: The Vitruvian Methods*"
- Grace Hinton, Institute for the Study of Classical Architecture
  "*Computer Drafting and Design with the Architectural Orders*"
- Peter Talty, Institute for the Study of Classical Architecture
  "*The Cornice: A Case Study in Classical Building Technique*"
- C. Allan Brown, University of Virginia
  "*Classical Garden Design: Principles and Techniques*"
- Bunny Williams, Bunny Williams, Inc.
  "*The Garden as Decoration*"

- Robert A.M. Stern, Robert A.M. Stern Architects
  "*Building and Landscape: The Work of Robert A.M. Stern Architects*"
- Mac Griswold, Author of *Pleasures of the Garden*
  "*New England, the South and California: The Garden Classics of the Early Twentieth Century*"
- Donald M. Rattner, Institute for the Study of Classical Architecture
  "*Principles of Traditional Interior Planning and Design*"
- Jeffrey Greene, Evergreene Studios
  "*Between Plaster and Paint: Resurrecting the Lost Crafts of Mural Decoration*"
- Richard Cameron, Institute for the Study of Classical Architecture
  "*Where to Find Your Inspiration: A Guide to 2,000 Years of Books on Classical Architecture, Gardens, and Interior Design*"

## EXHIBITIONS

The Institute participated in an exhibition mounted at the Chicago Cultural Center by the Classical Architecture League as part of its three-day conference THE ART OF BUILDING CITIES. The exhibition, which ran from July through August, 1995, presented works on the theme of traditionalist urban design from around the country and abroad. The Institute contributed five boards selected from the 1994 summer program: two *analytiques* of the Richard Morris Hunt Memorial on Fifth Avenue, executed by John Burge and William Brockschmidt; two designs for a monumental finish line for the New York City Marathon, as conceived by Robert Magrish and Mr. Brockschmidt; and one drawing for a medal for the winner of the race, rendered by John Barron Clancy.

## AWARDS

On May 8, 1995, the Institute received an Arthur Ross Award for its work in the field of education. The Arthur Ross Awards are given annually by Classical America, an organization founded in 1968 to further artistic and architectural classicism in this country. The Hon. Schuyler G. Chapin, Commissioner of Cultural Affairs for the City of New York, presented the awards at the National Academy of Design in New York. Among the other winners were Jaquelin Robertson, Architect; David Esterly, Craftsman; Raymond Kaskey, Sculptor; and the Metropolitan Museum of Art, Patron.

The premier issue of THE CLASSICIST received an American Graphic Design Award from Graphic Design: USA, and a Merit Award from the Society of Publication Designers, for excellence in graphic design. The journal vied with 10,000 and 5,000 entries in the two competitions, respectively. Selected pages from the journal are to be printed in the Society's annual publication featuring winners of the 1995 competition.

# THE CLASSICIST

ANNOUNCES

# A CALL FOR PAPERS AND PROJECTS

The editors of THE CLASSICIST announce a call for papers and projects to be published in issue number three. The work may be related to any theoretical or practical aspect of classical architecture and its allied disciplines, which include painting, sculpture, and the decorative arts. While design projects of all types are eligible for the portfolio section, of special interest this issue are schemes involving garden and landscape design. Contributions to the journal are welcome from architects, artists, educators, scholars, interior designers and decorators, builders, craftspeople, and students.

All papers must be accompanied by a 250 word abstract. Illustrations should be provided in the form of black-and-white 8 1/2" x 11" photocopies. If selected for publication, papers will need to be re-submitted on computer disk. Architectural projects may be built or unrealized, professional or student, involve new construction or the rehabilitation of existing structures, and should be accompanied by written documentation concerning site, program, etc. Drawings of projects submitted should be reproductions only and no larger than 11" x 17". Please do not send original materials or rolled drawings. Photographs may be prints up to 8" x 10" in size or 35mm slides. Materials for papers or projects will be returned only if a self-addressed and stamped envelope is provided.

Submissions should be addressed to:

## THE CLASSICIST
c/o
INSTITUTE FOR THE STUDY OF CLASSICAL ARCHITECTURE
111 FRANKLIN STREET NEW YORK NY 10013

SUBMISSION DEADLINE IS
JANUARY 15, 1996

# Summer Program In Classical Architecture

### NEW YORK CITY : JUNE 15 TO JULY 27, 1996

Survey of the Bryant Memorial, 1995 Summer Program. Photographic collage by Mitchell W. Campbell, student.

This intensive six-week study program in the classical building arts is open to students in the design and building fields, practicing architects, interior designers, preservationists, educators, builders, and craftspeople. Participants in the program receive advanced training in a wide range of subjects pertaining to classical design, including:

- The Elements of Classical Architecture • Literature and Theory •
- Proportion • Building and Craftsmanship • Studio Design •
- Traditional Wash Rendering • Figurative Drawing •

*Scholarships and academic credit options are available.*

FOR A CATALOGUE AND AN APPLICATION CONTACT:

## The Institute for the Study of Classical Architecture
### 111 Franklin Street  New York  NY  10013
### 212.570.7374 (telephone) 212.627.5740 (facsimile)

# BUTLER

## NEW YORK

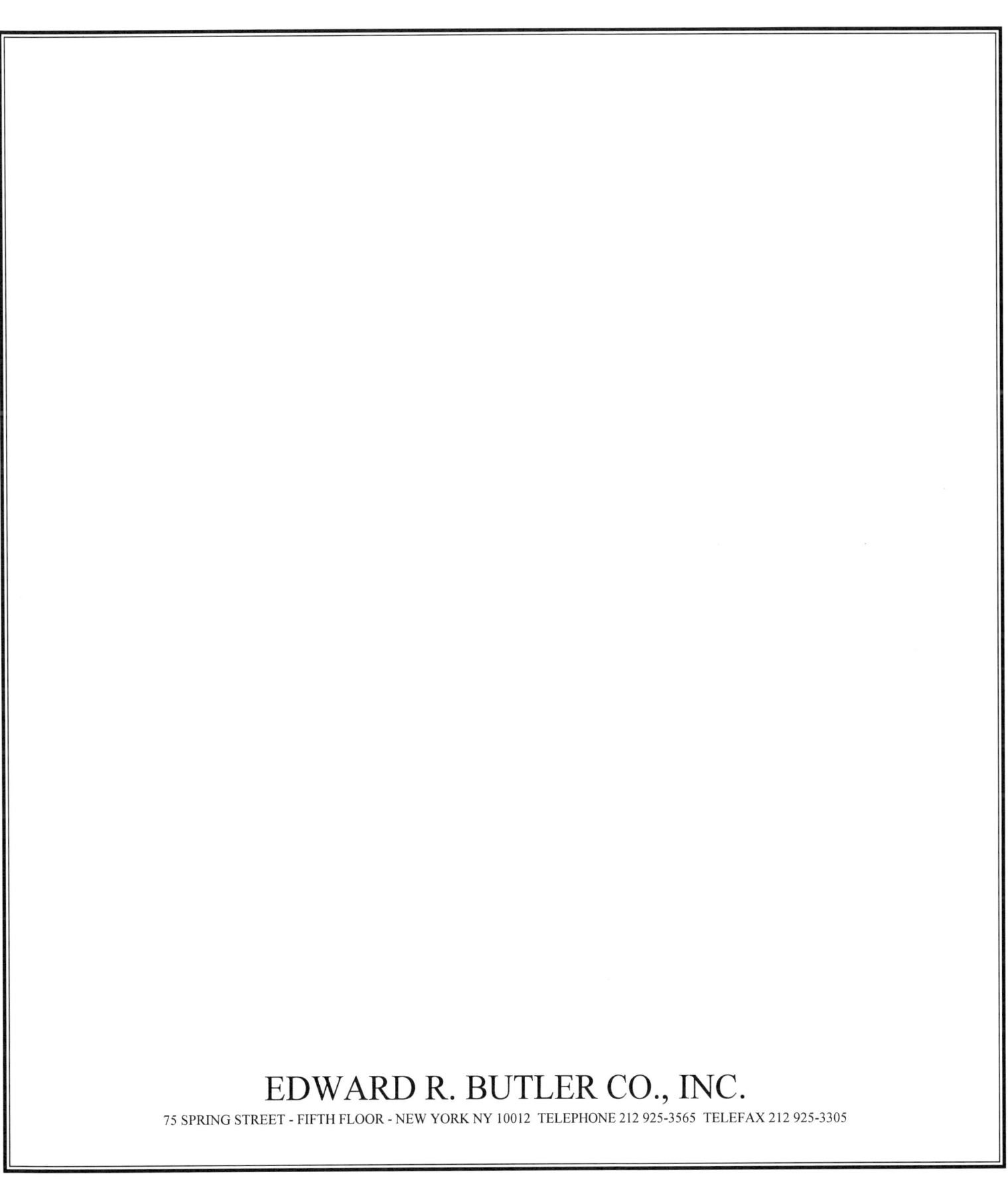

## EDWARD R. BUTLER CO., INC.

75 SPRING STREET - FIFTH FLOOR - NEW YORK NY 10012  TELEPHONE 212 925-3565  TELEFAX 212 925-3305

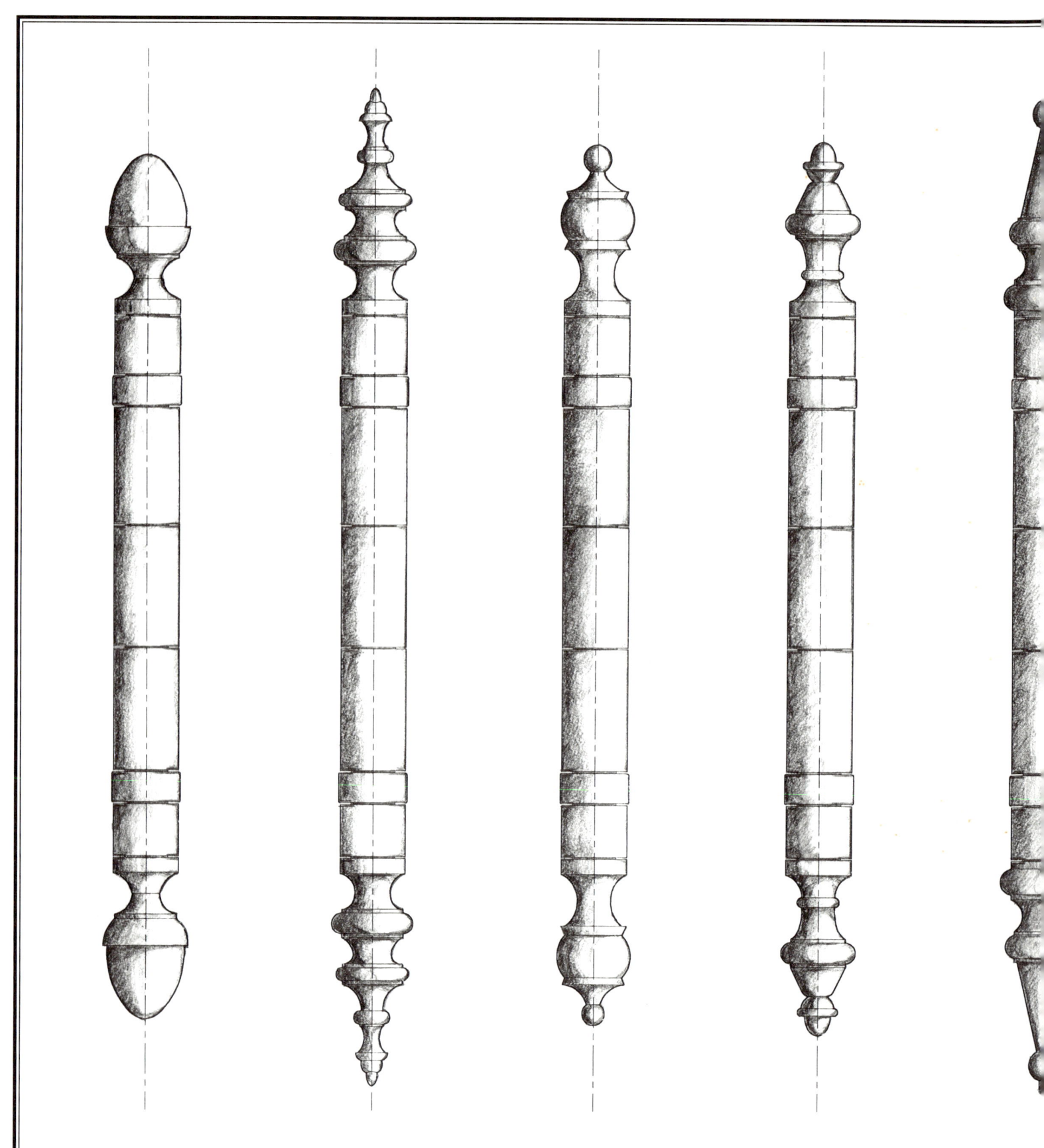

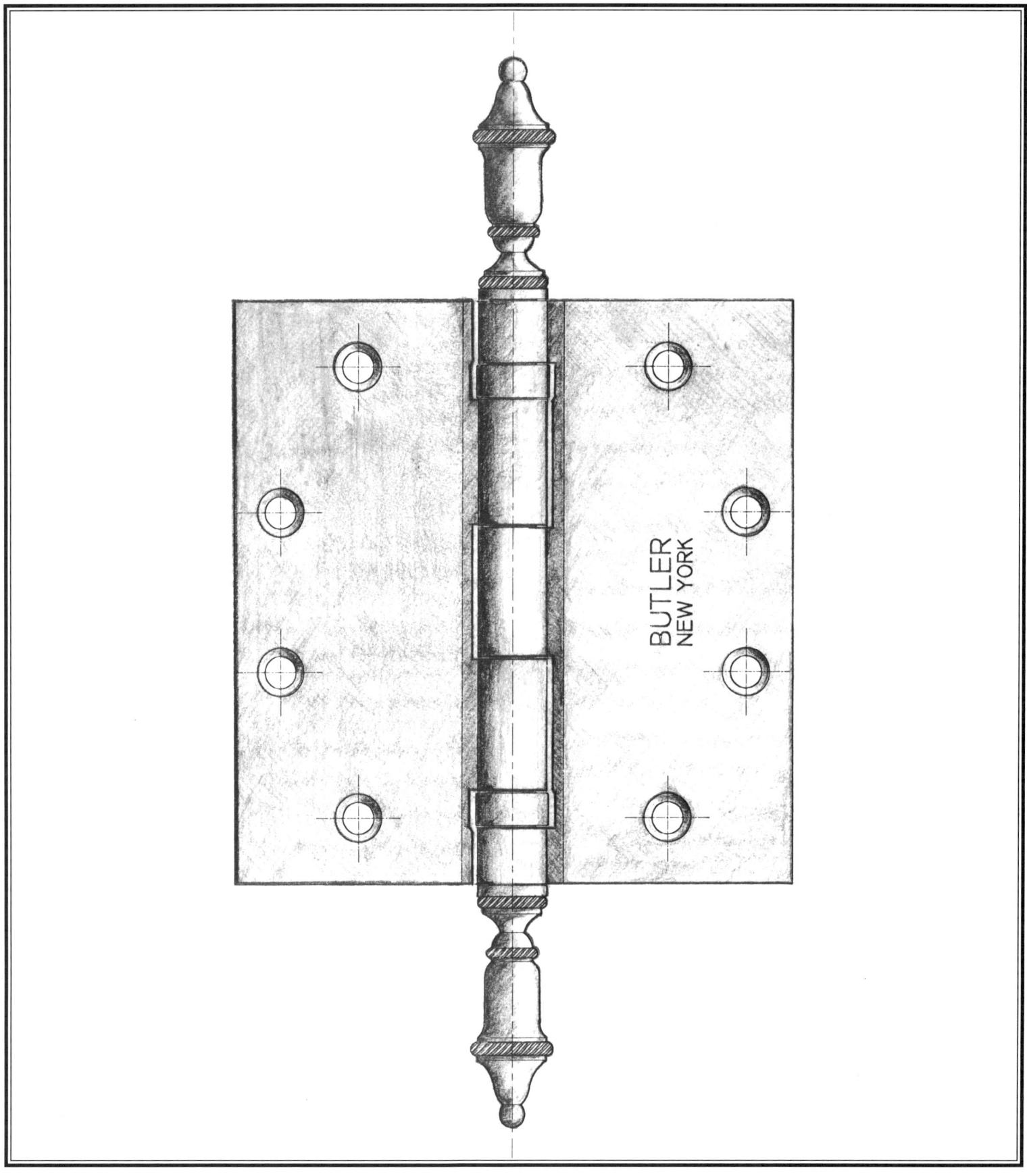

# FERGUSON MURRAY & SHAMAMIAN
## ARCHITECTS

# TRADITIONAL BUILDING MAGAZINE

◾ The Professional's Source for Historical Products ◾

DESIGNED FOR

**Architects □ Contractors □ Builders**

**Interior Designers □ Landscape Architects**

**Other Building Professionals**

**Each Edition is compiled from
our computerized database
of 6,556 suppliers —
the largest Historical Products File in the industry**

*By subscription only. $18/year.*

## TRADITIONAL BUILDING

69A SEVENTH AVENUE  BROOKLYN NY 11217 ◾ TEL (718) 636-0788  FAX (718) 636-0750

# Reid & Wright
# An Antiquarian
# Book Center

Fifty book dealers
Continually varying stock
Over 40,000 titles
Books in all fields
from the out-of-print
to the antiquarian book

At Reid & Wright we
specialize in books on
architecture and the
decorative arts.
We have over 4,000
titles in these areas.

Catalogue #1 to be issued Fall 1995
Make sure you are on our mailing list.

287 New Milford Turnpike, Route 202
New Preston, CT 06777   203-868-7706 FAX 203-868-1242
Hours: S & S 12-5:30; M W T F 10-5

# The I. Grace Company Inc.

## Builders & Construction Management

SUPPORTS THE
INSTITUTE FOR THE STUDY OF
CLASSICAL ARCHITECTURE

~ AND ~

# THE CLASSICIST

The I. Grace Company Inc.

403 East 91st Street

New York, NY 10128

212.987.1900 telephone

212.987.0900 telefax

David J. Cohen, President

# CHADSWORTH'S
# 1·800·COLUMNS

SALUTES THE

INSTITUTE FOR THE STUDY OF CLASSICAL ARCHITECTURE

ON THE

PUBLICATION OF THE SECOND ISSUE OF THE CLASSICIST

277 NORTH FRONT STREET WILMINGTON NORTH CAROLINA 28401

TEL: 1·800·COLUMNS 1·800·265·8667 FAX: 1·910·763·3191

# Bunny Williams
# Incorporated

4 East 77th Street
New York, New York 10021-1769

Tel. 212.772 8585

# NASSER NAKIB ARCHITECT

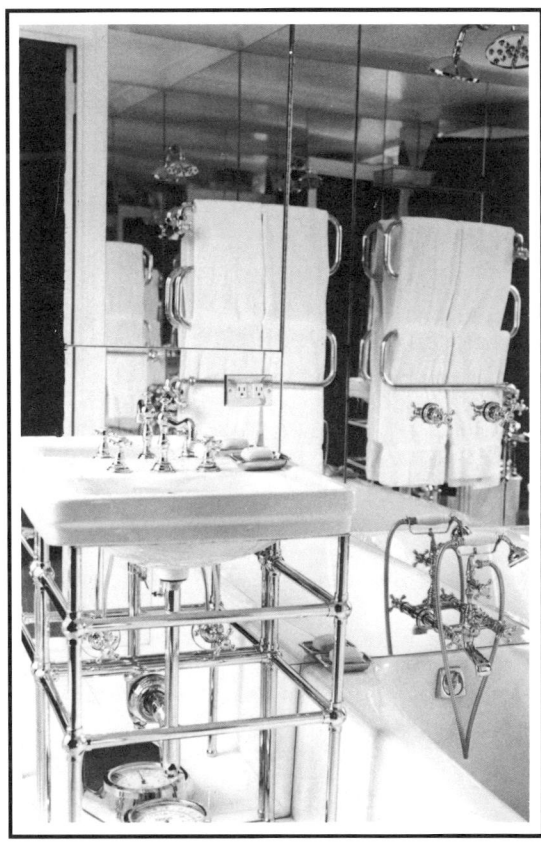

4 EAST 77 STREET
NEW YORK, NEW YORK 10021
(212) 717-1704

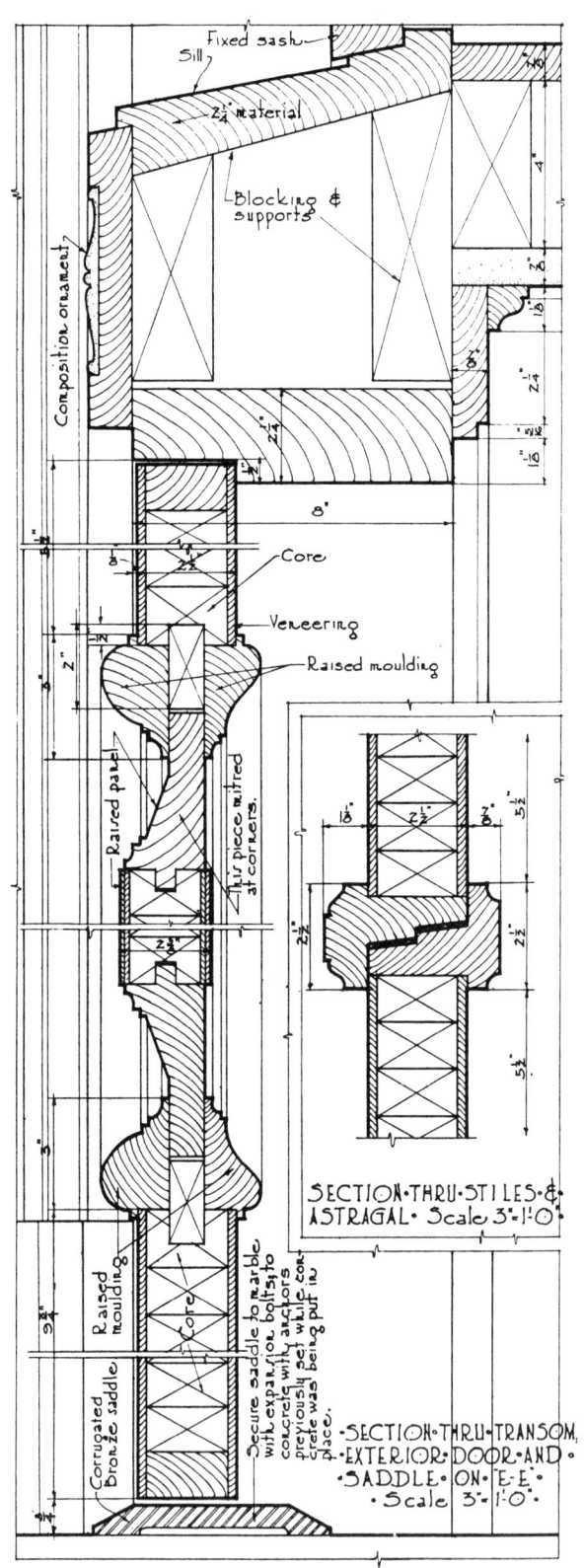

**MEADER ASSOCIATES INC.**

CUSTOM
BUILDERS
AND
CONSTRUCTION
MANAGERS

LOUIS E. MEADER,
PRESIDENT

CHARLES WOOD,
VICE PRESIDENT

270 LAFAYETTE STREET

SUITE 502

NEW YORK, NEW YORK

10012

PHONE:

212/966-0693

FAX:

212/966-2603

# Travers & co.

*Fine Fabrics and Wallpapers*

*979 Third Avenue*
*New York, New York 10022*
*(212) 888-7900*

Les Métalliers Champenois salutes the
Institute for the Study of
Classical Architecture.

**LMC CORP.**
**Les Métalliers Champenois, USA**

*Railings — Gates — Doors — Marquees*
*Fine Interior and Exterior Metalwork*

77 Second Avenue, Paterson, NJ 07514 ■ Tel: (201) 279-3573 ■ Fax: (201) 881-0235

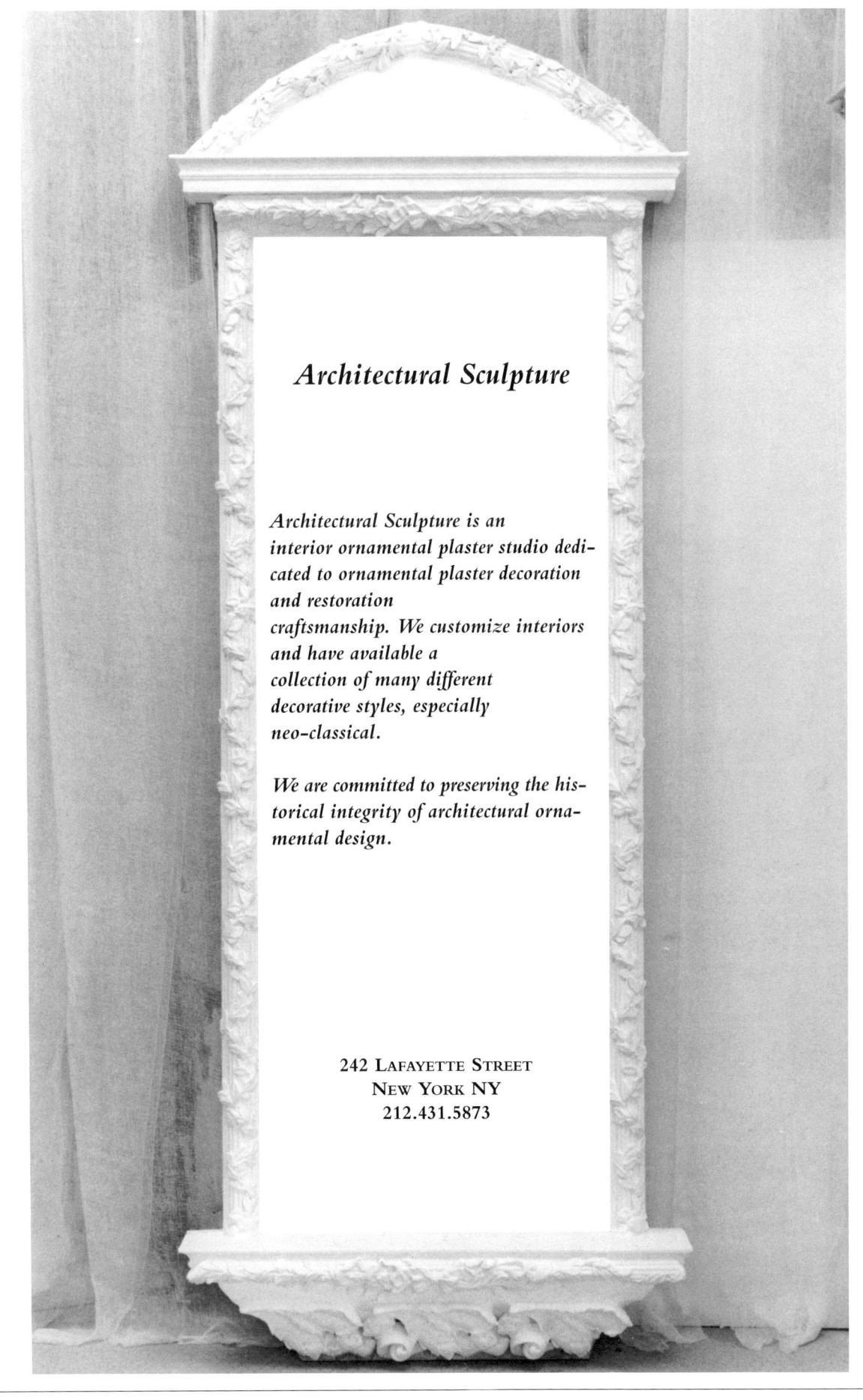

# Architectural Sculpture

*Architectural Sculpture is an
interior ornamental plaster studio dedicated to ornamental plaster decoration
and restoration
craftsmanship. We customize interiors
and have available a
collection of many different
decorative styles, especially
neo-classical.*

*We are committed to preserving the his-
torical integrity of architectural ornamental design.*

242 LAFAYETTE STREET
NEW YORK NY
212.431.5873

# Eisenhardt Mills Inc.

## CUSTOM ARCHITECTURAL MILLWORK IN THE CLASSICAL TRADITION

1510 RICHMOND ROAD • EASTON, PENNSYLVANIA 18040-8430

TELEPHONE (610) 253-2791 • FAX (610) 253-5994

*We support the*

**Institute for the Study of Classical Architecture**

*and welcome*

**"The Classicist"**

---

# DIMITRIOS KLITSAS

 *Fine* WOOD SCULPTOR

• 378 NORTH ROAD •
• HAMPDEN •
• MASSACHUSETTS • 01036 •
• TEL. 413.566.5301 •
• FAX. 413.566.5307 •

Discover custom-designed meticulously hand-carved pieces of elegance.

•

Carvings of any size, lovingly crafted for discriminating tastes and opulent surroundings.

•

Lavish works for private corporate and ecclesiastical applications.

# AHMAD SULEIMAN

ARCHITECTURAL SCULPTURE

RESTORATION

ORNAMENTAL PLASTER

PERIOD CEILINGS

SCAGLIOLA

MODELS FOR:
PLASTER, STONE, BRONZE

423 Horsham Road • P.O. Box 527
Horsham, Pennsylvania 19044
215-441-5767

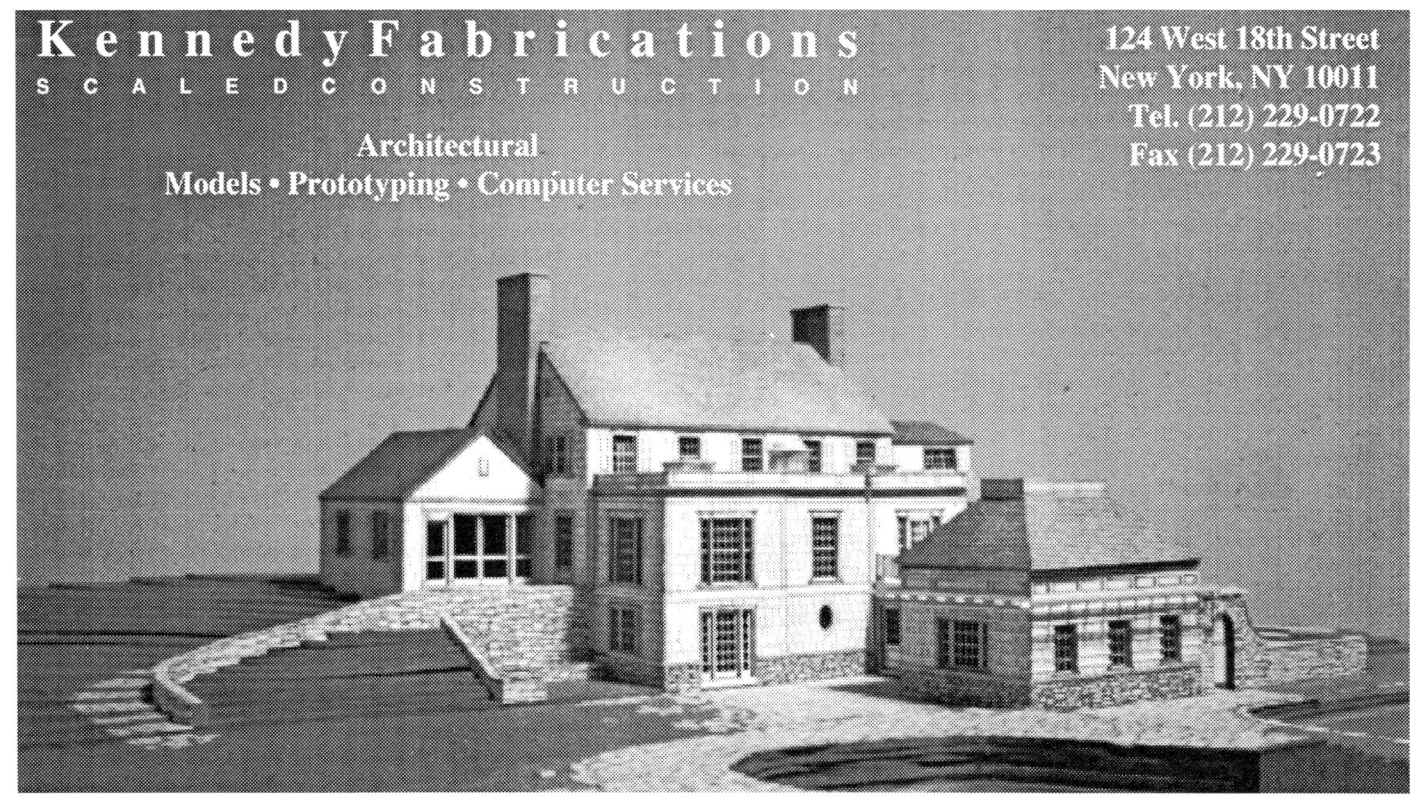

# Custom Furniture
# Architectural Woodwork

## Knipp & Company, Inc.

*Quality Cabinetry Since 1868*

3401 S. Hanover St. • Baltimore, MD 21225 USA
(410) 355-0440 • Fax: (410) 355-2866

*Cornice Detail* UNITED STATES CAPITOL

## ENDURING TRADITION

*Tradition in elegance, grace and durability is defined in every building designed with Dupuis Turned Concrete Columns. Custom-crafted to exact proportions, Dupuis Columns inspire any architectural style from contemporary to traditional and are well appointed for residential, commercial or religious buildings. Ask your architect about Dupuis Columns, or call 1-800-882-8667 for more information and a complimentary brochure.*

### DUPUIS
**TURNED CONCRETE**
## COLUMNS

1220 W. VIDRINE • OPELOUSAS, LA 70570
1-800-882-8667

Andrew Bordwin

# ✤ ARCHIVIA ✤

### THE DECORATIVE ARTS BOOK SHOP

❧

*DECORATIVE ARTS*
*ARCHITECTURE*
*LANDSCAPE AND GARDENS*
*INTERIOR DESIGN*

❧

944 Madison Avenue, New York, New York 10021
Tel [212] 439-9194
Fax [212] 744-1626

---

**CENTER LUMBER CO.**

**Fine Hardwoods**
**Custom Mouldings**
**Architectural Millwork**

*For a century Center Lumber Company has provided high quality wood products—from custom mouldings and architectural millwork to hardwood lumber and plywood—for industry and the building trades. For more information, including our brochure and moulding portfolio of over 2,500 existing profiles (also available in both DWG and DXF formats), please contact us.*

85 FULTON STREET, BOX 2242  PATERSON, NJ   07509
TELEPHONE  (201) 742-8300   FAX  (201) 742-8303

MEMBER OF AWI AND NHLA
SUPPORTER OF THE INSTITUTE FOR THE STUDY OF CLASSICAL ARCHITECTURE

# COLOPHON

This journal was composed in
QuarkXPress 3.2

———

Equipment used in the production
of this journal included:
Macintosh Quadra 610/System 7.5
Supermatch Platinum 20 monitor
Apple LaserWriter 320 printer for trial proofs

———

Text: Finch Opaque 80LB Smooth
Cover: Monadnock Astrolite 100LB Smooth
Text: custom black ink
Cover: black ink plus PMS 464 for duotone,
illustration and printer's red for logotype
Photographs: 300 line screen halftones
Printing: offset lithography
Binding: perfectbound
Edition: 1500